D0983161

COPING WITH COMPLEXITY

THEORY AND DECISION LIBRARY

AN INTERNATIONAL SERIES

IN THE PHILOSOPHY AND METHODOLOGY OF THE

SOCIAL AND BEHAVIORAL SCIENCES

Editors

GERALD EBERLEIN, *University of Technology, Munich*

WERNER LEINFELLNER, *University of Nebraska*

VOLUME 33

HANS W. GOTTINGER

Center for Environmental Research (G.S.F.)
Munich, F.R.G.

COPING WITH COMPLEXITY

Perspectives for Economics, Management
and Social Sciences

D. REIDEL PUBLISHING COMPANY

A MEMBER OF THE KLUWER ACADEMIC PUBLISHERS GROUP

DORDRECHT / BOSTON / LANCASTER

Library of Congress Cataloging in Publication Data

Gottinger, Hans-Werner.
  Coping with complexity.

  (Theory and decision library ; v. 33)
  Includes bibliographies and index.
    1. Decision-making—Mathematical models. 2. Economics—
Mathematical models. 3. Management—Mathematical models.
4. Social sciences—Mathematical models. 5. Computational
complexity. I. Title. II. Series.
HD30.23.G69 1983   001.53'8   83–3147
ISBN 90–277–1510–6

Published by D. Reidel Publishing Company,
P.O. Box 17, 3300 AA Dordrecht, Holland.

Sold and distributed in the U.S.A. and Canada
by Kluwer Boston Inc.,
190 Old Derby Street, Hingham, MA 02043, U.S.A.

In all other countries, sold and distributed
by Kluwer Academic Publishers Group,
P.O. Box 322, 3300 AH Dordrecht, Holland.

Printed in The Netherlands

TABLE OF CONTENTS

PREFACE   ix

CHAPTER 1   INTRODUCTION TO COMPLEX SYSTEMS   1

1.1   Finite Complex Systems   1
1.2   Some Concepts of Complexity   3
1.3   Fundamental Issues of Complexity   9
1.4   Multi-level System and Control   14
1.5   Design and Algebraic Systems   16
1.6   Models Using Catastrophe Theory   24
1.7   Aspects of FCS Modelling   29
1.8   Computer Models and Man Machine Interaction   31
     Note   35
     References   35

CHAPTER 2*   MATHEMATICS OF MACHINES, SEMIGROUPS
             AND COMPLEXITY   37

2.1   Finite State Machines   37
2.2   Definitions and Bounds of Complexity   39
2.3   Machines and Semigroups   44
2.4   The Krohn–Rhodes Prime Decomposition Theorem for
     Finite Semigroups and Machines   54
2.5   An Application of the Prime Decomposition Theorem –
     Some Results on Combinatorial Semigroups   62
2.6   Calculating the Complexity of a Transformation
     Semigroup   66
2.7   The Generalized Model   73
     References   75

CHAPTER 3   COMPLEXITY AND DYNAMICS   76

3.1   Introduction and Motivation   76
3.2   Competitive Processes and Dynamical Systems   79

3.3   Description of a Dynamic System   86
3.4   Axioms of Complexity   89
3.5   Evolution Complexity   91
3.6   Dynamic Systems of Resource Depletion   95
3.7   Complexity in Thom's Program   106
3.8   Policy Conclusions   108
      Notes   110
      References   111

CHAPTER 4   STRUCTURAL CHARACTERISTICS IN
            ECONOMIC MODELS   112

4.1   Introduction   112
4.2   Preliminary Considerations   112
4.3   Decomposable Systems   114
4.4   Systems Modelling and Complexity   115
4.5   Structure of the Model   119
4.6   The Model's Basic Set of Relationships   121
4.7   Evaluation of Complexity   125
4.8   Discussion   128
4.9   Comparison with some Studies on the Economics of
      Organization   131
      Note   132
      References   132

CHAPTER 5   COMPLEXITY, BOUNDED RATIONALITY
            AND PROBLEM-SOLVING   134

5.1   Introduction   134
5.2   Bounded Rationality   134
5.3   Problem Solving   139
5.4   An Overview of Algorithmic Complexity and Problem-
      Solving   144
5.5   A Case in Heuristics:
      General Problem-Solving (GPS)   147
5.6   Planning   151
5.7   Conclusions   152
      Appendix: Problem-Solving for Energy Technology
      Assessment   153

Notes   155
References   156

CHAPTER 6   COMPLEXITY AND DECISION RULES   157

6.1   Introduction   157
6.2   Background and Motivation   157
6.3   Choice Processes and Complexity   158
6.4   An Example of a Decision or Search Rule   161
6.5   A Social Choice Machine   162
6.6   Complexity of Decision Rules   164
6.7   A Construction of Compatible Decision Rules   167
6.8   Summary and Extension   170
      Notes   172
      References   173

CHAPTER 7   COMPLEXITY AND ORGANIZATIONAL
            DECISION-MAKING   175

7.1   Introduction   175
7.2   Organizational Structures and Performance   176
7.3   Organizations and Environments   178
7.4   A Real-time Organization   181
7.5   Information Technology   186
7.6   Costs of Information Processing   192
7.7   A Simple Machine Model of Organizational Design   194
7.8   Organizational Malfunctioning and Design   196
7.9   The Case of Line Organization   197
7.10 The Parallel Processing Line   201
7.11 The Case of Staff Organization   206
7.12 The Staff Acting as an Input Filter   206
7.13 Optimization Problem of the Staff Design   208
7.14 The Alternately Processing Staff   211
7.15 The Parallel Processing Staff   212
7.16 Some Practical Aspects of Organizational Design   216
      Notes   217
      References   218

INDEX OF NAMES   219
INDEX OF SUBJECTS   221

PREFACE

In this book I develop a theory of complexity for economics and management sciences. This book is addressed to the mathematically or analytically oriented economist, psychologist or management scientist. It could also be of interest to engineers, computer scientists, biologists, physicists and ecologists who have a constant desire to go beyond the bounds of their respective disciplines. The unifying theme is: we live in a complex world, but how can we cope with complexity?

If the book has made the reader curious, and if he looks at modelling, problem recognition and problem solving within his field of competence in a more "complex" way, it will have achieved its goal.

The starting point is the recognition that *complexity* is a well-defined concept in mathematics (e.g. in topological dynamics), computer science, information theory and artificial intelligence. But it is a rather diffuse concept in other fields, sometimes it has only descriptive value or even worse, it is only used in a colloquial sense.

The systematic investigation of complexity phenomena has reached a mature status within computer science.

Indices of computer size, capacity and performance root ultimately in John von Neumann's paradigmatic model of a machine, though other roots point to McCulloch and Pitts, not to forget Alan Turing.[1]

Offsprings of this development include:

– complexity of formal systems and recursiveness;
– cellular automata and the theory of self-reproducing machines;
– theory of program or computational complexity;
– theory of sequential machines;
– problem solving, cognitive science, pattern recognition and decision processes.

This book essentially treats the last two aspects of complexity phenomena within a well-defined framework. From this starting point the theory applies to economic dynamics, economic decision making and research, the economics of planning and decentralization, and the economics of organizational decision making. For motivational purposes let us start with the following basic identification problem.

ix

Suppose we are given some natural complex system, a 'black box', where we only observe outputs and inputs over time but are ignorant about what is happening 'inside', e.g. about local properties or parameters of transition. Is it possible to find an 'artificial' system that simulates the original natural system? The systems we have in mind in this context are those which respond in real time to their environments just to stay alive (bull fighting a bear). Ecological systems (bird colonies) or biological systems (metabolism of cells) constitute systems striving for survival, also all types of competitive economic systems challenged by adversary environments belong to this category. In general, extreme notions, such as survival or nonsurvival (death), which are characteristic for pure forms of competitive systems are involved. Here, interest is focused on global properties of dynamic systems. The design orientation follows from the identification process, e.g. by taking interconnecting parts of the artificial system, 'hooking' them together in order to simulate the 'black box'. The approach is algebraic, since it starts from finite-state dynamic systems, e.g. sequential machines.

There are some obvious advantages, theoretical and practical, to using an algebraic approach:

– Algebra is a natural tool because it emphasizes the design of a system as a collection of objects;

– Algebra is natural for computational work, and this is an important factor in applications. Modern computers accept digital instructions and those in turn require an algebraicization of systems;

– Algebraic system theory emphasizes qualitative aspects of systems to the extent that *we are interested in properties such as survival or breakdown*. This is achieved by determining complexity bounds of the system's design (design complexity). By the fact that algebraic system theory is related to computational structures we are in the position to construct a complexity theory for dynamic systems which is amenable to applications.

Systems of that sort reveal a natural bound of complexity. Complexity here has two facets, *computational complexity* and *structural complexity*.

Structural complexity refers to the inherent capability of parts, 'modules' basic 'intelligent' units of the system, as to what they are able to perform.

Computational complexity refers to the length of computations given by the extent of interconnection between parts. Another important distinction is that between *design* and *control* complexity, since it provides insight into its degree of manipulability.

Under design complexity is understood that complexity number associated with the transformation process in which full use of the system potential is made. Design complexity can only be achieved if the system is working without faults, if the components live up to computability requirements, if the parts function reliably. Under control complexity we understand that specific complexity number which keeps the entire system or at least part of it under complete control. Only if design and control complexity coincide will stable configurations in the state and output space result, or the system run smoothly. The relation between design and control complexity is an indication for stability or harmony of a dynamic system.

A starting point for our investigation is the observation that the behavior of complex systems can be reduced to certain structural characteristics of dynamic systems and these can be described by algebraic system models. In other words, the problem is that of simulating 'real' systems which due to their 'complexity' are subject to identification by appropriate 'artificial' systems (acting like finite automata).

Artificial systems are constructed in such a way that they enjoy similar structural properties relating to system dynamics (via state transition functions) and input–output processes as observed for real systems.

Modern large-scale socio-economic systems appear to reveal the following two characteristics:

(i) a high degree of complexity;
(ii) a lack of controllability and adaptability.

The second characteristic essentially appears to be a consequence of the first. Because of both characteristics, so far all scientifically established attempts have failed to determine real-world dynamic economic (or political) systems completely by policy changes. Therefore, it appears to be necessary to determine the complexity of dynamic systems before concluding anything more definite about *controllability, stability* and *adaptation* of these systems.

Without such qualification, construction and implementation of control policies remain dubious and vague.

Extending research by Krohn–Rhodes a complexity theory for dynamic systems is developed, and it is shown that complexity is a natural outcome of the evolution of such systems (design complexity). Complexity is a crucial notion for determining qualitative properties of dynamic systems. In contrast to traditional economic theory we do not aim at generating equilibrium properties of economic systems (say, of competitive systems), instead we are interested in those systems which could be characterized by qualitative properties such as *survival, breakdown, global instability, local instability, relative stability, relative instability, adaptability*, etc.

There are two reasons for studying complexity which have appeared earlier in the literature:

– If real-world systems are much more complex than is reflected by the models built to analyze them, then generalizations on the basis of these models appear to be impossible or at least so extremely biased that they would hardly serve any useful purpose. In this respect, B. Russell is quoted as saying 'thus we see how complexity can defeat science';

– Von Neumann[2] argued that in systems' behavior there is a kind of threshold of complexity below which the system may show regular, stable behavior, but above which entirely new modes of behavior can appear which is *qualitatively* completely different to the behavior of less complex systems. This may be translated in such a way as to saying that complex systems often appear to be counter-intuitive, e.g. that their behavior departs from what 'common sense' (i.e. simple systems) suggests their behavior ought to be.

In contrast to the *design complexity*, that is the complexity of the maximal potential of a system's design, we introduce *control complexity* as that particular complexity which yields all stable configurations under complete control of the system's evolution. The relationship between design and control complexity is called *evolution complexity*. From the knowledge of evolution complexity some conclusions can be drawn about the controllability of systems that are rooted in 'technological' or 'behavioristic' approaches to public policy (see Chaps. 1 and 3).

EXAMPLE. To illustrate the point, a public policy problem that can be treated in this dynamic system framework is the 'management of the commons'. The example of the 'tragedy of the commons' (G. Hardin) corresponds to the case of a 'common property resource', as treated in economics, for which no rent is charged and to which everyone has free access. If everyone has the right to fish in any river or lake, and pays no fee for this right, the river and lake will be overfished and the common property resource will be run down. Similarly, if anyone can swim at a beach, free of charge, there will be overcrowding; if anyone can use a freeway without paying for the facility of using it, there will be congestion on the freeways, etc.

By modelling this dynamic competitive situation as a dynamic algebraic system we find out that such systems are bound to break down if not properly designed or controlled.

A switch to a different design, for example, could involve the introduction of property rights for all participants to the effect that competitive behavior will bring the problems of externalities into appropriate balance. Instead of property rights one may design different disincentive schemes to lower the design complexity of the system such that the private decision of maximizing profit would be compatible with the socially optimal decision. On the other hand, a switch to a different control would involve, for example, a suitable limited access scheme or other regulatory devices via the price system that would induce a wise use of the common property resource. This effectively limits competition in order to husband common resources. Examples of this kind abound, they relate to limitation of professional or vocational activities, regulatory devices in urban and traffic systems.

In what follows, we present an overview of the individual chapters.

Chapter 1 (Introduction to Complex Systems) introduces the reader into various aspects of systems in relation to complexity. The central thesis in this chapter is that we have mature methods in handling 'simple' systems and in predicting infinitely large systems by stochastic methods, but that we are extremely poor in handling and predicting 'finitely complex systems'. A definition of this class of system is attempted and examples are given to approach them.

Chapter 2* (Mathematics of Machines, Semigroups and Complexity) presents the gist of all relevant mathematical results which culminate in the Krohn–Rhodes *Prime Decomposition Theorem*. Chapter 2* is starred since most results appear to be accessible only to readers with technical and mathematical background. The technically inexperienced reader is advised to browse over the material in order to get some intuitive grasp of the algebraic tools behind it. This might help him in assimilating unconventional results later on.

Chapter 3 (Complexity and Dynamics) describes common properties of various dynamic systems which cope with survival. For them we can find paradigms in biology, ecology as well as in economics and the social sciences. It appears that these systems belong to the class of competitive systems that may or may not possess a stable equilibrium. We argue that global stability can only be achieved in such systems if their design and control complexities coincide.

Chapter 4 (Structural Characteristics of Economic Models) provides an application of complexity theory to the design of economic systems and planning. It lends *an additional technical argument* to the support of F.A. Hayek's consistent claim that in general cases decentralized (market type) economic systems are far more efficient in communication and far less expensive in computation (economic adjustment) than their centralized (socialist type) counterparts. In principle, this result applies to all global, economy-wide organizational forms, for instance, pertaining to activities of resource and R&D planning.

In Chapter 5 (Complexity, Bounded Rationality and Problem-Solving) we show that complexity appears to be a structural property of any observable system, decision making mechanism, organization, bureaucracy which imposes constraints upon the computability, selectivity, control, decision-making power: hence, which limits its proper functioning, limits rationality. Complexity modifies the handling, manipulation, controllability of the system and its solution requires heuristic research, step-by-step procedures leading to problem-solving in a task environment.

Chapter 6 (Complexity and Decision Rules) applies the comprehensive algebraic measure of complexity as derived from automata theory (in Chapter 2*), to a program of 'limited rationality' regarding individual or social choices. It presents a continuation of the discussion started in Chapter 6. The complexity measure appears to be a natural consequence of looking at a decision rule as a finite-state machine that computes preferences bounded by computational constraints.

Chapter 7 (Complexity and Organizational Decision Making) investigates certain types of organizational forms, in addition to those discussed in Chapter 3, which are considered to be *sequentially* computable rather than Turing computable: i.e., we are considering those organizations which are subject to definite resource and time constraints and which can be split into elementary computational operations. As a starting point we choose the well-developed economic theory of optimal organizations and we attempt to translate some of the key notions into the language of sequential machine theory.

The practical aspects of sequential machine theory in the design of organizations would be two-fold.

First, given certain performance standards, is the design of a particular organization compatible with meeting these standards? If so, does there exist a 'better' design in terms of being more efficient and/or less costly? Second, given certain performance standards how would you design an organization which meets these standards in a most efficient and/or in a least costly way?

In the case of two different organizational designs it is shown that the computational load imposed on the organization members requires them to choose organizational designs that avoid overload or minimize the impact of overload. Overload bounds could be determined by psychometric experiments.[3]

The material presented in this book is the collection of work which started in the early seventies, interrupted by many other activities, yet once in a while returning to this topic. After attending a class of John Rhodes in Berkeley, I was 'turned on', excited an curious how this body of knowledge can be used for 'the sciences of decision-making' (to paraphrase H. Simon in his book *The Sciences of the Artificial*). Along this way, I have been encouraged by C.B. McGuire (Berkeley), Th. Marschak (Berkeley), L. Hurwicz (Minneapolis), J. Casti (IIASA), P. Albin (New York) and the late Jacob Marschak (Los Angeles). Discussions with L. Zadeh (Berkeley), T. Schelling (Cambridge, Mass.), R. Selten (Bielefeld), M. Kochen (Ann Arbor), and N. Luhmann (Bielefeld) have been very useful. Of course, may be none of them subscribes to the ideas presented in this book.

I have lectured on this material at the School of Organization and Management, Groningen University, the Summer School on Systems Analysis at the International Center of Theoretical Physics, Trieste, Italy, and at the Center for Game Theory and Mathematical Economics, Hebrew University, Jerusalem.

Last but not least it is my pleasure to thank Mrs. H. Guth for patching together draft notes and for typing part of the manuscript, and to Mrs. R. Gratz for drawing the figures.

Munich, April 13, 1981   HANS W. GOTTINGER

NOTES

[1] A nice treatment, in this regard, on the sociology of artificial intelligence and tracing these roots, is a book by Pamela McCorduck, *Machines Who Think*, H. W. Freeman and Co., San Francisco, 1979.

[2] Neumann von, J., 'Probabilistic Logics and the Synthesis of Reliable Organisms from Unreliable Components', in C.E. Shannon (ed), *Automata Studies*, Princeton Univ. Press, 1969.

[3] To effectively determine the bounds is beyond the competence of the author, but see A.J. Mackinnon and A.J. Wearing, 'Complexity and Decision Making', *Behavioral Science* 25 (1980), 285–296.

CHAPTER 1

INTRODUCTION TO COMPLEX SYSTEMS

1.1 FINITE COMPLEX SYSTEMS

In recent times there has been an increasing interest in analyzing the behavior and structure of large-scale systems. Here we report on some ideas for dealing with these systems in terms of problem-solving and for inplementing these systems on the basis of present day computer technology. We will come across some examples where it is far from obvious that large-scale systems can be seen simply as aggregated versions of small-scale systems but rather as revealing properties that lift them onto a different qualitative level (an observation already made by von Neumann [14]).

Mathematics has longtime held the prejudice that the only worthwhile model, the only one we should pay attention to, is the formal mathematical model. If we look at the situation of mathematical models in the social sciences, and evaluate their explanatory power, in particular in economics, this view can hardly be accepted if one cares for applications of strictly formal mathematical models. Still, to avoid misunderstandings, as 'social science' becomes more mature as a science, as it grows up and becomes more systematic and more unified in its scientific propositions, in the long run it eventually becomes fully 'mathematical'.[1] It has been predicted that entirely new branches of mathematics will have to be invented some day for the solution of societal problems, just as a new mathematics was necessary before significant progress could be made in physics. There is general agreement on this, but it is everybody's guess how long it will take to come about. However, nobody can content himself with the 'long run' only, and there is no question that decisions are required in the short run which concern problems of urban and economic planning, problems of far-reaching social and economic significance. These problems are extremely complex and require proper tools to handle, explain and control complex systems. What can be done? Why are present mathematical tools only of limited relevance.

First we ought to explain what has so far been achieved with mathematical modelling and then try to explain what has *not* been achieved and why not.

1

So far mathematics has been quite successful in dealing either with *small* or *infinitely large* systems. At one extreme there are a small number of parts to a system having fairly simple connections. Here mathematics is very helpful in exhausting all the possibilities by getting, say, a complete *analytic* solution of the set of equations. It is another matter whether we feel comfortable to model an essentially large scale (complex) system, an urban or environmental system, in simplistic terms by sharply reducing the dimension of a large number of connections virtually by manipulation of the aggregation procedure so that it fits analytic solution techniques. Many aggregate growth models in economics that use straight methods of optimal control to find analytic solutions can be quoted as evidence. Though it is a truism, there is a potential danger in the attitude of some model builders, namely that in order to understand we must throw away information. How much tolerance can we bear in 'throwing away' information and yet be able to understand and explain the behavior of a complex system?

At the other extreme, one works with a marvellous 'trick' when the number of particles (commodities, messages, actions) gets to be of some very high power of ten. If they are sufficiently homogeneous one pretends that there are infinitely many of them. Here certain properties of continuity, some sort of smoothness, may be invoked so that the whole power of classical analysis comes into play.

In fact, unfortunately, most of the large systems relating to societal problems fall into a range that is intermediate to these. The systems are much too 'complex' to get explicit solutions for them and yet the number of parts is not large enough, nor are the parts homogeneous enough, to be able to pass to the limit. We refer to these systems simply as 'systems of intermediate complexity', or more generally as finite complex systems (FCS). In summary, what is it, then, that makes a FCS so difficult to analyze, understand and predict in its behavior?

First, it is highly sensitive in responding to changes of its environment, the complexity of the environment is reflected in the system's behavior. Complexity is even increased if responsive actions have in turn an impact on the environment. Such situations occur in environmental or energy systems, when depletion of resources via price signals lead to responsive actions of consumers, e.g. by substituting materials or pursuing other energy options which in turn have an impact on the environment at some future date. This property may be referred to as *external interaction*.

Second, it is highly interdependent with regard to actions of its components. Private and social actions often generate a 'snow-ball' effect that leads to new actions, modification of existing ones, and generally triggering various feedback and feedforward mechanisms. This property is essentially a corollary of the first, and can be referred to as *internal interaction*.

Third, in contrast to 'simple' systems where behavioral rules can be relatively easily aggregated to form total systems' behavior, FCS is characterized by *'thresholds of complexity'*, below which the system may show a regular, stable pattern, but above which new and qualitatively different modes of behavior can occur for which there is a lack of understanding. Thresholds of complexity are reflected in empirical phenomena, such as aggression, panic, violent outbreak of conflicts, war, crowding, political unrest – common to all these situations is that 'things get out of hand'.

Fourth, an FCS appears to be only partially or locally controllable, so that effects of interventions are not fully understood and they produce global behavior which is not foreseen. Examples of this kind abound in the area of economic policy, where the trouble is that often local controls produce global results which counteract, even invalidate these controls, requiring new controls or modifying existing ones, etc.

If the FCS is basically self-adaptive, and competitive economic or ecosystems display this property, then in terms of management and under certain conditions one might be better off to utilize the intrinsic computational power (of self-adaptation) to achieve survival or long-run success of goal attainment.

In fact, this idea is intuitively supported by economic reasoning of the 'invisible hand' in classical economics which is supposed to direct the economic mechanism to self-adjustment.

1.2 SOME CONCEPTS OF COMPLEXITY

The study of complexity almost appears to be a futile enterprise. We know that almost everything is complex, in particular living systems or technological systems, the question is how complex?

In the case of technological systems, complexity appears to be an outgrowth, accumulation and effective bound of human knowledge: therefore we have proper methods of construction available to describe and understand such systems. In the case of natural or biological systems we are in a less fortunate position: hence, we try hard to understand interaction and modes of behavior in subsystems but our knowledge is necessarily limited. In fact, one obvious way to understand complexity in *natural* systems is by construction of analogy with *artificial systems*, e.g., by imitating a comparable kind of complexity in artificial systems in the hope that if we understand the latter systems sufficiently well we have at least some key to understanding the former one. It is therefore not surprising that great significance has been attached to the concept of complexity in the science of the artificial, i.e., in computer or system science where it has been considered as a key scientific problem warranted by the fact that complexity pertains to almost every aspect of model building, development and prediction. We try to overcome difficulties in dealing with complex systems by submitting them to simulation via simplified models in order to approximate their real behavior. In different connotations complexity is believed to assume different facets: among those we list largeness, size, multi-dimensionality or hierarchy – to name only a few. In particular, the concept of 'hierarchy' and that of 'complexity' seem to be intimately connected, and this relationship lends itself to a more intuitive understanding. H. Simon in his 'Architecture of Complexity' [23] says:

The fact, then, that many complex systems have a nearly decomposable hierarchic structure is a major facilitating factor enabling us to understand, to describe, and even to see such systems and their parts ... If there are important systems in the world which are complex without being hierarchic, they may to a considerable extent escape our observation and our understanding. Analysis of their behavior would involve such detailed knowledge and calculation of the interactions of the elementary parts that it would be beyond our capabilities of memory or computation.

One natural way, then, to describe a complex object is to structure (partition, decompose) it appropriately. Structured programming and decomposition methods of allocation systems using linear and non-linear programming may serve as examples among others. H. Simon puts it this way when describing complexity:

If you ask a person to draw a complex object – such as a human face – he will almost always proceed in a hierarchical fashion. First he will outline the face. Then he will add or insert features: eyes, nose, mouth, ears, hair. If asked to elaborate, he will begin to develop details for each of the features ... until he reaches the limits of his anatomical knowledge.([23], p. 107).

Clearly, the more we are able to describe the complexity of an object, the more we are able to obtain 'information' (to learn about) the object, hence complexity and information seem to be intrinsically related.

Knowing this there will be no basic difference between a human brain and a pattern-recognizing machine – both will proceed along the same lines, in a hierarchic or 'boxes-within-boxes' form.

Up to now we have a fairly broad and intuitively appealing description of what complexity really is and how it can be approached in general. However, there exist different theories of complexity which are valid for well-defined systems and these theories are not always natural or even compatible with each other.

One theory of complexity is proposed in connection with the construction of Turing machines and related algorithms generating computable functions, the structure and size of which pertains to computational complexity (see J. Hartmanis and J.E. Hopcroft [8]).

A Turing machine is essentially a number writer, working with paper and pencil. The paper it uses is a *long tape* divided into successive squares. The machine has a simple mind, there are no resource or time constraints involved, the machine can do virtually everything – even the most complex tasks – without bothering about time or resources. Turing gave his machine an infinite memory and an infinite tape, although this is not necessary for the working of this machine. It is a fairly general model of the human brain.

There is a long tradition to model the logical capabilities of the human brain by means of Turing machines. Turing machines are conceived to make precise the concept of algorithm. 'There exists an algorithm for a task' can be put into the equivalent statement: 'there exists a Turing machine and a program such that the Turing machine will acomplish the task and halt after finitely many operations'.

There exist Turing machines that are universal, which means that they can compute any function that any other Turing machine (with different internal states and state transitions) can compute. Since a Turing machine computes a function by means of a finite program it would seem reasonable to think that one could minimize the length of all programs that compute a given recursive function. A minimization of the program length, however, does not take into account differences in the speed of computation, which may vary from program to program. Optimizing for speed is not possible because of the *speed-up theorem*: there exist recursive functions such that for any program there exist other programs that are exponentially faster (almost everywhere). Another theorem says, according to Brainerd and Landweber [26]: there exist programs that compute the same recursive function but it *cannot* be proven that they do. Hence the complexity theory of *recursive functions* runs into difficulties. In view of these difficulties it has been suggested that we should abandon Turing machines and base complexity theory upon finite state automata. While Turing machines are an interesting mathematical object in their own right, and while they are of great importance for the foundations of mathematics, they are somewhat unrealistic as an actual brain model, or as a model of any real world computer. Hence a bounded, finite computing device is a more realistic model than an unbounded device like a Turing machine.

A complexity theory based on finite state automata *is not* a theory of the complexity of recursive functions, since such machines cannot compute all recursive functions. Instead it is a complexity theory of tasks and circuits. What finite state automata can compute can also be computed by Turing machines with bounded tapes. Thus one might try to base the complexity theory of finite state automata upon Turing machines with bounded tapes, taking the *program length* as a measure of complexity.

On the other hand, a Turing machine is not a good model for an economic organization or system, for any system which is striving to survive. Time, space and resources play a dominant role in this world!

Instead we conceive an economic system as a sequential machine which acts under resource and time constraints.

EXAMPLE. According to L. Hurwicz [10] we could talk about an 'economic system' in machine-like terms embedded in its environment (consisting of the initial resource endowment, technology and preferences). The state of the system would be constituted by *physical activities* such as consuming, producing, storing, obsolescence, ... and *informational activities* such as making bids, presenting economic plans, performing calculations, ... etc.

A particular organizational form, the competitive economy, has received most attention. Let an economy consist of agents (decision makers) acting competitively in reponse to a changing environment and to actions by other agents resulting in 'messages' (prices). Incidentally, this situation resembles one of activating 'switching circuits' or 'neurons' in a natural network.

One natural problem arising in this context is the problem of *informational minimality* of the message space generated by the competitive process where message spaces are usually considered to be topological spaces. Recent studies by S. Reiter [16]–[18] have attempted to approach this problem. Here is a sketch of his ideas. An *allocation process* consists of a message set and a response function mapping messages into actions for a given environment. Given two allocation processes for a fixed environment, that one is preferred which requires minimal information: such an allocation process is called *informationally efficient*. In particular, it can be proved that every competitive allocation process which is Pareto satisfactory (e.g. non-wasteful, unbiased and essentially single-valued) in a 'classical' (convex) environment is *informationally efficient* and at *least as good* as any other (Pareto-) satisfactory, informationally decentralized allocation process in the same environment. Complexity of message spaces is used in terms of the 'size' of the space which is topologically translated into its dimension reducing trivially to its cardinality if a discrete topology is taken. In other words, the competitive message space induced by the competitive process given the 'classical' (convex) environment has a topological dimension that is at most as large as the dimension of any other informationally decentralized message space sufficient for the class of Pareto-satisfactory allocation processes. This result is not generalizable and therefore a caution should be added here: for non-classical (in particular, nondecomposable) environments this does not hold; in fact, several examples exist – among others the 'tragedy of the commons' (see Chap. 3), which show that it is most unlikely to hold. The informational requirements of competitive systems have been studied empirically by P.L. Schmidbauer [22] using an elaborate computer model of some information transferring mechanism, the wheat market; however comparative empirical studies about informational requirements of various allocation processes in different economic environments are still lacking.

Such comparative studies would be likely to provide interesting results if we adopted a comprehensive methodological approach for devising allocation processes, e.g., sequential machine theory. A preliminary step in this direction has been made by showing that finite state sequential machine theory provides a natural organizational form for modelling structure and behavior of economic organizations and for treating allocation processes in terms of transformations on the set of states of a machine.

A sequential machine is a variant of a dynamic system (see Chap. 2). For introductory purposes we define: If A is a nonempty set, then let $\sum A$ represent the set of all strings whose members are elements of A, i.e.

$$\sum A = \{(a_1, \ldots, a_n) : n \geq 1 \text{ and } a_j \in A\}.$$

Then we define a sequential machine as a function $f: \sum A \to B$ where A is the basic input set, B is the basic output set and $f(a_1, \ldots, a_n) = b_n$ is the output at time n if b_j is the input at time $j (1 \le j \le n)$.

Next we look inside the machine (or 'black box') by defining a circuit C as a quintuple $(A, B, Z, \lambda, \delta)$, where A and B are as defined above, Z is the (nonempty) set of internal states, $\lambda: A \times Z \to Z$ is the next-state function, and $\delta: A \times Z \to B$ is the output function.

$$C_z(a_1) = \delta(a_1, z);$$
$$C_z(a_1, \ldots, a_n) = C_{\lambda(a_1, z)}(a_2, \ldots, a_n) \quad \text{for } n \ge 2.$$

This is all we need about a formal definition of a sequential machine. More than by formal definition we could illustrate the basic idea of a sequential circuit C.

$$C: z = z_0 \overset{a_1}{\to} z_1 \overset{a_2}{\to} z_2 \overset{a_3}{\to} \cdots \overset{a_n}{\to} z_n$$
$$\downarrow \quad \downarrow \qquad \quad \downarrow$$
$$b_1 \quad b_2 \qquad \quad b_n$$

The behavior of a finite state machine is represented by a concatenation of events or states over time. These events or states occur at discrete 'moments' between which nothing is going to happen (refractory period). One may imagine these moments as occurring regularly like the ticking of a clock, hence, 'real-time computation' – and we may identify the number of moments by integers $0, 1, 2, 3, \ldots$ or $-3, -2, -1, 0, +1, +2, +3, \ldots$ as we like. Hence, a computation is accomplished at every moment, when the machine has reached a new state via the state transition equation. Then the number of these transitions show the length of computations and therefore can be identified with its complexity. Hence complexity must be integer-valued. Modelling a sequential machine as a McCulloch–Pitts neural network, computational complexity could be looked upon as the number of logical elements multiplied by the number of cycles the machine is going to perform in order to compute some function (transformation) ϕ, known as the process. For instance, if the machine is constructed from x logical elements (e.g. neurons), and if it needs t cycles to compute ϕ the complexity of the sequential machine is given by xt. A natural way to define computational work carried out by the sequential machine is the following: Let $f: \sum A \to B$ be the sequential machine, let $|\sum A| \equiv |A^*|$ be the number of logical elements the set of which can be partitioned (via serial-parallel decomposition of the machine) into sets A_i^*. Let $p_i = |A_i^*|/|A^*|$ be the relative share of logical elements in the i-th submachine to process 'information' in terms of serial-parallel composition to realize f. Then computational work $w(f)$ – a counterpart of computational complexity – could be defined as

$$w(f) = \sum_{i=1}^{n} |A_i^*| \log \frac{|A^*|}{|A_i^*|} = |A^*| H(p_1, \dots, p_n)$$

where $p_i = |A_i^*|/|A^*|$ and H denotes the entropy of information theory. So computational work can be measured in terms of information.

As mentioned before, a natural approach to deal with complex objects is to break them down into primitive components and to see how they act individually and how they interact as parts of the whole. This idea is behind decomposition methods in planning and hierarchical model building in systems analysis. It also bears relations to sequential machine theory where – by emphasizing the organizational point of view – a system or a machine could be realized by a serial-parallel decomposition of component machines.

It is one of the great contributions of J.V. Neumann [14] to have proved the (not very intuitively plausible) fact that a reliable, i.e. predictable system can be built from unreliable parts. 'Unreliability' is not to be understood in an engineering sense of 'non-functioning'; rather it is meant in a logical sense of 'non-predictable'. To understand this situation we could be aided by the knowledge that any computer can be built from a small array of simple, basic elements. As von Neumann did we could take as primitive components McCulloch–Pitts neurons. These components are devised by analogy to neurons in the brain; however, more in view of hardware construction, we could look upon them as 'switching circuits' doing elementary computations in terms of 'and', 'or', 'not' constituting a Boolean algebra (of propositions or instructions). Now even if some of these components prove to be 'unreliable' in terms of being 'unpredictable' at some specified probability level, the behavior of the whole system, the organization of these parts, could be predicted.

This is a kind of modification of Heisenberg's uncertainty principle suitable for computer and system design.

1.3 FUNDAMENTAL ISSUES OF COMPLEXITY

Before approaching complexity in the context of specific models we should pause for a moment and first indicate why complexity is so crucial for the analysis of systems we encounter in real life. If we know the complexity we could possibly devise better (mathematical) methods of modelling and controlling real systems. So far our tools seem to be rather limited.

In light of the previous characterization of an FCS it seems useful to ask a couple of questions about the behavior of the system. One major question, for example, is about identification – or as R. Bellman [3] has put it: 'Given some information concerning the structure of a system, and some observations of inputs, outputs and internal behavior over time, deduce all the missing information concerning structure, inputs and outputs'.

The second question one may ask is: does it produce errors in the sense that its behavior is hard to predict?

As has been pointed out by R. Rosen [20], the concept of error is crucial and arises naturally in social and biological systems. In fact, error and complexity seem to be positively correlated, it is frequently the cause of sudden changes, mutations, perturbations, break-downs occurring within the system.

A third related question is: what is the level of control we can exert upon the system? Controllability seems to be a desirable property of systems independent of complexity. But 'independence' is sometimes not the case. It is useful to mention here that controllability is not always inversely related to complexity as one would intuitively expect. In the engineering field we observe systems operating that are highly complex (according to some standard) but they are also highly controllable. However, in the special economic and biological field the more interesting aspect is that these systems are only partially controllable if at all. This observation has given rise to the distinction between design and control complexity.

The level of controllability is really what matters in dealing with complex systems, and its relationship to complexity is not sufficiently well understood. A case in point is provided by our experience with the behavior of economic systems.

The fact that our economic system has responded to attempts to control it in surprising and unexpected ways has often been offered as an illustration that complex systems are counterintuitive. What does such a statement mean? It means simply that those intuitions regarding system behavior which we presently possess were formed on systems which are in some way simple, and that properties of these simple systems do not generalize in any obvious way (Rosen [19]).

One of the problems correlated with the level of controllability in complex systems is that of adaptability. In economics it has been widely presupposed as a kind of fact. All classical models of the competitive economy have assumed this built-in-process of adaptability. Of course, one may argue that these models have been derived from idealistic or simplistic assumptions, somewhat abstracted from the real world; however, they have often been chosen for policy recommendations. These recommendations are based naively on the assumption that the model is only an image of a real system and therefore that the basic properties of the system are simply preserved by the model which has more than once been contradicted in particular cases. Again this suggests that a real system basically differs in a qualitative way from any simplifying model attempting to describe it.

Of course, it would not be at all satisfactory to replace 'complexity' by some other more restrictive notions such as largeness, size, multi-dimensionality. Part of the problem is that complexity is not merely a quantitative property but foremost a qualitative one. Rather frequently complexity has been approached by putting models in simplistic terms, that is attempting to approximate the behavior of real systems by structuring the model in interconnected parts that seemed natural in a particular context. For example, hierarchical structuring has been used as a natural device to simulate the behavior of such systems (see H.A. Simon [23]). However, there may be many forms of hierarchical structuring; and what is necessary here is to find a decomposition of the system that takes care of its intrinsic complexity. There are certain observations that may help to detect when systems act in a way that is not sufficiently well understood, even being counterintuitive, and where a lack of predictability regarding the system's behavior arises. Of course, a system is never universally complex, a system may be complex in some respect (in some critical situation) but not in others, or it is complex if it is used for certain goals but not for others.

The problem of complexity is a scientific and intellectual challenge by its own, but one which has been neglected in the past. Rather there has been the customary attitude that complex processes could be understood in terms of simple underlying universal laws derived from comparatively simple model constructions of real systems. True, complexity has been approached in model building in various ways, e.g., by increasing the number of equations and/for variables and/or constraints as in mathematical programming or large-scale system theory, or by randomization in probabilistic modelling of large systems. However, the point is that complexity has always been handled in terms of increasing the dimension of the model, in a strict quantitative fashion, while hardly anything has been contributed to its qualitative-structural aspect. We cannot expect that the behavior of a small scale system is qualitatively the same as that of a large scale system. This is what von Neumann [14] presumably had in mind when he argued that there is a kind of 'threshold' of complexity below which the world behaves with its familiar regularities, but above which entirely new models of behavior appear (such as self-reproduction, evaluation and free will) which are *sui generis* with no counterparts in systems of lesser complexity. This idea has been further pursued with respect to socio-economic systems by P.S. Albin [27] on the basis of cellular automata theory.

For design purposes of a system we distinguish between *structural* and *computational* complexity. The first roughly indicates the complexity of the subsystems that hooked together (in a particular way to be explained) realize the entire system. The latter means the computational length that is required by (inter-) connecting subsystems to realize the entire system. (see Figure 1.) For conceptual purposes it would appear best to keep these two notions apart, in practice, however, one would like to be able to measure both characterizations of complexity simultaneously.

Another kind of complexity may occur when modelling FCS, namely if we assume linear relationships although nonlinearities are really present, or if certain states are assumed to be unconstrained although they are really constrained. Ignorance of these facts produces another source of error that is reflected in a lower level of control complexity. This kind

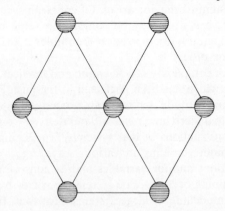

Fig. 1. The links represent computational, the circles structural complexity.

of complexity can also be treated within our system. It is demonstrated in our 'simulation process'. In the course of this process, if 'hooking together' does not realize the black box in any approximate way, then it is likely that we underrated the length of computations, or computational complexity. But non-linearities as compared to linerarities have the effect of increasing the length of computations. By changing the parameters to be computed we could increase the length of computations to such an extent that a satisfactory simulation procedure now becomes possible.

Our ideas of realizing a given real system by any appropriately structured artificial system corresponds to what G. Brewer [4] must have in mind when he speaks of increasing the analytic complexity of a model to cope with the complexity of the real system. His analytic complexity, in fact, plays the same role as our *control* complexity, whereas his empirical complexity is much akin to our *design* complexity. With respect to analytic complexity Brewer [4], p. 32 says:

One loses control. Confidence in the symbol system's structure decreases, as the number of elements, interconnections, relationships and measurement errors increases ... At some level of size for a given model we decidedly lose the ability to make structural revisions, i.e. to improve the model theoretically.

The time seems ripe for a mathematical theory of complexity being an intrinsic property of a dynamic system preserving the intuitive meaning of complexity in approaching real systems. Such a mathematical theory of complexity should obtain a similar status as probability theory. Whereas probability can be conceived as a measure of uncertainty, complexity can be considered as a measure of the level of understanding toward system behavior. The usefulness of this view can be demonstrated in discussing properties of dynamic systems.

Before discussing some difficulties arising in the handling of complex systems, we will briefly sketch three different types of approaches indicating avenues of research in dealing with FCS.

We may refer to these approaches as:
– the control-theoretic multilevel approach;
– the design-oriented algebraic approach;
– models using catastrophe theory.

While not mutually exclusive, they exhibit different philosophies on modelling and controlling complex systems. We shall also see that these approaches interact in very interesting ways.

1.4 MULTI-LEVEL SYSTEM AND CONTROL

The problem of optimal control of an object, 'black-box', machine, organization, or in general of any decision system, may be described as follows: the decision-maker is given the dynamic equations (differential or difference equations) characterizing the trajectory of the system, a set of permissible (feasible) controls, a set of observable data on the past and present states of the system's input-output structure and on the past history of the control actions. Given the information structure, a control action is selected out of the feasible controls in such a way as to minimize some index of performance (usually measured in terms of the cost of the system). Both the control and the observation mechanism may be subject to random disturbances and to the extent that those disturbances are statistically known or have to be estimated by some prior knowledge it may add further complications to the control task of the system.

The more general situation confronting the control system designer is this: he is given the equations of motion of the system, a set of unknown states of nature, an observation vector, and a performance index (a cost functional). This information, however, is not sufficient to enable him to choose an optimal control rule. If he had a priori information on the relative probability of the states of nature, he would seek to find the Bayes policy with respect to some prior judgment of the states. Without such information the problem is more complex. If we are very pessimistic we will assume that the system's response to unspecified parameter changes will cause a maximum of the performance measure. Then it is natural to investigate *minimax control rules*. The minimax policy especially applies to systems for which there is little a priori information. However, there are certain difficulties connected with this approach. First of all, a minimax approach destroys the (intuitively plausible) view that nature is somewhat neutral, e.g. is an indifferent and non-active agent. So why should nature act in such a way that it chooses a set of parameters which makes it most difficult for the controller's task. This lends itself to a kind of extreme pessimism on the side of the controller for which there may be no rational justification, and hence will be completely arbitrary.

In connection with this there is a second difficulty, not to be neglected: a minimax policy does not make use of any information at all. This, in fact, contradicts the Bayesian approach, and also violates the intuitively acceptable view that at least some vague prior information is available. At that point the control task and the system description may be formid-

able in view of random disturbances, even if it is still concerned with
relatively simplistic models. Realistic models are awfully complex. They
would involve the treatment of several controllers with limited and different information, and the control problem would be tremendously complicated because the interactions of the controls have to be taken into
account. If we (realistically) consider large-scale problems then the complexity of the problem may become computationally infeasible, and
therefore one has to deal with structural principles facilitating the control task. Hierarchical decompositions of large-scale systems may improve our ability to cope computationally with such problems. H.A.
Simon, in his 'Architecture of Complexity' [23] argues:

The fact ... that many complex systems have a nearly decomposable, hierarchic structure
is a major facilitating factor enabling us to understand, to describe, and even to see such
systems and their parts ... If there are important systems in the world which are complex
without being hierarchic, they may to a considerable extent escape our observation and
understanding.

In fact, the concepts of 'hierarchy' and of 'complexity' seem to be intimately connected and this relationship lends itself to intuitive understanding
in structuring large-scale systems. One natural way, then, to describe
a complex object, is to structure (decompose, partition) it appropriately.
    It is assumed that the system consists of a number of interacting sub-
systems each of which is under the control of one agent. The subsystems
are arranged in a hierarchy of levels. The subsystem(s) of each level communicates with several subsystems of the lower level and with one subsystem of the higher level. The design of stratification into levels is not
arbitrary. It is implied that the agents at different levels perform different
'tasks' or 'functions', described by the sequence planning-coordination-
control along the hierarchical ladder. The agents at the lowest level
perform routine-type control tasks while those above are assigned co-
ordination and strategic decision tasks.
    In a static context, structured programming and decomposition
methods of allocation systems using linear and non-linear programming
methods may serve as examples among many others. Most recently,
control theorists, having been overly concerned with the single controller-
centralized information case of the control problem, now have given
much thought to multi-person, decentralized (multi-level) control problems, which, they claim, ideally fit control problems of large-scale systems.
This looks like a marriage between control theory and organizational

theory (for example, 'the theory of teams' Marschak and Radner [12], Gottinger [6]). The introduction of an organizational design into the control problem adds realism to control-theoretic work as applied to economic or social problems. One critical point with this approach is that much information is needed on the local control level which, in general, is lacking in complex systems. This effect is mitigated but not excluded by using stochastic controls.

Another point is that there are no design philosophies of hierarchical forms which indicate that they could successfully cope with complexity – except for those which use historical analogs of bureaucratic organizations and those which relate to pattern recognition devices (see H. Simon [23], Minsky and Papert [13]). A more general theory of designs is needed and is presented in the next section.

1.5 DESIGN AND ALGEBRAIC SYSTEMS

Unfortunately, there has been a split in system theory in terms of the use of different mathematical tools. Discrete-time dynamic systems use algebraic techniques (those originating in abstract group theory, homological algebra, category theory) and much of automata theory is of that sort. Continuous-time dynamic systems are firmly embedded in analysis involving properties of continuity, differentiability, convergence, etc. Much of control theory is closely linked to the latter properties. On the other hand, many of the computational techniques such as dynamic programming are more closely related to the algebraicization of systems. A more unified view seems to be necessary.

The design-oriented algebraic approach starts with the basic identification problem. Given some natural complex system, a black box, where we only observe inputs, outputs and internal states over time but are ignorant about what is happening 'inside', e.g. about local properties or parameters of transition. Is it possible to find an 'artificial' system that simulates the original natural system. Systems we have in mind in this context are those which respond in real time to their environments just to stay alive (a bull fighting a bear). Ecological systems (bird colonies) or biological systems (metabolism of cells) constitute systems striving for survival; furthermore all types of competitive economic systems challenged by adverse environments belong to this category. In general, extreme notions, such as survival or non-survival (death), which are characteristic for pure forms of competitive systems are involved. Here interest is focused on global properties of dynamic systems. The design orientation follows from the identification process, e.g. by taking interconnecting parts of the artificial system, 'hooking' them together in order to simulate the 'black box'. The approach is algebraic, since it starts from finite-state dynamic systems, e.g. sequential machines, the general characteristics of which are described by:

1. *A set of inputs*, e.g. those changing parameters of the environment which will affect the system behavior in a predictable way.

2. *A set of outputs*, i.e. those parameters which act upon the environment leaving observable changes in the relationship between the system and the environment.

3. *A set of states*, i.e. those internal parameters which determine the relationship between inputs and outputs and which may reveal all necessary information embodied in the past.

4. *The state transition* function which determines the dynamics of how the state will change when the system is fed by various inputs.

5. *The output function* which determines what output the system will yield with a given input when in a given state.

Given these elements, a sequential machine is a function $f : \sum A \to B$ which maps a string of inputs $(a_1, \ldots, a_n)$ in $\sum A$ into single outputs $b_1, \ldots, b_n$ in B. Let then f be such a machine, then 'knowing the structure of the machine' means that we know f, e.g. that we can compute f. If we don't know f we first have to deal with the problem of identification of the system, i.e. we have to perform certain Gedanken experiments on sequential machines. In fact, this means we have to build a new system $f' : \sum A \to B$ where, in this case, f' is known and reveals the same input, output and state structure. In case of an inanimate (natural, humanistic) system, such as an economic or social system, this can be achieved by constructing an artificial system and simulating on that system in such a way that we approximate the input-output configurations as observed in the former system (see Figure 2). This is essentially the difference between normative system theory in which the design problem is basic, knowing f, and descriptive system theory, where f is not known or not observable and we simulate to approximate f.

There are some obvious advantages, theoretical and practical ones, to using an algebraic approach. *First*, algebra is a natural tool because it emphasizes the design of a system as a collection of objects – very similar to the formation of algebraic structures, by constructing new objects from given objects via algebraic operations. These operations again have an

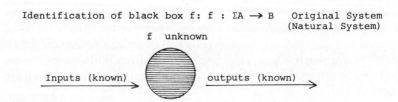

Identification of black box f: f : $\Sigma A \rightarrow B$ Original System
(Natural System)

f   unknown

Inputs (known)   outputs (known)

Simulation System
(Artificial System) f': $\Sigma A \rightarrow B$

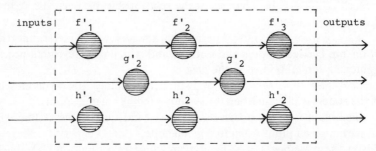

inputs | f'$_1$ f'$_2$ f'$_3$ | outputs

        g'$_2$ g'$_2$

        h'$_1$ h'$_2$ h'$_2$

f'$_1$,f'$_2$,f'$_3$,g'$_1$,g'$_2$,h'$_1$,h'$_2$,h'$_3$ known or partially known.

Representation: f'$_1 \otimes$ f'$_2 \otimes$ f'$_3 \oplus$ g'$_1 \otimes$ g'$_2 \oplus$ h'$_1 \otimes$ h'$_2 \otimes$ h'$_3$

by serial-parallel decomposition = f :$\Sigma A \rightarrow$ B

$\oplus$ = 'hooked in parallel',

$\otimes$ = 'hooked in serial'.

Fig. 2. Explanation: If with the given input configuration f' generates the same values of
state-output pairs as f, then f' 'simulates' f.

immediate intuitive appeal and significance in the design of systems such as
composition, partition, order (replacement). A good example is the *equivalence of an empirical object, such as a machine, and an algebraic object, such as a semigroup of transformations.* In fact, the equivalence is so natural
that any biological, ecological or economic system evolving in time can be
viewed as a transformation semigroup (tsg) in which time is an irreversible resource. (Some authors even went so far as to consider the tsg and
the associated notion of a machine as the key mathematical notions of this
century). *Second,* algebra is natural for computational work, and this is
an important factor in applications. Modern computers accept digital
instructions and those in turn require an algebraicization of systems.

Third, algebra is intuitively appealing, it starts with very simple structures for which common sense justification can be given, also it avoids requiring too much, for example, differentiability and continuity contain some idealization for which empirical justification may be hard to find. *Fourth,* algebraic system theory emphasizes qualitative aspects of systems to the extent that *we are interested in properties such as survival or break-down.* This is achieved by determining complexity bounds of the system's design (design complexity). By the fact that algebraic system theory is related to computational structures we are in the position to construct a complexity theory for dynamic systems which is also amenable to applications.

Systems of that sort reveal a natural bound of complexity. Complexity here has two facets, computational complexity and structural complexity.

Structural complexity refers to the inherent capability of parts of the system as to what they are able to perform. Computational complexity refers to the length of computation given by the extent of interconnection. The most important distinction is that between *design* and *control* complexity.

By 'design complexity' is understood that complexity (number) associated with the transformation process in which full use of the system potential is made. Design complexity can only be achieved if a system is working without faults, if the components live up to computability requirements, and if the parts function reliably. Under control complexity we understand that specific complexity number which keeps the entire system or at least part of it under complete control. Only if design and control complexity coincide will stable configurations in the state and output space result, or the system run smoothly. The relation between design and control complexity is an indication for stability or harmony of a dynamic system.

EXAMPLE. Divide a cell into two parts – Metabolism (M) and Genetic Control (G) – both of which are finite-state machines interacting with each other. One way to consider the interaction within a cell is as follows: G is attempting to control M where G samples the output of M and then puts a correction input into M. If G does it according to the design complexity then stable configurations will result, and design and control complexity coincide. On the other hand, if G commits serious errors, the evolution complexity will diverge and possibly a breakdown cannot be avoided.

In contrast to the design complexity, that is the complexity of the maximal potential of a system's design, we introduce '*control complexity*' as that particular complexity which yields all stable configurations under complete control of the system's evolution. The relationship between design and control complexity is called *evolution complexity*. From the knowledge of evolution complexity some conclusions can be drawn about the controllability of systems that are rooted in 'technological' or 'behavioristic' approaches to public policy (see Chap. 4 for elaboration).

EXAMPLE. A public policy problem that can be treated in this dynamic system framework is the 'management of the commons'. The example of the 'tragedy of the commons' (G. Hardin) corresponds to the case of a 'common property resource', as treated in economics, for which no rent is charged and to which everyone has free access. If everyone has the right to fish in any river or lake, and pays no fee for this right, the river and lake will be overfished and the common property resource will be run down. Similarly, if anyone can swim at a beach, free of charge, there will be overcrowding; if anyone can use a freeway without paying for the facility of using it, there will be congestion of the freeways.

By modelling this dynamic competitive situation as a dynamic system we find out that such systems are bound to break down if not properly designed or controlled.

A switch to a different design, for example, could involve the introduction of property rights for all participants to the effect that competitive behavior will bring the problems of externalities into appropriate balance. Instead of property rights one may design different disincentive schemes to lower the design complexity of the system such that the private decision of maximizing profit would be compatible with the socially optimal decision. On the other hand, a switch to a different control would involve, for example, a suitable limited access scheme or other regulatory devices via the price system that would induce a wise use of the common property resource. This effectively limits competition in order to husband common resources. Examples of this kind abound, they relate to limitation of professional or vocational activities, and regulatory devices in urban and traffic systems.

This gives rise to certain public policy options, in particular with respect to the following problem sets:

(1) Under which conditions can *qualitative global stability* of an economic system be achieved by explicitly taking into account non-renewable, limited substitutable resources and increasing environmental limitations?

(2) Does it make sense to talk about *structural stability or instability* of subsystems as in the case of increasing urban density and related environmental and infrastructural limitations in cities or other highly populated regions?

(3) Which *endogeneous* or *exogeneous* control mechanisms exist to achieve and maintain stable configurations in the global or local system dynamics?

Now, what is the structure of the model? We wish to indicate the nature of interdependence in societal systems, to show how systems might be decomposed into their component parts for analytic purposes and to relate the results to the choice of models in policy analysis and projection. According to what has been outlined previously we choose a kind of partition of the overall system into parts that comprise the main activities of complex societal systems. These are listed as follows:

PoP	–	Population Subsystem
E	–	Energy Subsystem
ECO	–	ECO– and Environmental Subsystem
EC	–	Economic Subsystem
G	–	Government Subsystem
P	–	Political Subsystem

The basic construction of the entire model can be schematically presented as in Figure 3.

Description of Figure 3: Each part enclosed in dotted lines is itself an automaton, called a component. The interaction of all components with feedbacks constitutes the realization of the entire system. The transformations relating to each component are each described by a set of structural equations taking into account input or feedback stimuli from other components. Each stimulus for a component is composed of an external stimulus together with all state-output configurations of all previous components plus the feedback responses of all subsequent components. The overall design complexity of the system is given by the structural complexity of the components and the computational complexity of interaction between components, the length of computational strings to arrive at solutions. The control complexity is that kind of complexity that satisfies some bounds in the performance boxes in order to keep the system in harmony or stability.

Summarizing, we can treat in this framework the following major aspects as represented in Chapters 3 and 4.

(1) Application of dynamic (algebraic) system theory for the derivation of global trajectories (of advanced economies) by explicit consideration of environmental, energy and urbanization factors that act exogeneously on the evolution of the system.

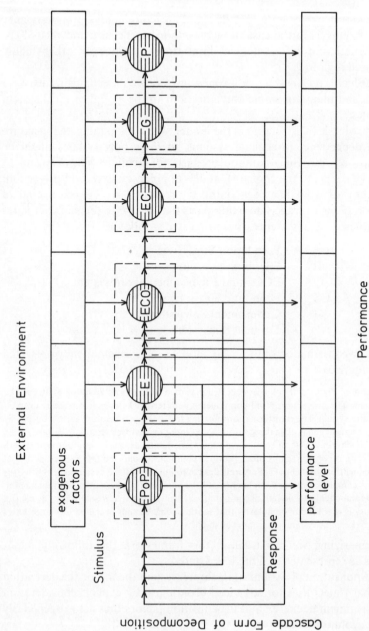

Fig. 3.

(2) Particular interest is focussed on qualitative properties of dynamic systems, e.g. by determining evolution complexity relations that indicate global stability or instability in the overall system's evolutionary performance.

(3) Problems of exhaustion of resources, of environmental limitations, of urbanization and migration, and of technology endowment can be introduced as structural constraints into various system models. Possible system transformations under varying parameter specifications will be computed. A simulation study is proposed.

(4) Stability problems of system's behavior for a sufficiently long time period could be discussed – using comprehensive data bases. Limitations imposed by institutional factors, behavioral patterns of social and economic forces, externalities and technological interdependences as well as legal controls will be taken into account.

(5) An algorithm is to be developed checking the degree of adaptability of sequential state-output processes.

There appear to be interesting ties between the design-oriented algebraic approach and the control-theoretic, multi-level approach.

For many years automata theory and control theory have developed quite separately, the main reason for this lies in the different mathematical tools which both theories have used. M. Arbib [1] deserves credit for having shown that there is a natural connection between automata and control theory. From the point of view of automata theory this enables us to add a new dimension. Controllability in terms of automata theory means that the state transition can be reversed. In this context we could speak of duality between the time-directed dynamics of a system and its counter clockwise directed control, revealing a dualism between automata and control theory. That is to say, controllability requires that it is always possible to find a control input that brings the system back into its zero state. This is an extreme notion of controllability and puts too much restriction on a potential use of controls in dynamic algebraic systems. However, the notion can be relativized by only applying 'local' controls, i.e. by modifying the above definition in such a way that the control(s) reset the transition to its present state.

The gap between automata and control theory, e.g. continuity, can be bridged by introducing the concept of a tolerance automaton (see Arbib). In this case the optimal control problem can be stated for automata with explicit reference to a performance index in terms of a cost function.

1.6 MODELS USING CATASTROPHE THEORY

Another approach which tries to analyze complex systems is provided by catastrophe theory. The underlying idea is that complex systems appear to be globally rigid but locally vague. This stems from the fact that an external observer knows very little about local interactions of systems components and that the global consequences of these postulates are then forced upon the system by the local dynamics. The conclusion therefore is that at the present stage we can only hope for a global understanding of systems behavior and this requires different mathematical tools rooted in differential topology.

The features which occur in such systems may be described first by discontinuity and divergence, i.e. that there is a sudden sharp change (jump) of the phase transition leading to a 'qualitatively' different behavior that may occur if a certain 'threshold' is reached or a certain bound is violated. This type of behavior gives rise to catastrophes. Second, there is an overwhelming interest for 'structurally stable' systems, i.e. those systems which under small perturbations conserve 'stability', and all such systems uniquely determined up to diffeomorphism are equivalent.

A mathematical theory of 'catastrophes' has been developed by R. Thom [25]; a survey of applications, in particular in the social science context, has been provided by Isnard and Zeeman [11], Beer and Casti [2]. Before discussing some aspects of Thom's work intrinsically related to complexity in dynamic systems we give a brief, mostly intuitive description of catastrophe theory.

We are seeking a simple way to describe a dynamic system that exhibits fast falls and slow recoveries. According to Thom's classification theorem, the simplest such system is described by the *cusp catastrophe*. Simplest means that the number of *slow* variables is as small as possible: the cusp catastrophe requires two slow variables. A consequence of Thom's theorem is that the cusp catastrophe is the unique description of 'fast fall-slow recovery' if we limit the number of slow variables to two. Let us consider a state variable z which evolves according to a differential equation parameterized by two slow variables, a and b:

$$\dot{z} = f(z, a, b)$$

The variables a and b also evolve but their motion will be described later.

Consider the short-run equilibrium set,

$$M = \{(z, a, b) \text{ in } R^3 : f(z, a, b) = 0\}$$

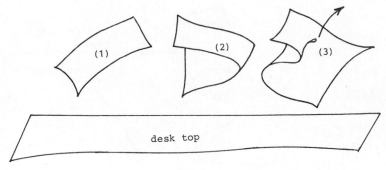

Fig. 4.

This is generically a two dimensional manifold that sits over R^2, and one could consider the projection map from M to R^2. The way in which M sits over R^2 may be globally very complicated, imagine, for example, a crumbled piece of paper sitting on a desk top.

Locally, however, the structure is extremely simple. According to Whitney's classification theorem it can be shown that generically the only possibilities are the projection from M to R^2 to be regular, a fold or a cusp, as presented in Figure 4.

The fold is just a two dimensional generalization of the fold catastrophe. The cusp is the point where a fold disappears. In suitable coordinates the cusp catastrophe can be described by

$$M = \{(z, a, b) \text{ in } R^3 : z^3 + az + b = 0\}.$$

Here the origin in R^3 is the actual cusp point.

The fold lines in (a, b) space are given by $\{(a, b) \text{ in } R^2 : 4a^3 + 27b^2 = 0\}$. We will call the region bounded by these fold lines the cusp, see Figure 5. Inside the cusp, the manifold is three-sheeted. As b gets large or small in absolute value, we move outside the cusp region and M becomes one-sheeted. As a gets small we also move outside the cusp region.

If we regard M as being the short-run equilibrium set of a dynamic system $\dot{z} = f(z, a, b)$ it is not too hard to see that the upper and lower sheets of M represent points of stable short-run equilibria while the middle sheet represents points of unstable equilibria.

Now how does the combination of fast and slow dynamics work to give fast falls and slow recoveries?

Suppose, as in the Figure, the long-run equilibrium of the system is

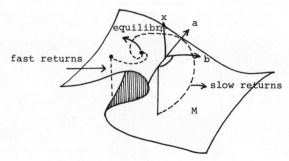

The Cusp Catastrophe

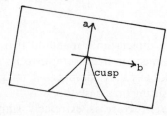

Fig. 5.

given by (z^*, a^*, b^*) and is located on the upper sheet of M. If we perturb the state of the system to the fold, we will 'drop off the edge' and move rapidly to the lower sheet. Now there are two ways to return to the upper sheet, which way the system moves depends on the slow dynamics for a and b. If b adjusts quickly relative to a, we find that b declines until we reach the lower fold and we hop quickly back to the upper leaf. This is just a two-dimensional version of the fold catastrophe which is one-dimensional. However, the cusp catastrophe allows for another possibility. If a adjusts quickly relative to b, the state of the system may have to move all the way around the cusp in order to return to the upper leaf. It is in this sense that the cusp catastrophe allows for fast falls and slow recoveries.

Example of a Cusp Catastrophe

An example of a cusp catastrophe, addressed to conflict theory, is derived from Isnard and Zeeman [11]. For this purpose, let a and b represent horizontal control axes, interpreted as 'threat' and 'cost', respectively, and let z be the behavior mode, e.g. military action.

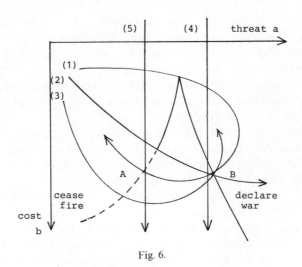

Fig. 6.

Consider the problem what happens under varying conditions of cost and threat upon a population whose government considers various combinations of 'hawk-dove' policy options, as displayed in Figure 6.

Option (1): A nation with plenty of resources feels increasingly threatened and, unified, gradually moves into moderate action. The resulting cost escalates, and as a consequence the action too gradually escalates. The threat subsides, and as a result opinion becomes divided between doves and hawks, but the government's policy is caught entrenched in the hawk opinion, and delays until *A* before making the (catastrophic) decision to withdraw, after which the cost subsides.

Option (2): A nation with more limited resources feels a similar increasing threat, but at the same time feels the escalating cost of military preparedness, and so delays any action until *B*, when it (catastrophically) declares war.

Option (3): A nation initially finds the cost of war prohibitive, but subsequently, due perhaps to the development or purchase of new weapon systems, may find that war becomes feasible. Therefore, to its enemy's surprise, it may suddenly declare war in the middle of a stable period of constant threat. This is called the *surprise reversal* phenomenon.

Options (4) and (5): Two nations confront each other, and, both feeling threatened, start a costly arms race. As a result opinion in both nations splits between 'hawks' and 'doves'.

Although they may both start in moderately hostile moods that are very close, in one nation the hawks prevail, because path (4) passes just to the right of the cusp, and so this administration gradually adopts a more aggressive stand. Meanwhile in the other nation the doves prevail, because (5) passes just to the left of the cusp, and the government gradually adopts an appeasement stand. Both changes are smooth, and this illustrates the phenomenon of divergence.

There exists an interesting interrelationship of 'growth' and 'form' in dynamic systems, and there is a possible interface between our approach (as described in the previous section) and Thom's theory of catastrophe. One of the main problems here is to relate discrete descriptions of the 'form' (via transformation semigroups: tsg) to differentiable models of the form (taken as point of departure by catastrophe theory). If we use it in the context of finite state machines, the form is generated by basic configurations of the states being transformed by a tsg, the tsg itself carries the dynamics of the process, being irreversible, generating growth or contraction and therefore changing the form.

On the other hand, one could describe the form analytically by referring to its geometric shape, its spatial structure (of elements contained in the form), and in terms of distance: this would be best achieved by constructing a topology of the form. The dynamic applied to this form is a differentiable dynamic (e.g. a gradient system) that irreversibly acts in carrying one topology of the form into another, and therefore produces changes of the form. This is very much in the spirit of catastrophe theory.

In the algebraic context, the complexity of the form does not apply directly to the form itself but to the machine that generates this form, i.e. the complexity of the associated tsg.

A catastrophe theory in state-space is in general a differentiable manifold or at least a finite dimensional manifold The corresponding dynamic is provided by a first-order ordinary differential equation on the manifold of states.

R. Thom [25, Chap. 7.2] talks about the topological complexity of a form that is measured by a metric between two forms, connected to each other by a differentiable path. One starts with a form that is topologically the most simple (ground form). The transformation from this form to a new form is measured in terms of a topological distance (the dimension), and constitutes the 'additional' complexity of the new form, more properly called *differential* complexity. He relates topological complexity to entropy in the sense that a system with high entropy is also a system of high topological complexity, and therefore is more sensitive to perturbations or disturbances. Thus the problem of complexity is discussed by Thom, though not in all details, as it appears to be embedded in the fundamental problem of theoretical biology (e.g. morphogenesis, or bio-dynamics), and the mathematical theory of topology. In the algebraic theory of dynamics, in contrast, complexity appears to be a natural outcome and is a crucial factor – determining control, adaptation, survival and breakdown of such systems. One of the most serious practical problems, I see, in applying catastrophe theory to FCS is that it is apparently not amenable to large-scale computation. This is more likely to be achieved by algebraic system models because of their intrinsic relation to computer systems.

1.7 ASPECTS OF FCS MODELLING

As indicated in the previous section(s) there has been a prejudice of mathematical modellers for the 'continuous', which finds its source in their preoccupation with infinitely large systems. One can caricature the situation as follows:

You start with a problem that is clearly discrete. The real system you wish to model has a finite number of parts, with a finite number of connections (links). You are dealing with a finite amount of time (finite horizon), the dynamics is in finite discrete time involving discrete stages.

However, you are so used or conditioned to working with continuous models ('continuity is elegance'), and, therefore, you pretend that you have a continuous model – to 'abstract from reality since you believe this is what modelling is all about' – and finally you come up with a very lovely partial differential equation (system). At this point, you, the model builder, are very happy, and you consult your colleague who is an expert on solving partial differential equations. Your colleague will look at the equation and say, of course, this cannot be solved in closed form. Therefore he opens his tool-box and picks up his great tool, which is to approximate the continuous equation by a nice discrete model, and he then goes and solves it on a computer. If someone happens to be there during the entire process, there are two things that would be disturbing. One disturbing observation is that the discrete model we end up with has significant differences from the discrete model problem (of the real system) we started with. And second it is not entirely clear in many of these applications how we were helped by the fact that we went through the stage of forming continuous equations.

Here again we observe that tools of 'infinite analysis' will not help in dealing with FCS. An example of that kind, but a more sophisticated one than the previous caricature suggests, is provided by equilibrium analysis in mathematical economies (see W. Hildenbrand [9]) which makes extensive use of measure theory and topology to derive equilibrium properties of an economic system.

Equilibrium properties, however, could be shown to be equivalent to the existence of fixed points in economic systems. Unfortunately, with the tools used such points cannot be computed. To compute such fixed points one has to retreat to digitalization, discretization and approximation, e.g. devising efficient combinatorial-algebraic algorithms. For approximation of such fixed points the innovating tools of H. Scarf [21] can be used relating to mathematical programming. But even then, it is still open to question whether the derivation of fixed points for very large systems of 'intermediate complexity' is more than of conceptual value (a mathematical exercise), since the complexity of such systems may well be beyond reasonable computation, as should be verified within an algebraic theory of complexity (see the previous section).

The second frequent prejudice which is worth discussing, but is often overlooked, is the long-standing tradition in mathematical modelling to come out with exact or optimal solutions. This point is very common in computing optimal controls in many complex control problems. As we know, H.A. Simon argued from a different angle against optimality programs, which are in his view behavioristically too restrictive and do not take into account the human's limited computational ability ('bounded rationality'). Part of the problem is that mathematicians tend to be 'lazy' and strive for optimality because it is most convenient for them. But there are good reasons *not* to follow their advice when analyzing complex humanistic systems. The use of the computer supports this view. If one has a good deal of practical experience with computers and has been finding out the difference between doing things in principle and doing them in practice, one discovers that the difference between an optimal solution and an outstandingly good solution can be one or two orders of magnitude in difficulty and in time. Here one is reminded to stop if the expected increase in accuracy is by far overcompensated by the expected increase of computational costs of time involved. In many practical situations of any significance one may come out with the conclusion that 'optimal stopping' is in violation to the rule of 'stopping at the optimal solution'.

This point of criticism, of course, has nothing to do with the valid argument that, in general, we must come up to prove that the solution is optimal. But in many complex systems, in particular in social science applications, we often do not know what the optimum is like or we do not bother to find the optimum because of exponentially increasing computational costs. In these problems, all we hope for is that we might with a reasonable amount of effort come up with an order of magnitude improvement. One should not wait until we can substitute for this an exact or optimal solution. Here we could establish a link to 'allocation of effort' models (see Radner and Rothschild [15]); that is to say, in modelling complex systems and finding feasible control strategies we should economically allocate our effort on computational activities that satisfy our needs most, given our 'effort budget'. In many instances, it is sufficient to improve but not to optimize.

1.8 COMPUTER MODELS AND MAN MACHINE INTERACTION

To what extent can computer models be of any use in describing complex social or economic behavior? In which sense is the word 'complex model' used? Why does it constitute an advantage over a fancy mathematical model that requires optimal, exact analytical solutions?

We should be reminded first that computer models are related to discrete systems requiring algebraic tools (those we encounter in automata theory, for example) rather than to continuous systems (firmly embedded in analysis involving properties of continuity, differentiability, convergence, etc.). Much of control theory invokes the latter properties.

Several stages in building a computer model will be involved. At some stage a model may have some sort of small physical system, at some later stage it may have been a verbal description of that system, and at a still later – and hopefully more advanced – stage, it may have consisted of mathematical equations that somehow described the behavior of the system. In this sense, we have to accept certain types of computer codes as models: and this is not even an extension of the way the word model has been traditionally used. However, using computer codes has one very obvious advantage: namely, that they are written in terms of a very simple language – which may be the new universal language of scientists, in particular of social scientists who need a common language to establish a more mature 'social science'.

Learning one of the standard computer languages, whether it is ALGOL, BASIC or FORTRAN, is vastly easier than, say, learning partial differential equations. Equally important, it is much more neutral as to types of mathematical approaches than is any single branch of relevant mathematics. (Of course, computer models are deeply rooted in algebra, but algebra is a most natural tool for designing and describing dynamic systems of 'intermediate complexity').

Moreover, computer codes are a great deal easier to modify than most systems of mathematical equations, and they are very well adapted to the introduction of random processes. The simulation of random processes on computers is quite well understood, and it is much easier to introduce a random process into a computer code than to introduce it into something that is described by a partial differential equation.

There are essentially four points on which one would like to see computer models developed in order to cope successfully with systems of 'intermediate complexity':

(1) As mentioned earlier, one should not try to find exact or optimal solutions to problems, because it may cost one or two orders of magnitude more time and money to come up with an optimal solution to a problem than to come up with something that is simply very good. We should be less fetishists of optimality and more willing to be pragmatic in this transitional phase in social science, and emphasize methods that give significant improvements rather than stick to methods that are known to be optimal.

Incidentally, we cannot resist pointing out that this 'computational program' finds its counterpart in the 'computational program' on behavior rules known as limited or bounded rationality (H.A. Simon [24]), or complexity-bounded search (C. Futia [5], H. W. Gottinger [7]) that in all cases stress *improvement-related* behavior rather than *optimizing* behavior of individual decision-makers or organizations. Such programs are intrinsically related to complexity of systems or decision rules.

(2) On the statistical side, on testing parameter stability or sensitivity, we are too much conditioned by the necessity of applying very complicated and powerful tests of significance to our models, where too much time is spent in checking the significance of what we are doing. This has become quite fashionable in large-scale-computer-based econometric models. The following situation, again caricaturing it, may easily arise in this context. Suppose you are worried about the question of how much effect the random variables had on the model. You are in the process of going through enormously complicated statistical analysis to try to estimate the effect of using a different set of random numbers. Someone may

suggest the 'childish' approach that instead you take the original problem and run it three times (or ten times if you have enough computer power and time available) using different sets of random numbers and simply looking at the results to see if they vary a great deal. If they do, it is clear that it is ridiculous to try to apply very detailed statistical tests. Similar kinds of tests can be applied to the question of the meaningfulness of parameters. One always worries about the fact that in social problems measurement is very difficult, that there is likely to be a very large error in measurement of parameters and of the data you are starting with. A simple-minded approach, but which often helps, is to take a guess as to how far off your data is likely to be and just run several examples of the same model, arbitrarily modifying data by about the right order of magnitude, and see whether the results you come out with are qualitatively different or not. If they are, as is very often the case, then your model is useless. You can then worry about getting better measurements or suggesting models that are not quite as sensitive to differences in the parameters. Despite all well-developed statistical methods that are naturally fit for well-behaved, small-scale models, in computer models one has still very much to rely on heuristic procedures, plausible reasoning and computational tricks to get the overall work done. On applying statistical analysis to computer models very much is based on *on-line* inductive rather than off-line deductive statistical procedures.

(3) To the extent that we developed more powerful and better computer models, we completely understimated the effect of man-machine interaction. Most people who have computer experience today have little or no experience in man–machine interaction. This could have some disastrous effect on implementing computer models or complex systems. Therefore, the third point is that we should stop thinking about building complicated models, which we work on for a long time and then give them to a computer to work on for a hundred hours. This is basically the wrong way to approach computer models. Since we cannot hope to cope with the complexity of FCS, at least for the time being, we should be as flexible as possible and should allow for active intervention at every stage of the computational process.

A computer model should consist of an interaction between a human being and a machine, the machine carrying out the millions or billions of steps of computations that are needed, but it must have frequent and significant interaction with a human being who is an expert in that particular field. In other words, we should depart from off-line computation and enter into on-line computation with a significant degree of man–machine interaction.

There are a number of cases where the programming time can be significantly reduced by man–machine interaction. But, much more important, there are a number of activities which human beings are extremely good at and there are others which they are miserable at explaining to other people. If they cannot explain it to other people they are much worse in explaining it to computers. Why then force the computer to do it? Much of what the *Club of Rome* has done in the past falls under this heading.

The problem today is that most computing systems are run as batch-processing systems, you simply don't have a chance to step in. But this is a purely temporary stage in the development of computers and eventually one would come out with interactive models, so that the scientist can provide the intuition, the value judgement and the decision on how to proceed. In fact, this is just what one is advised to do in Bayesian sequential decision making.

Let's give an oversimplified example that illustrates the point, which is not too far from the Club of Rome philosophy.

You may come up with a computer model where you extrapolate some highly simplified model as to how New York City is going to develop over the next 200 years. Because of some factors you have overlooked, the model does not note that, at the end of year 20, there would have been a revolt in the city with large-scale slaughter if things really went that way. If the modeller could once a year look at how things were going on in his model, he could step in and say: "No, no! At this point something completely different would happen." And he would not have been troubled by the facts that *should* have troubled the Club of Rome.

(4) The fourth and final point is emphasizing the potentials of dual- or multipurpose computer systems that are set up as interactive models.

Let us illustrate this again by means of a simple example, though many examples of this kind could be listed. Suppose again that New York City wanted to get into the act of doing something really intelligent in helping people to get jobs. Instead of having 3,000 employment agencies, each of which has a small fraction of the available jobs listed, each of which has many clerks not particularly trained for the job who have no ideas about the very difficult optimization problems involved of matching human beings with jobs, one could design a large time-sharing computing system for New York, which could operate with the same 3,000 employment agencies but where the agents would simply serve as an interface between the candidates and the machine. The machine could correlate the needs of thousands of individuals which could hopefully do, not an optimal, but a decent job in matching up human beings with job opportunities, where a person from either a very good neighborhood or from a very poor neighborhood would have access to the same list of jobs, and, most importantly, would be judged impartially as to his qualifications. In this way one could collect an immense amount of information on a real-time basis, with other people doing most of the work, as to what the major problems are, where there may be a major mismatch between the needs of the industry and the labor force, in what parts of the city they exist, whether change of the transportation system would help, where new education is needed etc. We could then, for the first time, reach the point where we have at least a chance, without up-setting the institutional structure of the whole system, of getting the kind of detailed, up-to-date data which would make intelligent, rational planning possible.

NOTE

[1] This in the sense that its major propositions can be derived by mathematical means. Being 'mathematical' may be subject to change in the future as mathematics may address itself more to complex problems of a problem-solving variety pertinent to artificial intelligence, for example.

REFERENCES

[1] Arbib, M.A., 'On the Relevance of Abstract Algebra to Control Theory', *Automatica* **5**, 1969.

[2] Beer, S. and Casti, J., 'Investment against Disaster in Large Organizations', *Journ. Oper. Res. Soc.* USA (also RM-75-16, International Institute for Applied Systems Analysis (IIASA), Laxenburg, Austria, 1975).

[3] Bellman, R., 'Mathematical Aspects of the Theory of Systems' Rand P-3031, Rand Corporation, Santa Monica-Ca., 1965.

[4] Brewer, G.D., 'Analysis of Complex Systems. An Experiment and its Implications for Policy Making'. Rand-P-4951, Rand Corporation, Santa Monica, Ca., 1973.

[5] Futia, C., 'The Complexity of Economic Decision Rules', Murray Hill, Bell Laboratories, unpublished report, 1975.

[6] Gottinger, H.W., 'Information in Teams', Rev. *francaise d'automatique, infor. et rech. oper.*, April 1976.

[7] Gottinger, H.W., 'Complexity and Social Decision Rules', *Decision Theory and Social Ethics*, H.W. Gottinger and W. Leinfellner (eds.), D. Reidel, Dordrecht, 1978.

[8] Hartmanis and J.E. Hopcroft, 'An Overview of the Theory of Computational Complexity', *Journ. of the Association for Computing Machinery* **18**, (1971), 444–475.

[9] Hildenbrand, W., *Core and Equilibria of a Large Economy*, Princeton Univ. Press, 1974.

[10] Hurwicz, 'Optimality and Informational Efficiency in Resource Allocation Processes', Ch. 3 in *Mathematical Methods in the Social Sciences*, Stanford Univ. Press, Stanford, Ca., 1959.

[11] Isnard, C.A. and Zeeman, E.C., 'Some Models from Catastrophe Theory in the Social Sciences', in L. Collings (ed.), *Use of Models in the Social Sciences*, Tavistock, London, 1974.

[12] Marschak, J., and Radner, R., *The Economic Theory of Teams*, Yale Univ. Press., New Haven, 1972.

[13] Minsky, M., and Papert, S., *Perceptrons*, M.I.T. Press, Cambridge 1970.

[14] Neumann von, J., 'Probabilistic Logics and the Synthesis of Reliable Organisms from Unreliable Components', in C.E. Shannon (ed.), *Automata Studies*, Princeton Univ. Press, 1969.

[15] Radner, R. and Rothschild, M., 'On the Allocation of Effort', *Journ. of Economic Theory* **10**, (1975), 358–376.

[16] Reiter, S., and Mount, K., 'The Informational Size of Message Spaces', Center for Mathematical Studies in Economics and Management Sciences, Northwestern Univ., Disc. No. 3, June 1972.

[17] Reiter, S., 'Informational Efficiency of Iterative Processes and the Size of Message Spaces', Center for Math. Stud. in Economics and Management Sciences, Northwestern Univ., Disc. No. 2, Oct. 1972.

[18] Reiter, S., 'The Knowledge Revealed by an Allocation Process and the Informational Size of the Message Space', Center for Math. Studies in Economics and Management Sciences, Northwestern Univ., Disc. No. 6, April 1973.

[19] Rosen, R., 'On Biological Systems as Paradigms for Adapation', Center for Theoretical Biology, unpublished Manuscript, 1974.

[20] Rosen, R., 'Complexity and Error in Social Dynamics', *International Journal of General Systems* **1**, (1975).

[21] Scarf, H., *The Computation of Economic Equilibria*, Yale Univ. Press, New Haven 1973.

[22] Schmidbauer, P.L., 'Information and Communications Requirements of the Wheat Market: An Example of a Competitive System', Parts I and II, Center for Research in Management Sciences Univ. of California, Berkeley, TR 21, Jan. 1966.

[23] Simon, H.A., 'The Architecture of Complexity', in *The Sciences of the Artificial*, M.I.T. Press, Cambridge, 1969.

[24] Simon, H.A., 'Bounded Rationality', in C.B. McGuire and R. Radner (eds.), *Decision and Organization*, North-Holland, Amsterdam, 1971.

[25] Thom, R., *Structural Stability and Morphogenesis*, W.A. Benjamin, Reading, Mass., 1975.

[26] Brainerd, W.S. and Landweber, L.H., *Theory of Computation*, Wiley, New York, 1974.

[27] Albin, P.S., *The Analysis of Complexity in Socioeconomic Systems*, D.C. Heath, Boston, 1977.

CHAPTER 2

MATHEMATICS OF MACHINES,
SEMIGROUPS AND COMPLEXITY

2.1 FINITE STATE MACHINES

Consider a large system with many units, each of which may receive messages from other units upon which it immediately acts producing new messages for other units, etc. A legitimate question to ask about such a process is what is its complexity (i.e. the complexity of the overall system)? In other words, what is the number of computations of a 'decision machine' such as a Perceptron [6], such that a decision (action) is made? The word *computation* refers to a special function (transformation), from a message space to an action space, or, from a message space to another (possibly biased or distorted) message space. A computation can be performed unconsciously, without reflection, as in stimulus-response representations.

Communication may be involved when 'information variables' are transmitted between persons or computers. Communication involves computation but not vice versa, for example, if messages are compiled and processed by one person only.

By an *element of a network* we mean a computing unit (a machine that transforms incoming messages into outgoing messages in a well-defined way). Messages from nature are observations, those going into nature are actions. The network itself consists of elements connected to nature and to each other in a logically consistent way. Elements of networks can be considered as microprocessors, i.e., persons, computing machines, departments (of organizations), relay stations, thermostates. These are building blocks from which alternative networks can be constructed, thus they are elements of designs or forms. The further elaboration of these 'primitives' and the construction of an analogy with computing machines is presented in Chapter 7.

A simple model suitable for determining the complexity would involve each unit as a two-state automaton and the economic system as a network of on-off automata. That is, each agent either receives the message as it is delivered to him or he does not receive or does not accept this message. The model, in fact, is taken from M.A. Arbib [2], as a basic model of the brain, where a nerve cell is considered to be a two-state automaton and the brain is a network of 'on-off' neurons. A finite state automaton can be used for modelling a competitive economic or biological system, that is a system that is bound to survive or break down. Notice that in this system only "global" qualitative properties of survival or breakdown are considered and they may substitute for much more restricted notions of classical economics such as equilibrium or disequilibrium. The results of this chapter have a direct bearing on all subsequent chapters.

We restate the definitions of Chapter 1 in the following way.

Let $C_z: A^* \to B$ be the machine configuration (abbreviated machine) given by starting the circuit

$C = (A, B, Z, \lambda, \delta)$ in state $z \in Z$, then C_z is defined inductively in a straight-forward way:

$$\begin{cases} C_z(a_1) = \delta(z, a_1) \\ C_z(a_1, \dots, a_n) = C_{\lambda(z, a_1)}(a_2, \dots, a_n) \text{ for } n \geq 2. \end{cases}$$

A fairly general organizational model of an economy, put in terms of a sequential machine, would be a serial-parallel decomposition of a large finite state automaton $(A, B, Z, \lambda, \delta)$ where each decision-making unit can be identified as a component machine connected in some serial-parallel fashion with other component machines. We call such a decomposition a cross connection (web). The pattern of connection resembles the construction of neural networks where every neuron acts as part of the network and is considered to be a finite-state automaton or a McCulloch-Pitts cell (cf. M. Minsky [6], Chapter 3).

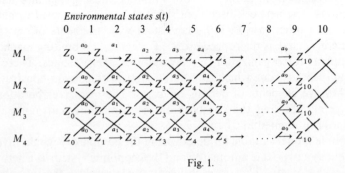

Fig. 1.

The output of any given subsystem affects the other subsystems by a unit time delay, let us assume for simplicity that all subsystems start working simultaneously. The stimulation by inputs (or by change of inputs) from the environment and its resulting generation of actions can be simply described in this network (cross connections).

An input (stimulus) $a(t)$ to Machine 1 (M_1) at time t changes its state by $\lambda_1(z(t), a(t)) = z(t + 1)$ and provides as output $\delta_1(z(t), a(t)) = a(t + 1) = b$. This in turn serves to stimulate M_2 at time $t + 1$ and so on down the line. It also works back the same way. By adopting the convention that the diagram

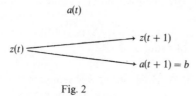

Fig. 2

represents the action of input $a(t)$ upon state $z(t)$ at time t, it is possible to build a matrix representation of the entire system. This matrix representation is illustrated in the network of cross-connection. In addition to the above scheme we may wish to include nature's states explicitly, and therefore split the output in essentially two parts:

$a_1(t + 1) = b_1$ acting on nature, and $a_2(t + 1) = b_2$ acting on some other subsystem (as illustrated below).

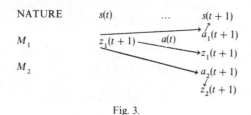

Fig. 3.

2.2 DEFINITIONS AND BOUNDS OF COMPLEXITY

The concept of mathematical complexity was introduced by K. Krohn and J. Rhodes in 1965 [9] as a natural outgrowth of the Krohn–Rhodes Prime Decomposition Theorem for Finite Semigroups and Machines. A survey of results in this field is provided in the present chapter. Some definitions are in order and the notation is borrowed from the first chapter of M.A. Arbib's book [1], another more recent reference source is Eilenberg [4].

DEFINITION 1. Let $f: A^* \to B$ be a machine. Then f^S, the *semigroup of f*, is given by the congruence $\equiv_f$ on A^* where for $t, r \in A^*$, $t \equiv_f r$ if and only if $f(\alpha t \beta) = f(\alpha r \beta)$ for all α, $\beta \in A^* \cup \{1\}$. Then, if $[t]_f$ denotes the equivalence class of the equivalence relation $\equiv_f$ containing t, we have $f^S = \{[t]_f : t \in A^*\}$ and $[t]_f \cdot [r]_f = [tr]_f$ (where tr denotes the product in A^* and $\cdot$ denotes the product in f^S).

DEFINITION 2. A semigroup S is combinatorial if and only if each subgroup of S is of order 1.

DEFINITION 3. A *right mapping semigroup* or *right transformation semigroup* is a pair (X, S), where X is a nonempty set, and S is a subsemigroup of $F_R(X)$ the semigroup of all mappings of X into X under the multiplication $(f \cdot g)(x) = g(f(x))$. For each $x \in X$, $s \in S$, let $xs = (x)s$. Then the following conditions are satisfied:

(1) $x(s_1 s_2) = (x s_1) s_2$.

(2) $s_1 s_2 \in S$ and $s_1 \neq s_2$ imply $x s_1 \neq x s_2$ for some $x \in X$.

DEFINITION 4. (Wreath Product) Let (X_j, S_j) be right mapping semigroups for $j = 1, \ldots, n$. Let $X = X_n \times \cdots \times X_1$. Let S be the subsemigroup of $F_R(X)$ consisting of all functions $\Psi: X \to X$ satisfying the two following conditions:

(1) (triangular action) If $p_k: X \to X_k$ denotes the kth projection map, then for each $k = 1, \ldots, n$ there exists $f_k: X_k \times \cdots \times X_1 \to X_k$ such that

$$p_k \Psi(t_n, \ldots, t_{k+1}, t_k, \ldots, t_1) = f_k(t_k, \ldots, t_1)$$

for all $t_i \in X_i$, $i = 1, \ldots, n$.

(2) (kth component action lies in S_k) We require $f_1 \in S_1$, and for all $k = 2, \ldots, n$ and all $\alpha = (t_{k-1}, \ldots, t_1) \in X_{k-1} \times \cdots \times X_1$, the function $g_\alpha \in F_R(X_k)$ given by $g_\alpha(y_k) = f_k(y_k, t_{k-1}, \ldots, t_1)$ is an element of S_k.

Then $(X_n, S_n) \circ \cdots \circ (X_1, S_1) = (X, S)$ is the *wreath product* of $(X_n, S_n), \ldots, (X_1, S_1)$, and $(X_n, S_n)w \ldots w(X_1, S_1)$ is the abstract semigroup determined by (X, S) (this notation is fully explained in Section 3.3). By definition, $(X_2, S_2) \circ (X_1, S_1) = (X_2 \times X_1, (X_2, S_2)w(X_1, S_1)) \equiv S$, 'w' being the wreath connection.

DEFINITION 5. Let (X, S) and (Y, T) be right mapping semigroups.

Then we write $(X, S)|(Y, T)$, read (X, S) divides (Y, T), if and only if

(1) there exists a subset Y' of Y and a subsemigroup T' of T such that Y' is invariant under the action of T' (i.e., $Y'T' \subseteq Y'$); and

(2) there exists a map $\theta: Y' \twoheadrightarrow X$ ($\twoheadrightarrow$ means onto) and an epimorphism (a one-to-one "onto" map)

$$\phi: T' \twoheadrightarrow S \text{ such that } \theta(yt) = \theta(y)\phi(t) \text{ for all } y \in Y', t \in T'.$$

DEFINITION 6. Finally, let S be a finite semigroup. Then by definition $\#_G(S)$, the (group) *complexity* of S is the smallest nonnegative integer n such that

$$S|(Y_n, C_n)w(X_n, G_n)w \dots w(Y_1, C_1)w(X_1, G_1)w(Y_0, C_0)$$

holds with $G_1, \dots, G_n$ finite groups and $C_0, \dots, C_n$ finite combinatorial semigroups.

It is obvious from the above definition that it would be futile to attempt to find the shortest wreath product representation for $(C'_{z_0})^S$, the semigroup of the machine C'_{z_0}. However, there are upper and lower bounds available which are computable; this is the route which will be taken in this section. But first it is necessary to look at the structure of $(C'_{z_0})^S$. As an example, I want to begin with C_{z_1} (the three-state model) and look at its semigroup in order to pave the way for an analysis of C'_{z_0}.

The elements of $C_{z_1}^S$ are equivalence classes of input strings, but they may be visualized more easily as transformations on the set of states $Z = \{z_1, z_2, z_3\}$. For example, let (131) represent $[(a_1)]C_{z_1}$, the class of inputs which sends z_1 to z_2, z_2 to z_3, and z_3 to z_1. By direct computation it is possible to establish that there are 24 such elements:

(111)	(211)	(311)
(112)	(212)	(312)
(113)	(221)	(313)
(121)	(222)	(322)
(122)	(223)	(323)
(123)	(231)	(331)
(131)	(232)	(332)
(133)	(233)	(333)

Since $C_{z_1}^S$ is a subsemigroup of $F_R(X_3)$, the full transformation semigroup on three letters, no two of these elements belong to the same equivalence class.

Furthermore, it is easy to see why $C_{z_1}^S \neq F_R(X_3)$, for the only elements of $C_{z_1}^S$ with rank three (i.e. taking three states to three different states) are those corresponding to combinations of inputs with rank three. This is because the product (composition) of a transformation of rank n and any other transformation (on either the right or the left) will always be a transformation with rank $\leq n$. So, since a_2 is the only rank-three input and since $C_{z_i}(a_2, a_2, a_2, a_2) = C_{z_i}(a_2)$ for $i = 1, 2, 3$, there are only three rank-three elements of $C_{z_1}^S$: $[(a_2)]C_{z_1} = (231)$, $[(a_2, a_2)]C_{z_1} = (321)$, and $[(a_2, a_2, a_2)]C_{z_1} = 123$.

Now there is an immediate upper bound for $\#_G(C_{z_1}^S)$, since (see [8])

$$\#_G(C_{z_1}^S) \leq |\operatorname{spec}(C_{z_1}^S)| = |\{r > 1 : r = \operatorname{rank}(t) \text{ for some } t \in C_{z_1}^S\}|$$
$$= |\{2, 3\}| = 2.$$

This also follows from the machine inequality

$$\#_G(C_{z_1}^S) = \theta(C_{z_1}) \leq |Z| - 1 = 3 - 1 = 2,$$

where $Z = \{z_1, z_2, z_3\}$.[5]

In order to apply any of the existing lower bounds to $C_{z_1}^S$, something must be known about the local structure of this semigroup. For this purpose it is convenient to define the Green relations:

DEFINITION 7. Let S be a semigroup. An *ideal* is a nonempty subset $I \subseteq S$ such that $IS \subseteq I$ and $SI \subseteq I$ (i.e. for all $i \in I$, $s \in S$, $is \in I$ and $si \in I$). I is a *right* or *left* ideal if the first or second, respectively, of these conditions holds.

For $s \in S$, $L(s) = S^1 s$, $R(s) = sS^1$, and $J(s) = S^1 s S^1$ are, respectively, the *principal left ideal*, *principal right ideal*, and *principal ideal* generated by s. Define binary relations $\mathcal{J}$, $\mathcal{L}$, $\mathcal{R}$, $\mathcal{H}$, and $\mathcal{D}$ on S as follows:

(1) $s_1 \mathcal{J} s_2$ if and only if $J(s_1) = J(s_2)$.
(2) $s_1 \mathcal{L} s_2$ if and only if $L(s_1) = L(s_2)$.
(3) $s_1 \mathcal{R} s_2$ if and only if $R(s_1) = R(s_2)$.
(4) $s_1 \mathcal{H} s_2$ if and only if $s_1 \mathcal{L} s_2$ and $s_1 \mathcal{R} s_2$.
(5) $s_1 \mathcal{D} s_2$. if and only if there exists $s \in S$ such that $s_1 \mathcal{L} s$ and $s \mathcal{R} s_2$ or, equivalently, if and only if there exists $t \in S$ such that $s_1 \mathcal{R} t$ and $t \mathcal{L} s_2$.

$\mathcal{L}, \mathcal{R}, \mathcal{J}$, and $\mathcal{H}$ are equivalence relations on S and L_s, R_s, J_s, and H_s denote the $\mathcal{L}, \mathcal{R}, \mathcal{J}$, and $\mathcal{H}$ equivalence classes, respectively, containing s.

Furthermore, the following orderings are defined on the $\mathcal{J}, \mathcal{R}$, and $\mathcal{L}$ classes of S:

(a) $J_a \leq J_b$ if and only if $J(a) \subseteq J(b)$.

(b) $R_a \leq R_b$ if and only if $R(a) \subseteq R(b)$.
(c) $L_a \leq L_b$ if and only if $L(a) \subseteq L(b)$.

Thus principal left ideals, principal right ideals, and principal ideals of $C_{z_1}^S$ are the following:

(1) principal left ideals:
$L[(111)] = \{(111)\}$
$L[(222)] = \{(222)\}$
$L[(333)] = \{(333)\}$
$L[(112)] = L[(121)] = L[(122)] = L[(211)] = L[(212)] =$
$\quad = L[(221)] = \{(111), (112), (121), (122), (211), (212), (221), (222)\}$
$L[(113)] = L[(131)] = L[(133)] = L[(311)] = L[(313)]$
$\quad = L[(331)] = \{(111), (113), (131), (133), (311),$
$\qquad\qquad (313), (331), (333)\}$
$L[(223)] = L[(232)] = L[(233)] = L[(322)] = L[(323)]$
$\quad = L[(332)] = \{(222), (223), (232), (233), (322),$
$\qquad\qquad (323), (332), 333)\}$
$L[(123)] = L[(231)] = L[(312)] = C_{z_1}^S$

(2) principal right ideals:
$R[(111)] = R[(222)] = R[(333)] = \{(111), (222), (333)\}$
$R[(112)] = R[(113)] = R[(221)] = R[(223)] = R[(331)]$
$\quad = R[(332)] = \{(111), (112), (113), (221), (222),$
$\qquad\qquad (223), (331), (332), (333)\}$
$R[(121)] = R[(131)] = R[(212)] = R[(232)] = R[(313)]$
$\quad = R[(323)] = \{(111), (121), (131), (212), (222),$
$\qquad\qquad (232), (313), (323), (333)\}$
$R[(122)] = R[(133)] = R[(211)] = R[(233)] = R[(311)]$
$\quad = R[(322)] = \{(111), (122), (133), (211), (222),$
$\qquad\qquad (233), (311), (322), (333)\}$
$R[(123)] = R[(231)] = R[(312)] = C_{z_1}^S$

(3) principal ideals:
$J[(111)] = J[(222)] = J[(333)] = \{(111), (222), (333)\}$
$J[(112)] = J[(113)] = J[(121)] = J[(122)] = J[(131)]$
$\quad = J[(133)] = J[(211)] = J[(212)] = J[(221)]$
$\quad = J[(223)] = J[(232)] = J[(233)] = J[(311)]$
$\quad = J[(313)] = J[(322)] = J[(323)] = J[(331)]$
$\quad = J[(332)] = C_{z_1}^S - \{(123), (231), (312)\}$
$J[(123)] = J[(231)] = J[(312)] = C_{z_1}^S$

From this information it is easy to see that the $\mathscr{L}$, $\mathscr{R}$, and $\mathscr{J}$ classes of $C^S_{z_1}$ are as follows:

(1) $\mathscr{L}$ classes:

$L_{(111)} = \{(111)\}$

$L_{(222)} = \{(222)\}$

$L_{(333)} = \{(333)\}$

$L_{(112)} = \{(112), (121), (122), (211), (212), (221)\}$

$L_{(113)} = \{(113), (131), (133), (311), (313), (333)\}$

$L_{(223)} = \{(223), (232), (233), (322), (323), (332)\}$

$L_{(123)} = \{(123), (231), (312)\}$

(2) $\mathscr{R}$ classes:

$R_{(111)} = \{(111), (222), (333)\}$

$R_{(112)} = \{(112), (113), (221), (223), (331), (332)\}$

$R_{(121)} = \{(121), (131), (212), (232), (313), (323)\}$

$R_{(122)} = \{(122), (133), (211), (233), (311), (322)\}$

$R_{(123)} = \{(123), (231), (312)\}$

(3) $\mathscr{J}$ classes:

$J_{(111)} = \{(111), (222), (233)\}$

$J_{(112)} = \{(112), (113), (121), (122), (131), (133), (211), (212),$
$\qquad\qquad (221), (223), (232), (233), (311), (313), (322), (323),$
$\qquad\qquad (331), (332)\}$

$J_{(123)} = \{(123), (231), (312)\}$

An examination of the above equivalence classes could be used for generalizations in calculating the complexity of transformation semigroups, see Section 3.6.

2.3 MACHINES AND SEMIGROUPS

DEFINITION 1. Recall the definition of a *machine* $f : \sum A \to B$, the *semigroup of a machine* f^S, and the *machine of a semigroup* S^f:

Let $f : \sum A \to B$ be a machine. Then define the *natural extension* f^σ: $\sum A \to \sum B$ of f by $f^\sigma(a_1, a_2, \ldots, a_n) = (f(a_1), (f(a_1, a_2), \ldots, f(a_1, \ldots, a_n))$.

Let $h: A \to B$ be a function. Then define the *unique extension* h^Γ: $\sum A \to \sum B$ of h by $h^\Gamma(a_1, \ldots, a_n) = (h(a_1), \ldots, h(a_n))$. h^Γ is a homomorphism of $\sum A$ into $\sum B$.

A homomorphism $H: \sum A \to \sum B$ is *length preserving* iff $H(a_1, \ldots, a_n)$ is a sequence of length n in $\sum B$ for all $(a_1, \ldots, a_n) \in \sum A$ and all $n = 1, 2, \ldots$.

Notice h^Γ is a length preserving homomorphism. Further, every length preserving homomorphism H can be uniquely written h^Γ, where $h: A \to B$ is given by $h(a)\cdot H(a)$ for all $a \in A$.

Let $\mathscr{F}$ be a collection of machines. Define $\mathscr{F}^S = \{f^S : f \in \mathscr{F}\}$. Similarly, let $\mathscr{S}$ be a collection of semigroups. Define $\mathscr{S}^f = \{S^f : S \in \mathscr{S}\}$.

The machine of the semigroup of the machine f, $(f^S)^f$ is written f^{ST}. The semigroup of the machine of a semigroup S, $(S^f)^S$ is written S^{fS}. Extend this notation in the obvious way. Thus f^{SfSf} is the machine of the semigroup f^{SfS}; the last letter on the right determines whether the object is a semigroup or a machine. However, since $S \cong S^{fS}$; the length of the superscripts will not get too long, for we have $f^{SfS} = f^S$ and $f^{SfSf} = f^{Sf}$ (after identifying f^{SfS} with f^S).

Remark 1. Let $f : \sum A \to B$ be a machine. Recall that f^S is the semigroup determined by the congruence $\equiv_f$ on $\sum A$, where for γ, $\delta \in \sum A$, $\gamma \equiv_f \delta$ iff $f(\alpha\gamma\beta) = f(\alpha\delta\beta)$ for all α, $\beta \in (\sum A)^1$.

Let $(\mathrm{mod}\, f)$ represent the partition that f places on $\sum A$. Then it is clear that the semigroup f^S is the minimal homomorphic image of $\sum A$ with respect to $\theta(\sum A, \mathrm{mod}\, f)$, i.e. $f^S = (\sum A)^{\mathrm{mod}\, f}$. Thus, if $\theta : \sum A \xrightarrow[\mathrm{mod}\, f]{} S$ is a $(\mathrm{mod}\, f)$-homomorphism then there exists an epimorphism $\varphi : S \twoheadrightarrow f^S$ such that $\varphi\theta$ is the canonical homomorphism associated with $\equiv_f$.

We denote the equivalence class (relative to $\equiv_f$) containing $\alpha \in \sum A$ by $[\alpha]_f$. Let $h_f : A \to f^S$ be defined by $h_f(a) = [a]_f$. Then $f^{Sf}h_f^\Gamma : \sum A \twoheadrightarrow f^S$ is the canonical homomorphism associated with $\equiv_f$. Let $j_f : f^S \to B$ be defined by $j_f[\alpha]_f = f(\alpha)$. Then f can be written $f = j_f \cdot f^{Sf} h_f^\Gamma$, and this is called the *fundamental expansion* of f.

In the following, all machines will be such that their semigroups have finite order.

DEFINITION 2. Division.

(a) Let $f : \sum A \to B$ and $g : \sum C \to D$ be machines. We say f *divides* g (write $f \mid g$) iff there exists a homomorphism $H : \sum A \to \sum C$ and a function $h : D \to B$ such that $f = hgH$. We say f *divides* g *(length preserving)* (write $f \mid g$ (lp)) iff H is a length preserving homomorphism. Notice that machine division and (lp) machine division are reflexive, transitive relations.

(b) Let S and T be semigroups. We say S *divides* T (write $S \mid T$) iff S is a homomorphic image of a subsemigroup of T, (i.e., there exists a subsemigroup $T' \subseteq T$ and a homomorphism φ such that $\varphi(T') = S$). Notice semigroup division is a reflexive, antisymmetric, transitive relation. (Antisymmetric in the sense $S \mid T$ and $T \mid S$ implies $S \cong T$.)

PROPOSITION 1.

(a) Let f be a machine. Then $f|f^{Sf}$.

(b) Let S, T be semigroups. Then $S|T$ implies $S^f|T^f$(lp)

(c) Let f, g be machines. Then $f|g$ implies $f^S|g^S$.

Proof: (a) follows from the fundamental expansion of f. (b) Suppose $S|T$. Let $T' \subseteq T$ be the subsemigroup of T and let φ be the homomorphism such that $\varphi(T') = S$. For each $s \in S$ pick a representative $\bar{s}$ in $\varphi^{-1}(s) \subseteq T'$. Define $h_1 : S \to T$ by $h_1(s) = \bar{s}$. Define $h_2 : T \to S$ by $h_2(t) = \varphi(t)$ if $t \in T'$ and arbitrarily if $t \notin T'$. Then $S^f = h_2 T^f h_1^{\Gamma}$, so $S^f|T^f$ (lp).

It is natural to ask the following question: Suppose we take two machines f and g and combine them to make new machines. Then how are the semigroups of the new machines related to f^S and g^S?

The two obvious ways to hook machines together are *series* and *parallel* composition.

DEFINITION 3. Let $f : \sum A \to B$ and $g : \sum C \to D$ be machines.

(a) Define the *series composition of f then g with connecting homomorphism* $H : \sum B \to \sum C$ to be the machine $gHf^{\sigma} : \sum A \to D$.

(b) Define the *parallel composition of f and g* to be the machine $f \times g$: $\sum(A \times C) \to B \times D$ given by

$$f \times g\left[(a_1, c_1), \dots, (a_n, c_n)\right] = \left[f(a_1, \dots, a_n), g(c_1, \dots, c_n)\right].$$

The series and parallel compositions of any finite number of machines are defined similarly.

(c) Suppose $f|g$. Then by (a) $f|g^{Sf}$, so $f = hg^{Sf}H$ where H is a homomorphism. Then $g^{Sf}H : \sum A \to g^S$ is a (mod f)-homomorphism, so we have $f^S|g^S$.

The series case is not as easy. Before addressing the problem, it is necessary to recall the definition of the *wreath product* of right mapping semigroups and the relation between wreath products and semidirect products.

To review, the wreath product of mapping semigroups (X_i, S_i), $i = 1, \dots, n$, is written $(X_n, S_n) \circ \dots \circ (X_1, S_1)$ and is the right mapping semigroup $(X_n \times \dots \times X_1, S)$, where $S \subseteq F_R(X_n \times \dots \times X_1)$ is the subsemigroup whose elements triangularize the action and whose i-th component action belongs to S_i for each $i = 1, \dots, n$.

The wreath product is an associative operation on mapping semigroups. The semigroup S is denoted $(X_n, S_n)w \dots w(X_1, S_1)$.

Let $F = gHf^{\sigma}$ be a series combination of machines $f : \sum A \to B$, g:

$\sum C \rightarrow D$, and, as above, let us consider how a string $(a_1, \ldots, a_n) \in \sum A$ acts on the set $g^{S_1} \times f^{S_1}$. More precisely, $F = j_g g^{Sf} h_g^\Gamma H j_f^\Gamma f^{Sf\sigma} h_f^\Gamma$ by the fundamental expansion of f and g. Then $f_1 = f^{Sf} h_f^\Gamma$ is a machine from $\sum A \rightarrow f^S$, and $g_1 = g^{Sf} h_g^\Gamma H j_f^\Gamma f^{Sf\sigma} h_f^\Gamma$ is a machine from $\sum A \rightarrow g^S$. Let θ be the homomorphism $g^{Sf} h_g^\Gamma H j_f^\Gamma : \sum f^S \rightarrow g^S$. Then $g_1 = \theta f^{Sf\sigma} h_f^\Gamma$. A certain amount of reflexion will reveal that if, at step $n-1$, s and t are the outputs of f_1 and g_1, respectively, then the output of f_1 and g_1 corresponding to a_n will be $s[a_n]_f$ and $t\theta(s[a_n]_f)$ respectively. For each $a \in A$ there corresponds $\hat{a} \in F_R(g^{S_1} \times f^{S_1})$ defined by $\hat{a} : (t, s) \rightarrow (t\theta(s[a]_f), s[a]_f)$. $\hat{a}$ is clearly a member of $(g^{S_1}, g^S) w(f^{S_1}, f^S)$. This leads to the Proposition

PROPOSITION 2.

(a) Let $F = gHf^\sigma$ as above. Then $F^S | (g^{S_1}, g^S) w(f^{S_1}, f^S)$.

(b) Let $F = f_n H_{n-1} f_{n-1}^\sigma \ldots f_2^\sigma H_1 f_1^\sigma$, where the f_i are machines and the H_i are connecting homomorphisms. Then $F^S | (f_n^{S_1}, f_n^S) w \ldots w(f_1^{S_1}, f_1^S)$.

Proof. (a) Let $\hat{a} \in (g^{S_1}, g^S) w(f^{S_1}, f^S)$ be defined as above. Let $\hat{A}$ be the subsemigroup of $(g^{S_1}, g^S) w(f^{S_1}, f^S)$ generated by the set $\{\hat{a} : a \in A\}$, and let φ be the unique extension of the map $a \rightarrow \hat{a}$ to an epimorphism of $\sum A$ onto $\hat{A}$. We will show that φ is a (mod F)-homomorphism, thus proving the assertion via Remark 1

Let $\alpha = (a_1, \ldots, a_n) \in \sum A$. Then

$$(t, s)\varphi(\alpha) = (t, s)\hat{a}_1 \circ \cdots \circ \hat{a}_n = (t\theta(s[a_1]_f)\theta(s[a_1, a_2]_f) \ldots$$
$$\theta(s[a_1, \ldots, a_n]_f), s[a_1, \ldots, a_n]_f)$$

Let $\beta = (b_1, \ldots, b_m) \in \sum A$ and suppose $\varphi(\alpha) = \varphi(\beta)$. Then $(1, 1)\varphi(\alpha) = (1, 1)\varphi(\beta)$ so

$$\theta([a_1]_f, \ldots, [a_1, \ldots, a_n]_f) = \theta([b_1]_f, \ldots, [b_1, \ldots, b_m]_f)$$

which is the same as saying $\theta f^{Sf\sigma} h_f^\Gamma(\alpha) = \theta f^{Sf\sigma} h_f^\Gamma(\beta)$. Since $F = j_\beta \theta f^{Sf\sigma} h_f^\Gamma$, we have $F(\alpha) = F(\beta)$. This proves part (a).

(b) Part (b) can be proven by extending the proof of (a) in the obvious way. No new ideas are involved, but the details are cumbersome and hence omitted.

We now wish to combine machines in a "loop free" manner by series and parallel composition. Let $\mathscr{F}$ be a collection of machines. We will define a family of machines containing $\mathscr{F}$ which is closed under the operations of series and parallel composition and division, however, restricting all homomorphism involved to be length preserving. (This restriction is desirable from an engineering point of view, since length preserving connecting homomorphisms correspond to simply running wires between machines.) This family will be defined in a manner which is convenient for inductive proofs.

DEFINITION 4. Let $\mathscr{F}$ be a collection of machines. Define $SP(\mathscr{F})$, the *series parallel closure* of $\mathscr{F}$ by $SP(\mathscr{F}) = \bigcup \{SP_i(\mathscr{F}): i = 1, 2, \ldots \}$, where $SP_1(\mathscr{F}) = \mathscr{F}$ and $SP_i(\mathscr{F}) = \{f_2 \times f_1, f_2 h^\Gamma f_1^\sigma, h_2 f h_1^\Gamma : f_1, f_2 \in SP_{i-1}(\mathscr{F})$ and h, h_1, h_2 are functions$\}$.

What can be said about the semigroups of the machines in $SP(\mathscr{F})$, that is, $SP(\mathscr{F})^S$? From the earlier discussion, we see that $SP(\mathscr{F})^S$ must be closed under *direct products, wreath products, and some division*. This leads to the following definitions.

DEFINITION 5. (a) Let (X, S) and (Y, T) be right mapping semigroups. We say (X, S) *divides* (Y, T) (write $(X, S)|(Y, T)$) iff

(1) there exists a subset Y' of Y and a subsemigroup T' of T such that Y' is left invariant under the action of T', that is $Y'T' \subseteq Y'$, and

(2) there exists a map $\theta: Y' \twoheadrightarrow X$ and an epimorphism $\varphi: T' \twoheadrightarrow S$ such that $\theta(yt) = \theta(y)\varphi(t)$ for all $y \in Y'$, $t \in T'$.

Notice that T' is not required to act faithfully on Y'. We write $(Y', T') \subseteq$ $\subseteq (Y, T)$ and $(Y', T') \twoheadrightarrow (X, S)$.

DEFINITION 6. Let $\mathscr{S}$ be a collection of semigroups. Define a family of mapping semigroups $\bar{W}(\mathscr{S})$, the *wreath divisor closure* of $\mathscr{S}$ by $\bar{W}(\mathscr{S}) =$ $= \bigcup \{\bar{W}_i(\mathscr{S}): i = 1, 2, \ldots\}$, where $\bar{W}_1(\mathscr{S}) = \{(S^1, S): S \in \mathscr{S}\}$ and $\bar{W}_i(\mathscr{S}) =$ $= \{(X, S): (X, S)|(X', S')$ for some $(X', S') \in \bar{W}_{i-1}(\mathscr{S}) \bigcup \{(X_2, S_2) \circ (X_1, S_1):$ $(X_j, S_j) \in \bar{W}_{i-1}(\mathscr{S}), j = 1, 2\}\}$

Let $\underline{W(\mathscr{S})}$ be the abstract semigroups associated with the family $\bar{W}(\mathscr{S})$.

We now define the direct product of mapping semigroups and prove some useful facts about the relations between wreath products, direct products, and division of mapping semigroups.

DEFINITION 7. Define the *direct product* $(X, S) \times (Y, T)$ to be the mapping semigroup $(X \times Y, S \times T)$ where $(x, y)(s, t) = (xs, yt)$. The direct product of a finite number of mapping semigroups is defined similarly.

REMARK 2. The following are easily verified:

(a) Mapping semigroup division is reflexive, antisymmetric, and transitive.

(b) If $(X, S)|(Y, T)$, then $S|T$.

(c) $S|T$ iff $(S^1, S)|(T^1, T)$.

(d) $(X_i, S_i)|(X_2, S_2) \times (X_1, S_1)$, $i = 1, 2$.

(e) Let $(X_i, S_i)|(Y_i, T_i)$, $i = 1, 2$. Then

$$(X_2, S_2) \times (X_1, S_1)|(Y_2, T_2) \times (Y_1, T_1)$$

REMARK 3. Suppose $(X, S)|(Y, T)$ and (Y', T') is as defined in Definition 5 (a). Define an equivalence relation $\equiv$ on T' by $t_1 \equiv t_2$ iff $yt_1 = yt_2$ for all $y \in Y'$. It is easy to show that $\equiv$ is a congruence and $T'/\equiv$ is the unique maximal homomorphic image, $\bar{T}$, of T' such that $(Y', \bar{T})$ is a mapping semigroup, i.e. such that $\bar{T}$ acts faithfully on Y'. Then it is easy to see that $(X, S) \leftleftarrows (Y', T'/\equiv)$.

PROPOSITION 3.

(a) $(X_2, S_2) \times (X_1, S_1)|(X_2, S_2) \circ (X_1, S_1)$

(b) $(X_i, S_i)|(X_2, S_2) \circ (X_1, S_1)$, $i = 1, 2$

(c) Let X be any set such that (X, S) is a mapping semigroup. Then $(S^1, S)|(X, S) \times \cdots \times (X, S)$ ($|X|$ times)

(d) Let $(X_i, S_i)|(Y_i, T_i)$, $i = 1, 2$. Then

$$(X_2, S_2) \circ (X_1, S_1)|(Y_2, T_2) \circ (Y_1, T_1).$$

Proof: (a) It is only necessary to prove that $S_2 \times S_1|(X_2, S_2)w(X_1, S_1) = F(X_1, S_2) \times_Y S_1$ since both act on the same set $X_2 \times X_1$. In fact, $S_2 \times S_1 \subseteq F(X_1, S_2) \times_Y S_1$, as evidenced by the monomorphism $\varphi(s_2, s_1) = (f_{s_2}, s_1)$, where $f_{s_2}(x) = s_2$ for all $x \in X_1$.

(b) follows from (a) and Remark 2 (d) by the transitivity of mapping semigroup division.

(c) Since (X, S) is a mapping semigroup, S is a subsemigroup of $F_R(X)$. Further, S^1 is a subsemigroup of $F_R(X)$, since if $1 \notin S$ we can adjoin to S the identity function of $F_R(X)$. Since X is finite, label its elements $1, \ldots, n$. Then for each $f \in F_R(X)$, f can be written $(i_1, \ldots, i_n)$, where $(k)f = i_k$. If $g = (j_1, \ldots, j_n)$, then $(i_1, \ldots, i_n) * (j_1, \ldots, j_n)$ is defined to be $(j_{i_1}, \ldots, j_{i_n})$. Then $F_R(X)$ can be identified with the semigroup $(X \times \cdots \times X, *)$.

Let $\hat{S}$ be the image of S^1 in $X \times \cdots \times X$. Then $(\hat{S}, \{(s, \ldots, s): s \in S\}) \subseteq (X \times \cdots \times X, S \times \cdots \times S)$. Further, it can easily be verified that $(\hat{S}, \{(s, \ldots, s): s \in S\}) \twoheadrightarrow (S^1, S)$. Hence $(S^1, S)|(X \times \cdots \times X, S \times \cdots \times S) = (X, S) \times \cdots \times (X, S)$.

(d) This proof is in four parts.

(1) Let $(Z_1, U_1) \subseteq (Y_1, T_1)$ and let (X, S) be any mapping semigroup. Then $(X, S) \circ (Z_1, U_1/\equiv)|(X, S) \circ (Y_1, T_1)$.

Proof. $V = F(Y_1, S) \times_Y U_1$ is a subsemigroup of $F(Y_1, S) \times_Y T_1$, so $(X \times Z_1, V) \subseteq (X \times Y_1, \ F(Y_1, S) \times_Y T_1)$. Define the epimorphism θ: $V \twoheadrightarrow F(Z_1, S) \times_Y U_1/\equiv$ by $\theta(f, u) = (\hat{f}, [u])$ where $\hat{f} = f$ restricted to Z_1 and $[u]$ is the image of u under the natural epimorphism associated with $\equiv$. Hence $(X \times Z_1, F(Z_1, S) \times_Y U_1/\equiv) \twoheadleftarrow (X \times Z_1, V)$. This proves (1).

(2) Let $(Z_2, U_2) \subseteq (Y_2, T_2)$. Then $(Z_2, U_2/\equiv) \circ (X, S)|(Y_2, T_2) \circ (X, S)$.

Proof. $(Z_2 \times X, \ F(X, U_2) \times_Y S) \subseteq (Y_2 \times X, \ F(X, T_2) \times_Y S)$. Define θ: $F(X, U_2) \times_Y S \twoheadrightarrow F(X, U_2/\equiv) \times_Y S$ by $\theta(f, s) = (\lfloor f(\cdot) \rfloor, \ s)$. θ is an epimorphism. This proves (2).

(3) Let (Y_1, T_1) be a mapping semigroup and suppose $(X_1, S_1) \twoheadleftarrow$ $\twoheadleftarrow (Y_1, T_1)$. Then $(X, S) \circ (X_1, S_1)|(X, S) \circ (Y_1, T_1)$.

Proof. Let $\theta: Y_1 \twoheadrightarrow X_1$ and $\varphi: T_1 \twoheadrightarrow S_1$ be the maps involved. Define the subsemigroup $V = \{(f, t) \in F(Y_1, S) \times_Y T_1: f(y_1) = f(y_2)$ whenever $\theta(y_1) = \theta(y_2)\}$. Then $(X \times Y_1, V) \subseteq (X \times Y_1, \ F(Y_1, S \times_Y T_1)$. Define ψ: $V \twoheadrightarrow F(X_1, S) \times_Y S_1$ by $\psi(f, t) = (\hat{f}, \varphi(t))$ where $\hat{f}(x) = f(\bar{x})$, $\bar{x} \in \theta^{-1}(x)$. $\hat{f}$ is well-defined by the definition of V. ψ is an epimorphism and it is easy to verify that $(X \times X_1, F(X_1, S) \times_Y S_1) \twoheadleftarrow (X \times Y_1, V)$ when $\hat{\theta}: X \times Y_1 \twoheadrightarrow$ $\twoheadrightarrow X \times X_1$ is given by $\hat{\theta}(x, y_1) = (x, \theta(y_1))$. This proves (3).

(4) Let (Y_2, T_2) be a mapping semigroup and suppose $(X_2, S_2) \twoheadleftarrow$ $\twoheadleftarrow (Y_2, T_2)$. Then $(X_2, S_2) \circ (X, S)|(Y_2, T_2) \circ (X, S)$.

Proof. Let θ, φ be as in (3). Define $\hat{\theta}: Y_2 \times X \twoheadrightarrow X_2 \times X$ by $\hat{\theta}(y_2, x) =$ $= (\theta(y_2), x)$. Define $\psi: F(X, T_2) \times_Y S \twoheadrightarrow F(X, S_2) \times_Y S$ by $\psi(f, s) = (\varphi \cdot f, s)$. ψ is an epimorphism and it is easy to verify that

$$(X_2 \times X, F(X, S_2) \times_Y S) \twoheadleftarrow (Y_2 \times X, F(X, T_2) \times_Y S)$$

This proves (4).

Now by (1)–(4), Remark 3, and transitivity of division, we have $(X_2, S_2) \circ (X_1, S_1)|(Y_2, T_2) \circ (Y_1, T_1)$ whenever $(X_i, S_i)|(Y_i, T_i)$, $i = 1, 2$. This proves Proposition 3.

PROPOSITION 4. Let $\mathscr{S}$ be a family of semigroups. If $(X, S) \in \bar{W}(\mathscr{S})$ then $(X, S)|(S_n^1, S_n) \circ \cdots \circ (S_1^1, S_1)$ where each $S_i \in \mathscr{S}$, $i = 1, \ldots, n$ and $n \geq 1$. In particular, if $S \in W(\mathscr{S})$, then $S|\{S_n^1, S_n)w \ldots w(S_1^1, S_1)$, each $S_i \in \mathscr{S}$, or $S/T \in \mathscr{S}$.

Proof. The second statement follows from the first. We prove the first assertion by induction on the i of $\bar{W}_i(\mathscr{S})$. For $i = 1$ the assertion is trivially true. Assume true for $i = n$, and let $(X, S) \in \bar{W}_{n+1}(\mathscr{S})$. Then either

(1) $(X, S)|(Y, T) \in \bar{W}_n(\mathscr{S})$ or

(2) $(X, S)|(Y_2, T_2) \circ (Y_1, T_1), (Y_i, T_i) \in \bar{W}_n(\mathscr{S}), i = 1, 2.$

For case 1, the assertion follows by induction and transitivity of division. For case 2, the assertion follows by induction, transitivity and Proposition 3.

REMARK 4. It is in the interest of notational convenience that we now introduce the shorthand $S_2 w S_1$ for the semigroup $(S_2^1, S_2) w (S_1^1, S_1)$. However, this notation must be used with care, since the operation "w" on *semigroups* is *not associative*, although the operations "$\circ$" and "w" on mapping semigroups are associative.

The difficulty arises because "w" requires the use of S_2^1 and S_1^1 as the sets that S_2 and S_1, respectively, act upon. Thus,

$$(S_3 w S_2) w S_1 = F\big[S_1^1, F(S_2^1, S_3) \times_Y S_2\big] \times_Y S_1$$

while

$$S_3 w (S_2 w S_1) = F\big[(F(S_1^1, S_2) \times_Y S_1)^1, S_3\big] \times_Y \big[F(S_1^1, S_2) \times_Y S_1\big].$$

Since the cardinality of the two are not equal, it follows that "w" is not associative.

However, the semigroup $(X_2, S_2) w (X_1, S_1)$ depends on S_1, S_2, and X_1, but not X_2. Because of this it is easy to show that

$$(S_3 w S_2) w S_1 = (S_3^1, S_3) w (S_2^1, S_2) w (S_1^1, S_1)$$

which is what we want.

DEFINITION 8. Let $\mathscr{S}$ be a family of semigroups. Define the family of semigroups $\hat{W}(\mathscr{S})$ by $\hat{W}(\mathscr{S}) = \bigcup \{\hat{W}_1 : i = 1, 2, \ldots\}$ where $\hat{W}_1(\mathscr{S}) = \mathscr{S}$ and $\hat{W}_i(\mathscr{S}) = \{S : S | T$ for some $T \in \hat{W}_{i-1}(\mathscr{S}) \cup \{S_2 w S_1 : S_1, S_2 \in \hat{W}_{i-1}(\mathscr{S})\}\}$. Clearly $\hat{W}(\mathscr{S}) = W(\mathscr{S})$.

For the most part, the characterization of $W(\mathscr{S})$ as given by Definition 8 will be used.

We now repeat the results of Proposition 3 in terms of "w" for convenience.

Properties
   (a) $S_2 \times S_1 | S_2 w S_1$
   (b) $S_i | S_2 w S_1, i = 1, 2$
   (c) If $S_i | T_i, i = 1, 2$, then $S_2 w S_1 | T_2 w T_1$
   (d) If $S \in W(\mathscr{S})$, then $S | S_n w \ldots w S_1$ where each $S_i \in \mathscr{S}, i = 1, \ldots, n$ and $n \geq 1$.

PROPOSITION 5. Let $\mathscr{F}$ be a collection of machines. Then

$$SP(\mathscr{F})^S \subseteq W(\mathscr{F}^S).$$

Proof: The proof is by induction on i of SP_i. Certainly, for $i = 1$, $SP_1(\mathscr{F})^S \subseteq W(\mathscr{F}^S)$ since $SP_1(\mathscr{F}) = \mathscr{F}$. Suppose $SP_n(\mathscr{F})^S \subseteq W(\mathscr{F}^S)$. Let $f \in SP_{n+1}(\mathscr{F})$. Then either
   (1) $f = h_2 g h_1^\Gamma$ where $g \in SP_n(\mathscr{F})$,
   (2) $f = f_2 \times f_1$ where $f_2, f_1 \in SP_n(\mathscr{F})$ or
   (3) $f = f_2 h^\Gamma f_1^\sigma$ where $f_2, f_1 \in SP_n(\mathscr{F})$.
In case 1, $f^S | g^S$ and by induction $g^S \in W(\mathscr{F}^S)$ so $f^S \in W(\mathscr{F}^S)$. In case 2, $f^S | f_2^S \times f_1^S$ and by property (a), $f_2^S \times f_1^S | f_2^S w f_1^S \in W(\mathscr{F}^S)$ by induction, so $f^S \in W(\mathscr{F}^S)$. In case 3, $f^S | f_2^S w f_1^S$ by Proposition 2 so $f^S \in W(\mathscr{F}^S)$. Hence $SP_{n+1}(\mathscr{F})^S \subseteq W(\mathscr{F}^S)$. This proves Proposition 5.

What about the converse idea? That is, given a family of semigroups $\mathscr{S}$, is $W(\mathscr{S})^f \subseteq SP(\mathscr{S}^f)$? The answer is no in general, but with the inclusion of certain basic machines in SP and a basic semigroup in W, the statement is true.

To develop this idea we need to define certain semigroups and machines which play a special and important role in this theory.

DEFINITION 9
   (a) Let A be a non-empty set.
   (b) Define the semigroup $U_3 = \{r_0, r_1\}^{r_1}$, $U_2 = \{r_0\}^1$, $U_1 = \{r_0, r_1\}^r$ and $U_0 = \{1\}$. U_0, U_1, and U_2 are all the proper subsemigroups of U_3 (up to isomorphism). If $S | U_3$, then $S = U_i$ for some $i = 0, 1, 2, 3$.
   (c) The *delay machine* $D_A: \sum A \to A \cup \{*\}$ is defined by $D_A(a_1) = *$ (an arbitrary action) and $D_A(a_1, \ldots, a_n) = a_{n-1}$.
   (d) The *delay machine* D_1 is D_A with $A = \{r_0, r_1\}$ and $* = 1$.
   (e) The *machine* $2_A: \sum A \to (A \cup \{*\}) \times A$ is defined by $2_A(a_1) = (*, a_1)$ and $2_A(a_1, \ldots, a_n) = (a_{n-1}, a_n)$.

REMARK 5. Let A be a non-empty set. The natural extension of the machine A^{rf} is the identity map on $\sum A$. The semigroup A^r can be written as a subsemigroup of a direct product of a suitable number of semigroups U_1. Hence $A^{rf} | U_1^f \times \cdots \times U_1^f$ (lp), so $A^{rf} \in SP(U_1^f)$.

PROPOSITION 6. Let $U_1^f \in \mathscr{F}$. Then $SP(\mathscr{F})$ is the set of all machines f written

$$f = h_{n+1} f_n h_n^\Gamma f_{n-1}^\sigma \cdots h_2^\Gamma f_1^\sigma h_1^\Gamma$$

where each f_i is a finite parallel composition of members of $\mathscr{F}$ and the h_i are functions.

Proof. Once again the proof goes by induction on i of SP_i. The critical step is as follows. Suppose the statement is true for $SP_n(\mathscr{F})$ and suppose $f \in SP_{n+1}(\mathscr{F})$ is written $f = f_2 \times f_1$, f_1, $f_2 \in SP_n(\mathscr{F})$. Let $f_1: \sum A \to B$, $f_2: \sum C \to D$. Then $f = (f_2 \times B^{rf})i^\Gamma(C^{rf} \times f_1)^\sigma$ where i is the identity function on $C \times B$. Since $f_1 \in SP_n(\mathscr{F})$, write

$$f_1 = h_{n+1} g_n \bar{h}_n^\Gamma \dots h_2^\Gamma g_1 h_1^\Gamma.$$

Then it is not difficult to see that $C^{rf} \times f_1$ can be · written $\bar{h}_{n+1}(C^{rf} \times g_n)\bar{h}_n^\Gamma \dots \bar{h}_2^\Gamma(C^{rf} \times g_1)^\sigma \bar{h}_1^\Gamma$. Now $C^{rf} \times g_i$ is a finite parallel composition of members of $\mathscr{F}$ since $U_1^f \in \mathscr{F}$. Doing the same for $f_2 \times B^{rf}$, it follows that f satisfies the condition of the statement. The other parts of the proof are trivial. This proves Proposition 6.

PROPOSITION 7. Let A be a non-empty set.
  (a) $A^{rf} \in SP(U_1^f)$
  (b) $D_A \in SP(D_1)$
  (c) $2_A \in SP(D_1, U_1^f)$.
Proof. (a) was shown in Remark 5.

  (b) As in Remark 5, write A as a subset of the direct product of a suitable number of sets $\{r_0, r_1\}$. Then it is easy to see that D_A is the parallel composition of that same number of D_1 machines. Hence $D_A \in SP(D_1)$.

  (c) Verify that $2_A = (D_A \times A^{rf})h^\Gamma$ where $h: A \to A \times A$ with $h(a) = (a, a)$. Hence by (a) and (b), $2_A \in SP(D_1, U_1^f)$. This proves Proposition 7.

We are now ready to prove a converse to Proposition 2 and an important corollary:

PROPOSITION 8. Let S_1, S_2 be semigroups, and let $S_2 \times_Y S_1$ be any semidirect product of S_1 by S_2. Then $(S_2 \times_Y S_1)^f \in SP(S_1^f, S_2^f, D_1, U_1^f)$.
Proof. Verify that

$$(S_2 \times_Y S_1)^f = (S_2^f \times S_1^{rf})h^\Gamma 2_{S_2 \times S_1}^\sigma (S_2^{rf} \times S_1^f)^\sigma$$

where $h:[(S_2 \times S_1) \cup \{*\}] \times (S_2 \times S_1) \to S_2 \times S_1$ with $h[*, (s_2, s_1)] = (s_2, s_1)$ and $h[(s_2, s_1), (t_2, t_1)] = (Y(s_1)t_2, t_1)$. Hence by the previous Facts and Remarks, Proposition 8 is proven.

COROLLARY 9. Let (X_1, S_1) and (X_2, S_2) be right mapping semigroups.

Then

$$[(X_2, S_2)w(X_1, S_1)]^f \in SP(S_1^f, S_2^f, D_1, U_1^f).$$

Proof. The proof follows since $(X_2, S_2)w(X_1, S_1) \cong F(X_1, S_2) \times_Y S_1$ and $F(X_1, S_2) \cong S_2 \times \cdots \times S_2(|X_1|$ times). This proves Corollary 9.

PROPOSITION 10. $D_1^S, U_1 \in W(U_3)$.

Proof. Clearly $U_1 \in W(U_3)$ since $U_1 | U_3$. Verify that $D_1 = $
$= U_3^f h^\Gamma (U_3^f \times U_1^f)^\sigma H$ where
(1) $H: \sum U_1 \to \sum (U_3 \times U_1)$ is a homomorphism given by $H(x) = $
$= [(1, r_0), (x, r_1)]$ for all $x \in U_1$,
(2) $h: U_3 \times U_1 \to U_3$ where $h(x, r_0) = x$ and $h(x, r_1) = 1$ for all $x \in U_3$.
Hence by Proposition 10 we have $D_1^S | U_3 w(U_3^f \times U_1^f)^S | U_3 w(U_3 \times U_1)$.
Therefore $D_1^S \in W(U_3)$. This proves Proposition 10.

REMARK 6. Notice that the machine equation $D_1 = U_3^f h^\Gamma (U_3^f \times U_1^f)^\sigma H$ *does not* imply $D_1 \in SP(U_3^f)$ since the homomorphism H is not length preserving. In fact it is true that $D_1 \in SP(U_3^f)$.

PROPOSITION 11. Let $\mathscr{S}$ be a collection of semigroups:
Then

$$W(\mathscr{S} \cup \{U_3\}) = SP(\mathscr{S}^f \cup \{D_1, U_3^f\})^S$$

Proof. By the obvious induction argument, show that $W(\mathscr{S})^f \subseteq$ $\subseteq SP(\mathscr{S}^f \cup \{D_1, U_1^f\})$ using the corollary to Proposition 8. Using Proposition 5 and the fact that $W(\mathscr{S})^{fs} = W(\mathscr{S})$, we find that

$$W(\mathscr{S}) \subseteq SP(\mathscr{S}^f \cup \{D_1, U_1^f\})^s \subseteq W(\mathscr{S} \cup \{D_1^s, U_1\}).$$

But by Proposition 10, $W(\mathscr{S} \cup \{D_1^S, U_1\}) \subseteq W(\mathscr{S} \cup \{U_3\})$. So by adding a U_3 to $W(\mathscr{S})$ on the left and changing the U_1^f to U_3^f in the SP, we obtain

$$W(\mathscr{S} \cup \{U_3\}) = SP(\mathscr{S}^f \cup \{D_1, U_3^f\})^S.$$

This proves Proposition 11.

2.4 THE KROHN-RHODES PRIME DECOMPOSITION THEOREM FOR FINITE SEMIGROUPS AND MACHINES

Let f be a machine and $f^s = S$, its semigroup. A natural question to ask is what are the "basic" semigroups that would have to be in a collection $\mathscr{S}$

in order for S to belong to $W(\mathscr{S})$, i.e., what are the smallest necessary ingredients (semigroups) that must be in $\mathscr{S}$ so that $S \in W(\mathscr{S})$? Or analogously, what are the "basic" machines $\mathscr{F}$ such that $f \in SP(\mathscr{F})$?

Certainly $S \in W(S)$. Suppose there exists S_1, S_2 such that $S | S_2 w S_1$ but S does not divide either S_1 or S_2. Then $S \in W(S_1, S_2)$. Suppose, in turn, that $S_i | T_i w W_i$ but S_i does not divide T_i or W_i, $i = 1, 2$. Then since $S | S_2 w S_1 |$ $(T_2 w W_2) w (T_1 w W_1)$, we have. $S \in W(T_1, T_2, W_1, W_2)$. Suppose we continued on in this manner until we could no longer do so.

DEFINITION 1. S is an *irreducible* semigroup if $S | S_2 w S_1$ implies either $S | S_1$ or $S | S_2$ for all semigroups S_1, S_2. IRR denotes the set of all irreducible semigroups.

Then it is clear that given a semigroup S, there exists a collection of semigroups $\mathscr{S} \subseteq$ IRR such that $S \in W(\mathscr{S})$. So the questions now are

(1) Which semigroups are irreducible?

(2) Given S, what are the necessary and sufficient conditions for a collection of irreducible semigroups $\mathscr{S}$ to be such that $S \in W(\mathscr{S})$?

In what follows, we discuss the relationship between primitives of machines or semigroups.

DEFINITION 2.

(a) PRIMES denotes the collection of finite non-trivial simple groups.

(b) UNITS denotes all divisors of U_3, i.e., UNITS $= \{U_0, U_1, U_2, U_3\}$.

(c) Let S be a semigroup. PRIMES $(S) = \{P \in$ PRIMES$: P | S\}$. If $\mathscr{S}$ is a collection of semigroups, define PRIMES $(\mathscr{S}) = \{$PRIMES$(S): S \in \mathscr{S}\}$.

(d) IRR $(S) = \{S' \in$ IRR $: S' | S\}$.

THEOREM (*Krohn–Rhodes*)

(a) Let f be a machine with f^S of finite order. Then $f \in SP(\mathscr{S}^f \cup \cup \{D_1, U_3^f\})$ iff PRIMES $(f^S) \subseteq$ PRIMES $(\mathscr{S})$. In particular,

(1) $f \in SP($PRIMES$(f^S)^f \cup \{D_1, U_3^f\})$

(b) Let S be a finite semigroup. Then $S \in W(\mathscr{S} \cup \{U_3\})$ iff PRIMES $(S) \subseteq$ $\subseteq$ PRIMES $(\mathscr{S})$. In particular,

(2) $S \in W($PRIMES$(S) \cup \{U_3\})$

(c) IRR $=$ PRIMES $\cup$ UNITS

(d) In general $s \notin W($IRR$(S))$.

REMARK 1. Part (d) of the theorem justifies both the distinction between PRIMES and UNITS and the inclusion of U_3 in the above equations.

COROLLARY. Let S be a finite semigroup. Then $S \mid S_n w \ldots w S_1$ for some sequence $S_1, \ldots, S_n$ where $S_i \in \mathrm{PRIMES}(S) \cup \mathrm{UNITS}$, $i = 1, \ldots, n$.

Proof. This follows from (2) and properties (c) and (d), Section 3.3, p. 86.

The proof of the theorem proceeds via several lemmas. The first lemma shows that PRIMES and UNITS are irreducible.

LEMMA 1. $\mathrm{PRIMES} \cup \mathrm{UNITS} \subseteq \mathrm{IRR}$.

We next prove that equation (1) is valid. This is done by induction on the order of f^S. The critical induction step separates into three cases as follows.

LEMMA 2. Let S be a finite semigroup. Then either

(a) S is left simple.

(b) S is cyclic.

(c) There exists a proper left ideal $V \subset S$ and a proper sub-semigroup $T \subset S$ such that $S = V \cup T$.

Proof. Throughout this proof we utilize the "picture" of a $\mathscr{J}$ class as provided by Green's and Rees' relations (Section 5). Let J be a maximal $\mathscr{J}$ class of S. Either J is regular or is a one point null class. Suppose J is regular and has only one $\mathscr{J}$ class. Then J is a subsemigroup of S. Let $F(J)$ be the ideal $S - J$. If $F(J) = \varnothing$, $J = S$ is left simple, case (a). If $F(J) \neq \varnothing$, let $V = F(J)$ and $T = J$, case (c).

Suppose J is regular and has more than one $\mathscr{L}$ class. Let L be one. If $F(J) = \varnothing$, let $V = L$ and $T = J - L = S - L$, case (c). If $F(J) \neq \varnothing$, let $V = L \cup F(J)$ and $T = (J - L) \cup F(J)$, case (c).

Suppose J is a one point null $\mathscr{J}$ class. Let $J = \{q\}$, and let Q be the semigroup generated by q. Either $Q = S$, case (b), or let $V = F(J)$ and $T = Q_{,\alpha}$ case (c). This exhausts the possibilities and proves Lemma 2.

LEMMA 3. Let f^S be left simple. Then equation (1) is valid for f.

Proof. Since f^S is left simple, $f^S = G \times A^l$, for some group G and nonempty set A, also $\mathrm{PRIMES}(f^S) = \mathrm{PRIMES}(G)$, for if $P \in \mathrm{PRIMES}(f^S)$, then $P \mid f^S = G \times A^l$, so either $P \mid G$ or $P \mid A^l$ since P is irreducible. But A^l contains no non-trivial groups, so $P \mid G$ and $P \in \mathrm{PRIMES}(G)$. Conversely, let $P \in \mathrm{PRIMES}(G)$. It is clear that $P \mid G$ implies $P \mid G \times A^l$, so $P \in \mathrm{PRIMES}(f^S)$. Thus $\mathrm{PRIMES}(G) = \mathrm{PRIMES}(f^S)$.

Let $L = \{r_0, r_1\}^l$. Then verify that

$$L^f = h_3 U_3^f h_2^\Gamma (D_1 \times U_1^f)^\sigma h_1^\Gamma \quad \text{where}$$

(1) $h_1 : L \to U_1 \times U_1$ with $h_1(r_i) = (r_i, r_i)$, $i = 1, 2$.
(2) $h_2 : U_3 \times U_1 \to U_3$ with $h_2(1, x) = x$ and $h_2(r_i, x) = 1$, $i = 1, 2$.
(3) $h_3 : U_3 \to L$ with $h_3(r_i) = r_i$, $i = 1, 2$. $h_3(1)$ does not occur.

So $L^f \in SP(D_1, U_3^f)$. Now A^l is a subgroup of the direct product of a suitable number of semigroups L, so it follows that $A^{lf} \in SP(D_1, U_3^f)$.

Hence we need only verify that equation (1) is valid for G^f. For, if it is, we have

$$f^{Sf} = G^f \times A^{lf} \in SP(\text{PRIMES}(G)^f \cup \{D_1, U_3^f\});$$

and since $f | f^{Sf}(lp)$ and $\text{PRIMES}(G) = \text{PRIMES}(f^S)$, this proves the assertion.

Claim $G \in W(\text{PRIMES}(G))$. This is certainly true if G is simple. Suppose G is not simple and let G_1 be a normal subgroup of G. Let $H = G/G_1$ and let $N : G \twoheadrightarrow H$ be the natural epimorphism. Let $\{\bar{h} \in N^{-1}(h) : h \in H\}$ be a set of representatives of the cosets of G_1 with the condition that $\bar{1} = 1$. Let $(g_1, h) \in G_1 \times H$. For each $\hat{g} \in G$, define $\hat{g} \in F_R(G_1 \times H)$ by

$$(g_1, h)\hat{g} = (g_1 \bar{h} g \overline{hN(g)}^{-1}, hN(g)).$$

It is easy to verify that $\hat{g} \in G_1 w H$ and that the map $g \to \hat{g}$ is an isomorphism. Therefore $G | G_1 w H$.

Let $G = G_0 \supseteq G_1 \supseteq \cdots \supseteq G_n = \{1\}$ be a composition series for G with factors $H_i = G_{i-1}/G_i$, $i = 1, \ldots, n$. Then $G | G_1 w H_1$ and $G_1 | G_2 w H_2$, etc. Hence $G | H_n w \ldots w H_1$ and $G \in W(H_1, \ldots, H_n)$. By an inductive argument on the order of G, we have $H_i \in W(\text{Primes}(H_i))$ for each $i = 1, \ldots, n$, so $G \in W(\text{PRIMES}\{H_1, \ldots, H_n\})$. However, $\text{PRIMES}(G) = \text{PRIMES}\{H_1, \ldots, H_n\}$, for if $P \in \text{PRIMES}(G)$ then $P | G | H_n w \ldots w H_1$ which implies $P | H_i$ for some i. Hence $P \in \text{PRIMES}\{H_1, \ldots, H_n\}$. Conversely, let $P \in \in \text{PRIMES}\{H_1, \ldots, H_n\}$, so $P | H_i$ for some i. But $H_i = G_{i-1}/G_i$ is a homomorphic image of the subsemigroup G_{i-1} of G so $P | H_i | G$. Hence $P \in \text{PRIMES}(G)$. Thus $G \in W(\text{PRIMES}(G))$ and $G^f \in SP(\text{PRIMES}(G)^f \cup \cup \{D_1, U_3^f\})$. This proves Lemma 3.

LEMMA 4. Let f^S be a cyclic semigroup. Then equation (1) is valid for f.

Proof. Let $C_{(n,m)}$ denote the cyclic semigroup of index n and period m. All finite cyclic semigroups are of this form.

Let Z_m be the cyclic group of order m. Then $C_{(n,m)} \subseteq Z_m \times C_{(n,1)}$ and is generated by (a, b) where a generates Z_m and b generates $C_{(n,1)}$. Further,

$C_{(n,1)} \subseteq T_n = U_2 w \dots w U_2$ (n times). This is established by induction on n and the fact that the wreath product of monoids is a monoid. Let q_k generate $C_{(k,1)}$; let 1_k be the unit of T_k. For $n = 1$, let $C_{(1,1)} = \{r_0\} \subseteq U_2$. Now suppose $C_{(n-1,1)} \subseteq T_{n-1}$. Let $q_n = (f, r_0) \in T_{n-1} w U_2 = T_n$, where $f : U_2 \to T_{n-1}$ with $f(r_0) = q_{n-1}$ and $f(1) = 1_{n-1}$. It follows that q_n generates $C_{(n,1)} \subseteq T_n$.

Thus we have $C_{(n,m)} | Z_m \times T_n \in W(\mathrm{PRIMES}(Z_m), U_2)$ since $T_n \in W(U_2)$ and Z_m is a group. But $\mathrm{PRIMES}(Z_m) = \mathrm{PRIMES}(C_{(n,m)})$. Thus $f^{Sf} = C_{(n,m)}^f \in SP(\mathrm{PRIMES}(f^S)^f \cup \{D_1, U_3^f\})$ and since $f | f^{Sf}(lp)$, this proves Lemma 4.

In considering case (c) of Lemma 2 we require the following definitions.

DEFINITION 3. Let $f : \sum A \to B$ be a machine and let c be a symbol not belonging to A or B. Define the machine *partial product f*, written $\mathrm{PP}f$: $\sum(A \cup \{c\}) \to B \cup \{c\}$ by $\mathrm{PP}f(\alpha) = f(\alpha_c)$ where α_c is the element of $(\sum A)^1$ obtained by striking out all members of the sequence α occurring before the last c and that last c itself. Set $f(1) = c$.

DEFINITION 4. Let $f : \sum A \to B$ be a machine and let e be a symbol not belonging to A or B. Define the machine $ef : \sum(A \cup \{e\}) \to B \cup \{e\}$ by $ef(\alpha) = p(\alpha_e)$ where α_e is the element of $(\sum A)^1$ obtained by striking out all occurrences of e in α. Set $f(1) = e$.

LEMMA 5. Let S be a semigroup with a proper left ideal V and a proper subsemigroup T such that $S = V \cup T$. Then

$$S^f \in SP(eV^f, \mathrm{PPT}^f, D_1, U_1^f).$$

Proof. Verify that

$$S^f = h_3(eV^f \times T''^{rf})h_2^{\Gamma} 2_{V' \times T'}^{\sigma}(V''^{rf} \times \mathrm{PP}\, T^f)^{\sigma} h_1^{\Gamma}.$$

where $T' = T \cup \{c\}$, $V' = V \cup \{e\}$ and where

(1) $h_1 : S \to V' \times T'$ with $h_1(s) = \begin{cases} (s, c) & \text{if } s \in V \\ (e, s) & \text{if } s \in S - V \subseteq T \end{cases}$;

(2) $h_2 : [(V' \times T') \cup \{*\}] \times (V' \times T') \to V' \times T'$ with $h_2[*, (v, t)] = (v, t)$ and

$$h_2[(v_1, t_1), (v_2, t_2)] = \begin{cases} (t_1 v_2, t_2) & \text{if } t_2 = c \text{ and } t_1 \neq c \\ (v_2, t_2) & \text{otherwise} \end{cases};$$

(3) $h_3 : V' \times T' \to S$ with $h_3(v, t) = vt$ where e and c act like identities. The element (e, c) will never occur.

This verification proves Lemma 5.

LEMMA 6. If equation (1) is valid for a machine f, then it is valid for ef.

Proof. We first show if $U_1^f \in \mathscr{F}$, then $\{ef : f \in \mathscr{F}\} \subseteq SP(\mathscr{F})$ implies $\{ef : f \in SP(\mathscr{F})\} \subseteq SP(\mathscr{F})$ by using the usual induction argument. Let $f \in SP_n(\mathscr{F})$. Either (1) $f = f_2 h^\Gamma f_1^\sigma$, (2) $f = f_2 \times f_1$, or (3) $f = h_2 f_1 h_1^\Gamma$ where $f_1, f_2 \in SP_{n-1}(\mathscr{F})$. By induction, $ef_1, ef_2 \in SP(\mathscr{F})$.

In case (1), suppose $f_1 : \sum A \to B$ and $f_2 : \sum C \to D$. Then verify that

$$ef = (ef_2) h_2^\Gamma (ef_1 \times A'^{rf})^\sigma h_1^\Gamma$$

where $A' = A \cup \{e\}$, $B' = B \cup \{e\}$, $C' = C \cup \{e\}$, and $h_1 : A' \to A' \times A'$ with $h_1(a) = (a, a)$ for all $a \in A'$.

$h_2 : B' \times A' \to C'$ with $h_2(b, a) = \begin{cases} e & \text{if } a = e \\ h(b) & \text{otherwise} \end{cases}$.

Hence $ef \in SP(\mathscr{F})$ in this case.

Cases (2) and (3) are handled in the obvious manner.

Now if (1) is valid for f, by the above we need only show that $\{eD_1, eU_3^f, eG^f : G \in \text{PRIMES}(f^S)\} \subseteq SP(\text{PRIMES}(f^S)^f \cup \{D_1, U_3^f\})$. A monoid is a semigroup with unit element, see Tilson [10].

(a) First, let S be a monoid. Then $eS^f \in SP(S^f, U_3^f)$. Verify that

$$eS^f = h_2(S^f \times U_3^f) h_1^\Gamma$$

where $h_1 : S \cup \{e\} \to S \times U_3$ with $h_1(e) = (1, 1)$ and $h_1(s) = (s, r_0)$ and $h_2 : S \times U_3 \to S \cup \{e\}$ with $h_2(s, 1) = e$ and $h_2(s, r_0) = s$.

(b) $eD_1 \in SP(D_1, U_3^f)$. Verify that

$$eD_1 = h_4(U_3^f \times U_3^{rf} \times U_3^f) h_3^\Gamma 2_A^\sigma (U_3^f \times U_3^f \times U_3^{rf})^\sigma h_2^\Gamma 2_A^\sigma h_1^\Gamma$$

where

(1) $h_1 : U_1 \cup \{e\} \to A$ with $h_1(e) = (1, 1, 1)$, $h_1(r_i) = (1, 1, r_i)$, $i = 0, 1$;

(2) $h_2 : A \times A \to A$ with $h_2(*, (1, 1, x)) = (1, 1, x)$
$h_2((1, 1, x), (1, 1, y)) = (1, x, y)$ for all $x, y \in U_3$;

(3) $h_3 : A \times A \to A$ with

$$h_3[(1, x_1, y_1), (1, x_2, y_2)] = \begin{cases} (1, x_2, y_2) & \text{if } y_1 = 1 \\ (x_1, x_2, y_2) & \text{if } y_1 \neq 1 \end{cases}$$

$$x_i, y_i \in U_3$$

$$h_3[*, (1, x_1, y_1)] = (1, x_1, y_1);$$

(4) $h_4 : A \to U_3 \cup \{1\}$ with

$h_4(1, 1, 1) = e$

$h_4(1, 1, r_i) = h_4(1, r_i, 1) = 1$

$h_4(r_k, r_j, r_i) = h_4(1, r_j, r_i) = h_4(r_j, r_i, 1) = r_j \qquad i, j, k = 0, 1.$

Since U_3 and groups are monoids, by (a) and (b) we have proven Lemma 6.

LEMMA 7. If equation (7.1) is valid for f, it is valid for PPf.

Proof. We first show that $\{PPf : f \in \mathcal{J}\} \subseteq SP(\mathcal{J})$ implies $\{PPf : f \in SP(\mathcal{J})\} \subseteq SP(\mathcal{J})$ using the usual induction. Let $f \in SP_n(\mathcal{J})$. Then either (1) $f = f_2 h^{\Gamma} f_1^{\sigma}$, (2) $f = f_2 \times f_1$ or (3) $f = h_2 f_1 h_1^{\Gamma}$ where $f_1, f_2 \in SP_{n-1}$ $(\mathcal{J})$. By induction, $PPf_1, PPf_2 \in SP(\mathcal{J})$. In case 1, $PPf = PPf_2 h_c^{\Gamma}(PPf_1)\sigma$ where h is extended to h_c by $h_c(c) = c$. Cases 2 and 3 are handled in a similar manner.

Now if equation (1) is valid for f, by the above, we need only show that

$$\{PPD_1, PPU_3^f, PPG^f : G \in PRIMES(f^S)\} \subseteq SP(PRIMES(f^S)^f \cup \{D_1, U_3^f\}).$$

(a) Let G be a group. Then $PPG^f \in SP(G^f, U_3^f)$. Verify that

$$PPG^f = h_3(G^{rf} \times G^{rlf} \times \{c, *\}^{rf}) h_2^{\Gamma}(G^f \times (G \cup \{c\})^{rf})^{\sigma} h_1^{\Gamma}$$

where

(1) $h_1 : G \cup \{c\} \to G \times (G \cup \{c\})$ with $h_1(g) = (g, g)$ and $h_1(c) = (1, c)$.

(2) $h_2 : G \times (G \cup \{c\}) \to G \times (G \cup \{1\}) \times \{c, *\}$ with 1 the identity of G^{rl} and $h_2(g, c) = (g, g, c)$ and $h_2(g, g') = (g, 1, *)$.

(3) $h_3 : G \times (G \cup \{1\}) \times \{c, *\} \to G \cup \{c\}$ with

$h_3(x, y, c) = c$ for all x, y,

$$h_3(x, y, *) = \begin{cases} x & \text{if } y = 1 \\ y^{-1}x & \text{if } y \neq 1. \end{cases}$$

Now G^{r1} is a subsemigroup of a suitably large finite direct product of U_3^f with itself. Hence $G^{rlf} \in SP(U_3^f)$ and $PPG^f \in SP(G^f, U_3^f)$.

(b) $PPU_3^f \in SP(U_3^f)$. Verify that

$PPU_3^f = h_2(A^{rlf} \times U_1^f) h_1^{\Gamma}$ where $A = \{r_0, r_1, c\}$ and

(1) $h_1 : U_3 \cup \{c\} \to (A \cup \{1\}) \times U_1$ with $h_1(c) = (c, r_1)$ and $h_1(u) = (u, r_0)$ for all $u \in U_3$.

(2) $h_2 : (A \cup \{1\}) \times U_1 \to U_3 \cup \{c\}$ with $h_2(c, r_1) = c$, $h_2(c, r_0) = h_2(1, r_0) = 1$, and $h_2(r_i, r_0) = r_i$, $i = 1, 2$.

(c) $PPD_1 \in SP(D_1, U_1^f)$. Verify that

$PPD_1 = h_2(D_1 \times D_1 \times U_1^f)h_1^\Gamma$ where

(1) $h_1 : (U_1 \cup \{c\}) \to U_1 \times U_1 \times U_1$ with $h_1(c) = (r_0, r_1, r_1)$ and $h_1(r_i) = (r_i, r_0, r_0)$.

(2) $h_2 : U_3 \times U_3 \times U_1 \to U_3 \cup \{c\}$ with $h_2(x, y, r_1) = c$ for all $x, y \in U_3$, $h_2(r_0, r_1, r_0) = h_2(1, 1, r_0) = 1$, and $h_2(r_i, r_0, r_0) = r_i$, $i = 1, 2$. Other inputs to h_2 do not occur.

Thus with the proofs of (a), (b) and (c) we have proved Lemma 7.

LEMMA 8. Equation (1) is valid.

Proof. It is sufficient to prove (1) valid for f^{Sf} since $f \mid f^{Sf}(1p)$. Hence it is sufficient to prove (1) for S^f where S is a finite semigroup.

We proceed by induction on the order of S. The case $|S| = 1$ is trivial. Suppose (1) is valid for all semigroups with order less than n. Let $|S| = n$. Then apply Lemma 2 to S. In cases (a) and (b), Lemmas 3 and 4, respectively, apply, and we have finished. In case (c), apply Lemmas 5, 6, and 7 using induction. Hence

$$f \in SP(\text{PRIMES}(f^S)^f \cup (D_1, U_3^f\}).$$

LEMMA 9. If $S \in \text{IRR}$ and $S \in W(\mathscr{S})$, then $S \mid S'$ for some $S' \in \mathscr{S}$.

Proof. Follows immediately by induction and the definition of IRR.

Proof of the Krohn–Rhodes Decomposition Theorem

Equation (1) applied to S^f gives equation 2. Equations 1 and 2 prove that $\text{PRIMES}(f^S) \subseteq \text{PRIMES}(\mathscr{S})$ implies $f \in SP(\mathscr{S}^f \cup \{D_1, U_3^f\})$ and $\text{PRIMES}(S) \subseteq \text{PRIMES}(\mathscr{S})$ implies $S \in W(\mathscr{S} \cup \{U_3\})$, respectively.

To finish (a) and (b), assume $f \in SP(\mathscr{S}^f \cup \{D_1, U_3^f\})$. Then $f^S \in W(\mathscr{S} \cup \{U_3\})$. Let $P \in \text{PRIMES}(f^S)$. Then $P \mid f^S$ so $P \in W(\mathscr{S} \cup \{U_3\})$, which by Fact 8.11 implies $P \mid S$ for some $S \in \mathscr{S}$ (P cannot divide U_3). Hence $P \in \text{PRIMES}(\mathscr{S})$. This proves (a) and (b) of the theorem.

To prove (c) we must show $\text{IRR} \subseteq \text{PRIMES} \cup \text{UNITS}$. Let $S \in \text{IRR}$. Then by (b) $S \in W(\text{PRIMES}(S) \cup \{U_3\})$, so either $S \mid G$ a group, or $S \mid U_3$. If $S \mid G$, then S is a group. We know from the proof of Lemma 3 that the only groups that are irreducible are simple groups. Hence $S \in \text{PRIMES}$ or $S = \{1\}$, a UNIT. If $S \mid U_3$, S is a UNIT. This proves (c).

For (d) consider the semigroup $L = \{r_0, r_1\}^l$. $\text{IRR}(L) = \{U_0\}$ and since U_0 is the trivial one point semigroup, clearly $L \notin W(U_0)$. The proof of

Lemma 3, however, shows that $L \in W(U_3)$. This proves the *Prime Decomposition Theorem*.

2.5 AN APPLICATION OF THE DECOMPOSITION THEOREM – SOME RESULTS ON COMBINATORIAL SEMIGROUPS

We first recall the definition and some facts about combinatorial semigroups.

DEFINITION 1. A semigroup S is *combinatorial* iff each subgroup of S is of order 1.

PROPOSITION 1

(a) S is combinatorial iff each $\mathscr{H}$ class contains exactly one element.

(b) Homomorphic images, subsemigroups, and finite direct products of combinatorial semigroups are combinatorial.

PROPOSITION 2

(a) There exists a positive integer $r = r(S)$ such that $s^r = s^{r+1}$ for all $s \in S$ iff S is combinatorial.

(b) PRIMES$(S) = \varnothing$ iff S is combinatorial.

(c) Combinatorial semigroups are closed under wreath and semidirect products. That is, if S_1, S_2 are combinatorial then $S_2 w S_1$ and $S_2 \times_Y S_1$ are combinatorial. Further if $S_2 w S_1$ is combinatorial then both S_1 and S_2 are.

Proof. (a) and (b) are left as exercises. To prove (c) notice if $P \in \text{PRIMES}(S_2 w S_1)$ or PRIMES$(S_2 \times_Y S_1)$ then $P \in \text{PRIMES}(S_1)$ or PRIMES(S_2). If the latter are empty, the former are. This proves the first assertion. Since $S_i | S_2 w S_1$, $i = 1, 2$, we have PRIMES$(S_i) \subseteq$ PRIMES $(S_2 w S_1)$, so if $S_2 w S_1$ is combinatorial, S_1 and S_2 must be. This proves Proposition 2.

THEOREM. *Principle of Induction for Combinatorial Semigroups*
Let $\mathscr{S}$ be any property of finite semigroups such that
(1) $\mathscr{S}$ is closed under division.
(2) $U_3^{(n)} \equiv U_3 w \ldots w U_3$ (n times) satisfies $\mathscr{S}$.
Then every combinatorial semigroup satisfies $\mathscr{S}$.

Proof. Let $\mathscr{S}$ be a property of finite semigroups satisfying (1) and (2), and let S be combinatorial. Then PRIMES$(S) = \varnothing$ so $S \in W(U_3)$ and

$S \mid U_3^{(n)}$ for some n, by the Prime Decomposition Theorem. Hence S satisfies $\mathscr{S}$.

For reasons of notation we introduce:

(a) Let A be a non-empty set. Let $\Pi(A)$ denote the set of all infinite sequences of elements of A. (That is, $\Pi(A) = F(\{1, 2, \dots\}, A)$.)

(b) Let S be a semigroup. Define the *nth iteration of the machine S^f* by $(S^{f\sigma})^n : \sum S \to \sum S$ where $(S^{f\sigma})^2 = S^{f\sigma}S^{f\sigma}$ and $(S^{f\sigma})^n = S^{f\sigma}(S^{f\sigma})^{n-1}$.

(c) Let S be a semigroup and let $X \in \Pi(S^1)$, $X = (x_1, x_2, \dots)$. Then $P_X : \sum S \to \sum S$ is defined by $P_X(s_1, \dots, s_n) = (x_1 s_1, \dots, x_n s_n)$.

Next we give the main result of this section which says if the machine of a combinatorial semigroup is iterated long enough, the $n + 1$-th iterated machine is the same as the n-th iterated machine. Further, if the output of the combinatorial machine is altered as a function of time by left multiplication, the same thing happens.

PROPOSITION 3 The following statements are equivalent.

(a) S is a combinatorial semigroup.

(b) There exists a positive integer $m = m(S)$ such that

$$(S^{f\sigma})^m = (S^{f\sigma})^{m+1}.$$

(c) There exists a positive integer $q = q(S)$ such that for all $X \in \Pi(S^1)$

$$(P_X S^{f\sigma})^q = (P_X S^{f\sigma})^{q+1}, \text{ and}$$

$$(S^{f\sigma} P_X)^q = (S^{f\sigma} P_X)^{q+1}.$$

Proof. (c) implies (b) by taking $X = (1, 1, \dots)$.

(b) implies (a): Suppose S is a semigroup with a non-trivial subgroup G (i.e., S is non-combinatorial). Let $g \in G$, $g \neq 1$, the identity of G. Then $(S^{f\sigma})^n(g, 1) = (g, g^n)$ for all $n = 1, 2, \dots$. Since $g \neq 1$, there exists no positive integer m such that $(S^{f\sigma})^m = (S^{f\sigma})^{m+1}$.

(a) implies (c): First we note that (2) and (3) are equivalent. Assume (2) is true. Then

$$(S^{f\sigma} P_X)^{q+1} = S^{f\sigma}(P_X S^{f\sigma})^q P_X = S^{f\sigma}(P_X S^{f\sigma})^{q+1} P_X = (S^{f\sigma} P_X)^{q+2}.$$

Similarly, (3) implies (2).

Let $\mathscr{S}$ be the collection of all semigroups satisfying equation (2). We will show $\mathscr{P}$ is closed under division and $U_3^{(n)} \in \mathscr{S}$ for all n, thus applying the Principle of Induction for Combinatorial Semigroups to prove the Proposition.

(1) $\mathscr{S}$ *is closed under division.* Let $S\,|\,T$ and $T\in\mathscr{S}$ Write $S\overset{\varphi}{\leftarrow} T'\subseteq T$. Then $S^f\,|\,T^f$ and $S^{f\sigma} = h_2^\Gamma T^{f\sigma} h_1^\Gamma$ where $h_1 : S\to T'$, $h_1(s)=\bar{s}$ where $\bar{s}$ is a fixed representative of $\varphi^{-1}(s)$, and $h_2 : T'\twoheadrightarrow S$, $h_2(t)=\varphi(t)$. (Refer to the proof of Proposition 1, Section for this notation.) Let $X\in\Pi(S^1)$, $X = = (x_1, x_2, \ldots)$, and let $q = q(T)$. Then

$$(*)\qquad (P_X S^{f\sigma})^{q+1} = (P_X h_2^\Gamma T^{f\sigma} h_1^\Gamma)^{q+1} = P_X h_2^\Gamma (T^{f\sigma} h_1^\Gamma P_X h_2^\Gamma)^q T^{f\sigma} h_1^\Gamma$$

Now we claim

$$(**)\qquad h_2^\Gamma (T^{f\sigma} h_1^\Gamma P_X h_2^\Gamma)^p = h_2^\Gamma (T^{f\sigma} P_Y)^p \quad\text{for all } p = 1, 2, \ldots$$

where $Y\in\Pi(T^1)$, $Y = (\bar{x}, \bar{x}_2, \ldots)$. For $p = 1$, $(*)$ is easy to verify. Suppose $(**)$ true for $p - 1$. Let

$$(t_1, \ldots, t_n) = h_2^\Gamma (T^{f\sigma} h_1^\Gamma P_X h_2^\Gamma)^{p-1}(t'_1, \ldots, t'_n)$$
$$= h_2^\Gamma (T^{f\sigma} P_Y)^{p-1}(t'_1, \ldots, t'_n).$$

Then to prove $(**)$ it is sufficient to show that

$$h_2^\Gamma T^{f\sigma} h_1^\Gamma P_X(t_1, \ldots, t_n) = h_2^\Gamma T^{f\sigma} P_Y(u_1, \ldots, u_n)$$

where u_i is any element of $\varphi^{-1}(t_i)$, $i = 1, \ldots, n$. This is easily verified.

Now since $(T^{f\sigma} P_Y)^q = (T^{f\sigma} P_Y)^{q+1}$ it follows easily by $(**)$ and $(*)$ that $(P_X S^{f\sigma})^{q+1} = (P_X S^{f\sigma})^{q+2}$. Thus $\mathscr{S}$ is closed under division.

(2) $U_3^{(n)}\in\mathscr{S}$. Verify that $(P_X U_3^{f\sigma})^2 = (P_X U_3^{f\sigma})^3$ for all $X\in\Pi U_3$. Also verify that $\mathscr{S}$ is closed under finite direct product. Both are easy. Further, if S_1, S_2 are combinatorial, then $q(s_1 \times s_2) = \max\{q(s_1), q(s_2)\}$.

Now assume there exists q_n such that (2) holds for $U_3^{(n)}$. We will find a q_{n+1} in terms of q_n such that (2) holds for $U_3^{(n+1)} = F(U_3, U_3^{(n)}) \times_Y U_3$. Notice that q_n is the integer such that (10.2) holds for $F(U_3, U_3^{(n)})$. Let $X\in\Pi(U_3^{(n+1)})$ with $X = [(g_1, b_1), (g_2, b_2), \ldots]$, $b_i\in U_3$, $g_i\in F(U_3, U_3^{(n)})$. Let $M = P_X U_3^{(n+1)f\sigma}$ and let $Y\in\sum U_3^{(n+1)}$ with $Y = [(f_1, a_1), \ldots, (f_k, a_k)]$.

We want to get into a position where we can apply the induction hypothesis. We can do this if we can get the semidirect product acting like the direct product. If all the a_i's and b_i's equal 1, this is the situation. Let r be the largest integer such that $a_1, \ldots, a_{r-1}, b_1, \ldots, b_{r-1}$ all equal 1. Then on the first $r - 1$ terms of Y, M^p acts exactly like $[P_{X'}, F(U_3, U_3^{(n)})^f \times \times U_3^f]^{\sigma p}$, where $X'\in\Pi F(U_3, U_3^{(n)})$ with $X' = (g_1, g_2, \ldots)$. So after q_n iterations of M, the first $r - 1$ terms of Y do not change. Write $M^{q_n}(Y) = = [(h_1, 1), \ldots, (h_{r-1}, 1), (h'_r, c_r), \ldots, (h'_k, c_k)]$. Note that each $c_i\in\{r_0, r_1\}$ after the second iteration and q_n is certainly ≥ 2.

Now after another $q_n + 1$ iterations the r-th term will become stable.

To see this, start with $M^{q_n}(Y)$ and iterate p times. The new r-th term will be $(g_r[^{b_r}(h_1 \ldots h_{r-1} g_r)]^{p-1} {}^{b_r}(h_1 \ldots h_r'), c_r)$. Now for all $f \in F(U_3, U_3^{(n)})$, we have $f^{q_n} = f^{q_n+1}$. (Consider $(F(U_3, U_3^{(n)})^{f\sigma})^{q_n}(f, f)$.) Thus when $p = q_n + 1$, the r-th term is stabilized. Write $M^{2q_n+1}(Y) = [(h_1, 1), \ldots, (n_r, c_r), \ldots, (h_k, c_k)]$.

We will now show that after another $q_n + 1$ iterations all the terms become stable so that $q_{n+1} \leq 3q_n + 2$, proving the assertion. Let c_1 denote the identity of $F(U_3, U_3^{(n)})$. Define the machine $f: \sum U_3^{(n+1)} \to U_3^{(n+1)}$ by

$$f[(k_1, d_1), \ldots, (k_n, d_n)] = \begin{cases} (^{d_{n-1}}k_n, d_n) & \text{if } n \geq 2 \text{ and } d_{n-1} \neq 1 \\ (c_1, d_n) & \text{otherwise} \end{cases}$$

Also define $X_1 \in \Pi F(U_3, U_3^{(n)})$ by

$$X_1 = (j_1, \ldots, j_r, {}^{c_r}g_{r+1}{}^{c_r b_{r+1}}(h_1 \ldots h_r), \ldots,$$
$$\quad {}^{c_{k-1}}g_k{}^{c_{k-1} b_k}{}_{(h_1 \ldots h_r)}, j_{k+1}, \ldots)$$

where each $j_i = c_1$. Define $X_2 \in \Pi(U_3^{(n+1)})$ by

$$X_2 = [(h_1, 1), \ldots, (h_1, 1), (g_{r+1}{}^{b_r+1}(h_1 \ldots h_r), 1), \ldots$$
$$\quad \ldots, (g_k{}^{b_k}(h_1 \ldots h_r), 1), (j_{k+1}, 1), \ldots]$$

where once again each $j_i = c_1$. Note that X_1 and X_2 are functions of X and Y. Let $F = (F(U_3, U_3^{(n)}))^f$. Then by direct computation verify that

$$M^{2q_n+2+p}(Y) = P_{X_2} U_3{}^{(n+1)f\sigma}[P_{X_1} F \times U_3^f]^{\sigma p_f \sigma_M 2q_n+1}(Y)$$

for $p = 1, 2, \ldots$. But by induction $[P_{X_1} F \times U_3^f]^{\sigma q_n} = [P_{X_1} F \times U_3^f]^{\sigma(q_n+1)}$ for all $X_1 \in \Pi F(U_3, U_3^{(n)})$. Thus $M^{3q_n+2}(Y) = M^{3q_n+3}(Y)$ for all $Y \in \sum U_3^{(n+1)}$. This proves Proposition 3.

	$s_1 = a_{01}$	$s_2 = a_{02}$	$s_3 = a_{03}$	$\ldots$
$x_1 = a_{10}$	$x_1 s_1 = a_{11}$	$x_1 s_1 s_2 = a_{12}$	$x_1 s_1 s_2 s_3 = a_{13}$	$\ldots$
$x_2 = a_{20}$	$x_2 x_1 s_1 = a_{21}$	$x_2 x_1 s_1 x_1 s_1 s_2 = a_{22}$	$a_{22} \cdot a_{13} = a_{23}$	$\ldots$
$x_3 = a_{30}$	$x_3 x_2 x_1 s_1 = a_{31}$	$a_{31} \cdot a_{22} = a_{32}$	$a_{32} a_{23} = a_{33}$	$\ldots$
$\cdot$	$\cdot$	$\cdot$	$\cdot$	
$\cdot$	$\cdot$	$\cdot$	$\cdot$	
$\cdot$	$\cdot$	$\cdot$	$\cdot$	

Fig. 4. Pascal Array of S^1

Remark. A way of visualizing $(S^{1f\sigma})^p$ is by the 'Pascal Array' of the multiplication table of S^1. Let $X = (x_1, x_2, \dots)$ and $Y = (s_1, s_2, \dots) \in \Pi(S^1)$. Consider Figure 4. Let $a_{0i} = s_i$, $a_{j0} = x_j$ and compute the entries in the array by the formula $a_{mn} = a_{m(n-1)} \cdot a_{(m-1)n}$. If $x_1 = x_2 = \cdots = 1$, then $(a_{p1}, a_{p2}, \dots)$ will be the output of $(S^{1f\sigma})^p(s_1, s_2, \dots)$. Thus Proposition 3 (b) says that S is combinatorial iff there exists $m = m(S^1)$ such that for all $Y \in \Pi(S^1)$ the $m, m+1, \dots$ rows of the array are identical

Let $f_i = S^{1f}L_{x_i}$, where $L_{x_i}(s_1, \dots, s_n) = (x_i, s_1, \dots, s_n)$. Then $a_{jk} = f_j f_{j-1}^\sigma \dots f_1^\sigma(s_1, \dots, s_k)$.

We have the following "duality". Transposition in Figure 1 about the diagonal, i.e., the transformation taking a_{jk} to a_{kj}, may be effected by interchanging X and Y and replacing S^1 by $r(S^1)$, the reverse semigroup of S^1. The dual result of Proposition 3 (b) is:

PROPOSITION 4. S is combinatorial if there exists an integer $n = n(S)$ such that if

$$b_{jk} = f_j f_{j-1}^\sigma \dots f_1^\sigma(1, \dots, 1) \ (k \text{ times})$$

then $b_{jn} = b_{j(n+1)} = \cdots$ for all $j = 1, 2, \dots$ and for all $(x_1, x_2, \dots) \in \Pi(S^1)$.

Proof. Let $a'_{kj} = f'_k f'^\sigma_{k-1} \dots f'^\sigma_1(x_1, \dots, x_j)$, where $f'_i = r(S^1)^f L_{s_i}$, represent the k-jth entry in the 'Pascal Array' of $r(S^1)$. Then since $r(S^1)$ is combinatorial, if $S_1 = S_2 = \cdots 1$, there exists an integer n such that $\overline{a'_{nj}} = \overline{a'_{(n+1)j}} = \cdots$ for all $j = 1, 2, \dots$ and for all $(x_1, x_2, \dots)$. But $\overline{a'_{kj}} = a_{jk}$ as defined in the above remark. Writing $b_{jk} = a_{jk}$ when $s_1 = s_2 = \cdots = 1$ we have the assertion.

2.6 CALCULATING THE COMPLEXITY OF A TRANSFORMATION SEMIGROUP

PROPOSITION 1. Let $X = \{1, 2, 3\}$. With each element t of $C^S_{z_1}$ we associate three things (1) the *range* $t(X)$ of t, (2) the *partition* $\pi_t = t \cdot t^{-1}$ of X corresponding to t, i.e. the equivalence relation on X defined by $x\pi_t y, x, y \in X$, if $t(x) = t(y)$, and (3) the *rank* $|t(X)|$ of t. Then we may describe the $\mathscr{L}$, $\mathscr{R}$, and $\mathscr{J}$ classes of $C^S_{z_1}$ as follows:

(1a) Two elements of $C^S_{z_1}$ are $\mathscr{L}$ related if and only if they have the same range.

(1b) Two elements of $C^S_{z_1}$ are $\mathscr{R}$ related if and only if they have the same partition.

(1c) Two elements of $C^S_{z_1}$ are $\mathscr{J}$ related if and only if they have the same rank.

Proof. Clifford and Preston [3, pp. 51–52] prove the above proposition for $F_R(X_n)$. It generalizes to $C_{z_1}^S$, however, due to the fact that $L_{(123)} = R_{(123)} = J_{(123)}$ (the highest $\mathscr{L}$, $\mathscr{R}$, and $\mathscr{J}$ classes of $C_{z_1}^S$, respectively, in the sense that $L_t \leq L_{(123)}$, $R_t \leq R_{(123)}$, and $J_t \leq J_{(123)}$ for all $t \in C_{z_1}^S$) is a cyclic subgroup of $C_{z_1}^S$ of order three. It is not true in general for any subsemigroup of $F_R(X_n)$. Clifford and Preston prove (1c) for $\mathscr{D}$ equivalence rather than $\mathscr{J}$ equivalence, but for finite semigroups $\mathscr{J} = \mathscr{D}$ (M.A. Arbib [1, p. 153]).

This proposition may be further generalized as follows:

PROPOSITION 2. Call $t \in F_R(X_n)$ an *order-preserving transformation* if $t = (x_i \ldots x_n x_1 \ldots x_{i-1})$ for $x_1, \ldots, x_n \in X_n = \{1, \ldots, n\}$ and $x_1 \leq \ldots \leq x_n$. An *order-preserving partition* is defined analogously, i.e. π is order-preserving if and only if there exists an order-preserving transformation with partition π. Let S be the subsemigroup of $F_R(X_n)$ consisting of all of the order-preserving elements.

(2a) There is a one-to-one correspondence between the set of all $\mathscr{J}$ classes of S and the set of all cardinal numbers $r \leq n$ such that the $\mathscr{J}$ class J_r corresponding to r consists of all elements of S of rank r.

(2b) Let r be a cardinal number $\leq n$. There is a one-to-one correspondence between the set of all $\mathscr{L}$ classes in J_r and the set of all subsets Y of X of cardinality r such that the $\mathscr{L}$ class corresponding to Y consists of all elements of S having range Y.

(2c) Let r be a cardinal number $\leq n$. There is a one-to-one correspondence between the set of all $\mathscr{R}$ classes contained in J_r and the set of all order-preserving partitions π of X_n for which $|X_n/\pi| = r$ such that the $\mathscr{R}$ class corresponding to π consists of all elements of S having partition π.

(2d) Let r be a cardinal number $\leq n$. There is a one-to-one correspondence between the set of all $\mathscr{H}$ classes in J_r and the set of all pairs (π, Y), where π is an order-preserving partition of X_n and Y is a subset of X_n such that $|X_n/\pi| = |Y| = r$, such that the $\mathscr{H}$ class corresponding to (π, Y) consists of all elements of S having partition π and range Y.

Proof. Cf. Clifford and Preston [3, p. 52–53], and Proposition 1 above. These facts will be used later in the analysis of $(C'_{z0})^S$.

One last fact which is obtainable by generalization from the discussion of $F_R(X_n)$ by Clifford and Preston is the following:

PROPOSITION 3. Let S be the set of all order-preserving elements of $F_R(X_n)$, let Y be a subset of the set $X_n = \{1, \ldots, n\}$, and let π be an order-

$J_{(123)}$	{123}
{1} {2} {3}	(123)* (231) (312)

$J_{(1\,1\,2)}$	{23}	{13}	{12}
{2} {13}	(232) (323)*	(231) (313)	(121)* (212)
{3} {13}	(223)* (332)	(113)* (331)	(112) (221)
{1} {23}	(233) (322)	(133)* (311)	(122)* (211)

$J_{(111)}$	{3}	{2}	{1}}
{123}	(333)*	(222)*	(111)*

Fig. 5. 'Eggbox' representations of the $\mathscr{J}$ classes for $C_{z_1}^S$. Starred elements are idempotents (i.e. elements e such that $e^2 = e$). They show which $\mathscr{H}$ classes are subgroups of $C_{z_1}^S$. Column headings represent the range of each $\mathscr{L}$ class, while row headings represent the partition corresponding to each $\mathscr{R}$ class (i.e. {1} {23} means that 1 goes to a unique element of {1, 2, 3}, but 2 and 3 are mapped to the same element).

preserving partition of X_n such that $|Y| = |X_n/\pi|$. Let H be the $\mathscr{H}$ class of S determined by the pair (π, Y) as in Proposition (2d). If H contains an idempotent, than H induces and is isomorphic with the cyclic group $Z_{|Y|}$ of order $|Y|$.

Proof. See Clifford and Preston [3, p. 53–54].

It is now possible to illustrate each of the $\mathscr{J}$ classes of $C_{z_1}^S$ by an "eggbox picture", where each row is an $\mathscr{R}$ class, each column is an $\mathscr{L}$ class, and the intersection of each row and column is an $\mathscr{H}$ class (Figure 5).

Associated with every $\mathscr{J}$ class of a semigroup S is a semigroup $J^{\cdot} = (J \cup \{0\}, \cdot)$ where

$$x \cdot y = \begin{cases} xy \text{ if } xy \in J \\ 0 \text{ otherwise.} \end{cases}$$

In other words, if the product of two elements x, y of J is again in J, $x \cdot y$ is defined to be xy, but if the product xy "drops" to a lower $\mathscr{J}$ class (i.e. has rank less than the rank of x and y, in the case of $C_{z_1}^S$), then $x \cdot y$ is defined to be 0. Furthermore, $J^{\cdot}$ is either *null*, $(J^{\cdot})^2 = 0$, or *0-simple* (not null and having no ideals other than 0 and itself) (Arbib [1, p. 15]). J is called *regular* if J ' is 0-simple and *null* if J ' is null. In the case of the semigroup consisting of all of the order-preserving transformations of $F_R(X_n)$, it is obvious that all $\mathscr{J}$ classes will be regular, for each $\mathscr{J}$ class $J_m(m \leq n)$ will contain the idempotent $(1 \ldots m \ldots m)$. Thus, since $C_{z_1}^S$ is a special case of this semigroup for $n = 3$, it must have all regular $\mathscr{J}$ classes.

PROPOSITION 4. Let S be the semigroup consisting of all of the order-preserving elements of $F_R(X_n)$. If J is a $\mathscr{J}$ class of S, then J is isomorphic to a regular Rees matrix semigroup (Arbib [1, p. 7]).

Proof: All of the $\mathscr{J}$ classes of S are regular. Thus J is 0-simple for each $\mathscr{J}$ class J and is isomorphic to a regular Rees matrix semigroup (Arbib [1, p. 157]).

Now with each $\mathscr{J}$ class J of $C_{z_1}^S$ it is possible to associate the structure matrix of the Rees matrix semigroup isomorphic to J.

This is done as follows:

Select an $\mathscr{H}$ class of J containing an idempotent e, denoting R_e and L_e by R_1 and L_1, respectively, and consequently H_e by H_{11}. This amounts to moving any $\mathscr{H}$ class with an idempotent into the upper left hand corner of the "eggbox picture" of J, simultaneously adjusting the rows and columns accordingly. Let $\{R_a : a \in A\}$ and $\{L_b : b \in B\}$ be the sets of $\mathscr{R}$ classes and $\mathscr{L}$ classes, respectively, of $C_{z_1}^S$ contained in J. For each $a \in A$ and $b \in B$, select and fix an element r_a of H_{a1} and an element z_b of H_{1b}. Define the $|B| \times |A|$ matrix $C = (c_{ba})$ over H_{11}^0 as follows:

$$c_{ba} = \begin{cases} z_b r_a & \text{if } z_b r_a \in H_{11} \\ 0 & \text{otherwise.} \end{cases}$$

It is clear that a different choice of representatives z_b and r_a would yield a different structure matrix; however, the Rees matrix semigroups so obtained would be isomorphic.

The structure matrices for $J_{(111)}$, $J_{(112)}$, and $J_{(123)}$ of $C_{z_1}^S$ are as follows:

$$J_{(123)} : [(123)^*]$$

$$J_{(112)} : \begin{bmatrix} (323)^* & (312)^* & 0 \\ 0 & (323)^* & (323)^* \\ (232) & 0 & (323)^* \end{bmatrix}$$

$$J_{(11)^*} \begin{bmatrix} (333)^* \\ (333)^* \\ (333)^* \end{bmatrix}$$

Now let 1 represent the idempotent of each *structure* group H_{11} and let $g = (232)$; thus the above matrices become

$$J_{(123)} : [1]$$

$$J_{(112)} : \begin{bmatrix} 1 & 1 & 0 \\ 0 & 1 & 1 \\ g & 0 & 1 \end{bmatrix}$$

$$J_{(111)} : \begin{bmatrix} 1 \\ 1 \\ 1 \end{bmatrix}$$

PROPOSITION 5. Let S be a finite semigroup and let $J_1 > J_2 > \cdots > J_n$ be a chain of regular $\mathscr{J}$ classes of S. For each $i \varepsilon \{1, \ldots, n\}$ let G_i be the structure group of the Rees matrix representation of J_i (i.e. the group in the H_{11} position of each $\mathscr{J}$ class). Furthermore, define the structure matrix C_i of J_i to be *normalizable to zeros and ones* (the identity of G_i) if and only if it is possible to obtain from it a matrix consisting only of zeros and ones by a process of multiplying rows and columns by elements of G_i. Let G_i' be the subgroup of G_i generated by the idempotents of J_i. Finally, define the *orbit* of G_i' on J_{i+1} to be the set of $\mathscr{L}$ classes of J_{i+1} obtained by a right group action of G_i' on J_{i+1} (i.e. the $\mathscr{L}$ classes whose elements are of the form $j_{i+1} g_i'$ where $j_{i+1} \in J_{i+1}$ and $g_i' \in G_i'$ and where j_{i+1} is fixed by the identity of G_i'). If C_{i+1}, the structure matrix of J_{i+1}, restricted to the orbit of G_i', is not normalizable to zeros and ones, call C_{i+1}' (of the restricted J_{i+1}) *essential*, and let k be the largest non-negative integer such that there exists a chain of essential groups

$$G_1 > G_2' > \cdots > G_k'$$

where $G_i' > G_{i+1}'$ if and only if $J_i > J_{i+1}$. Then $k \le \#_G(S)$.

Proof. $k \le \#_I(S)$, defined by Rhodes and Tilson in [8] as follows:

Let L_i be the $\mathscr{L}$ class of J_i containing G_i, and let S_i be the semigroup generated by the chain $L_i > L_{i+1} > \cdots > L_n$ of $\mathscr{L}$ classes. Now let $L_i', \ldots, L_n'$ be the $\mathscr{L}$ classes obtained by deleting from $L_i, \ldots, L_n$ those elements belonging to $\mathscr{R}$ classes which yields only zeros in their respective structure matrices restricted to the orbit of the preceding essential group, and let S_i' be the subsemigroup of S_i generated by $L_i', \ldots, L_n'$. Define $EG(S_i')$ to be the subsemigroup of S_i' generated by its idempotents. Then

$$S \ge S_1' \ge EG(S_i') \ge S_2' \ge EG(S_2') \ge \ldots \ge S_k' \ge EG(S_k')$$

is a chain of subsemigroups of S such that S'_i is a non-combinatorial "T_1" semigroup (i.e. generated by a chain of its $\mathcal{L}$ classes) contained in $EG(S'_{i-1})$, for $i = 1, \ldots, k$. This is guaranteed by the fact that each structure matrix C_i, $i = 2, \ldots, k$, is not normalizable to zeros and ones. $\#_I(S) =$ = maximum of the lengths of all such chains of subsemigroups of S.

Thus $k \leq \#_I(S) \leq \#_G(S)$.

In the case of $C^S_{z_1}$ notice that, if $J_{(123)}$ is denoted by J_1, $J_{(112)}$ by J_2, and $J_{(111)}$ by J_3, then $G_1 > G'_2 = G_2$ is such a chain. $G_2 = G'_2$ here due to the fact that $g = (232) = (121) \cdot (133) \cdot (223)$ and $G_2 = \{1, g\}$. Thus $k = 2 \leq$ $\leq \#_G(C^S_{z_1})$, but it was already shown that $\#_G(C^S_{z_1}) \leq 2$, so $\#_G(C^S_{z_1}) = 2$.

Let us now discuss C'_{z_0}, the ten-state model. $(C'_{z_0})^S$ contains as elements equivalence classes of input strings, but as in the discussion of $C^S_{z_1}$, they will be considered here as transformations on $Z' = \{z_0, \ldots, z_9\}$.

PROPOSITION 6. $(C'_{z_0})^S$ is the subsemigroup of $F_R(X_{10})$ consisting of all of its order-preserving elements.

Proof. (a) Notice that the transformations corresponding to each of the unit length input strings are order-preserving. Thus $(C'_{z_0})^S$ is a subsemigroup of $F_R(X_{10})$ and consists only of order-preserving transformations, since the product (composition) of two order-preserving transformations is another order-preserving transformation and since every element of $(C'_{z_0})^S$ corresponds to a product (concatenation) of unit length input strings.

(b) Now notice that $(C'_{z_0})^S$ contains (1234567890), the transformation representing $[(a_2)]C'_{z_0}$. This element generates all other order-preserving transformations of rank ten (i.e. taking ten states to ten different states), the collection of which is a cyclic group isomorphic to Z_{10}. Now multiplying any rank-nine element (say $(2234567801) = [(a_3)]C'_{z_0}$) on the right by each of the elements of rank ten gives a rank-nine transformation of any desired range. Similarly, by multiplying a rank-nine element on the left by all of the rank-ten elements, all possible order-preserving partitions of X_{10} of order nine may be obtained. In order to get a rank-nine transformation of range Y and partition π, choose one of the already existing rank-nine elements with partition π and multiply it on the right by an appropriate rank-ten transformation. Thus all order-preserving elements of $F_R(X_{10})$ of rank nine and ten are included in $(C'_{z_0})^S$.

Now all order-preserving elements of $F_R(X_{10})$ of rank $n(n = 1, \ldots, 8)$ are obtained in like manner from the elements of higher rank.

PROPOSITION 7. $\#_G[(C'_{z_0})^S] \le 9$.

Proof. As for $C^S_{z_1}$, there are two ways to show this, one by thinking of $(C'_{z_0})^S$ as a semigroup and the other by considering the machine C'_{z_0}:

(a) $\qquad \#_G[(C'_{z_0})^S] \le |\text{spec}[C'_{z_0}]^S|$

$\qquad\qquad\qquad = |\{r > 1 : r = \text{rank}(t) \text{ for some } t \in (C'_{z_0})^S\}|$

$\qquad\qquad\qquad = |\{2, 3, \ldots, 10\}| = 9$.

(b) $\qquad \#_G[(C'_{z_0})^S] = \theta(C'_{z_0}) \le |Z'| - 1 = 10 - 1 = 9$.

By proposition 2 it is now possible to go directly to the "eggbox picture" of each of the $\mathscr{J}$ classes of $(C'_{z_0})^S$. However, since in this case the $\mathscr{J}$ classes are quite large (in comparison to those for $C^S_{z_1}$), it is advantageous to look only at the "relevant" portion of each $\mathscr{J}$ class. This is accomplished in two ways:

(1) Included are only those $\mathscr{L}$ classes of J_i which are in the orbit of the essential group G'_{i-1} belonging to J_{i-1} (as defined in Proposition 5).

(2) All $\mathscr{R}$ classes of J_i which yield only zeros in the structure matrix for J_i (when restricted as described in (1)) are excluded.

Since all of these $\mathscr{J}$ classes are regular, each J_i is isomorphic to a regular Rees matrix semigroup (Proposition 4) and so, in particular, it is possible to compute their structure matrices C_i (i.e. the structure matrices of the "reduced" $\mathscr{J}$ classes).

PROPOSITION 8. $\#_G[(C'_{z_0})^S] = 9$.

Proof. Notice that $C_2, \ldots, C_9$ are not normalizable to zeros and ones. Furthermore, $G'_i = G_i$ in each of these cases, since a generator of G_i is obtainable as the product of idempotents as follows:

$$e_{(1,12-i)} \cdot e_{(12-i,11-i)} \cdot e_{(11-i,10-i)} \cdots e_{(3,2)} \cdot e_{(2,1)}$$

$$= e_{(1,12-i)} \cdot \prod_{n=-12}^{-i-2} e_{(-i-n,-i-n-1)}$$

$$= g_{11-i}^{-1},$$

where g_{11-i} is the non-normalizable element of C_i. For example, if $i = 2$, then

$$e_{(1,12-i)} \cdot \prod_{n=-12}^{-i-2} e_{(-i-n,-i-1)}$$

$$= e_{(1,10)} \cdot e_{(10,9)} \cdot e_{(9,8)} \cdots e_{(2,1)}$$

$$= (0123456780) \cdot (0123456799) \cdot (0123456889) \cdot$$
$$\cdot (0123457789) \cdot (0123466789) \cdot (0123556789) \cdot$$
$$\cdot (0124456789) \cdot (0133456789) \cdot (0223456789)$$
$$\cdot (1123456789) \cdot$$
$$= (1234567891) =$$
$$= g_9^{-1}.$$

Hence $\langle g_{11-i}^{-1} \rangle = G_i' = G_i$, since G_i is cyclic.
Thus G_i' is essential for $i = 2, \dots, 9$, and

$$Z_{10} \equiv G_1 \cdot G_2' = G_2' > G_3' = G_3 > \cdots > G_9' = G_9$$

is a chain of essential groups with length $k = 9$. Therefore $9 \leq \#_G(C_{z_0}')^S$ and by Proposition 7, $\#_G[C_{z_0}']^S \leq 9$. Thus $9 \leq \#_G(C_{z_0}')^S \leq 9$ and $\#_G[(C_{z_0}')^S] = 9$.

2.7 THE GENERALIZED MODEL

In fact, the set of internal states Z' could be enlarged in order to simulate the action potential with more quantitative accuracy. It will be shown now that as $|Z'| = n$ is increased, the complexity of the model remains $n - 1$. Let $C_{z_0}^n$ represent the n-state machine simulation. The elements of $(C_{z_0}^n)^S$, the semigroup of $C_{z_0}^n$, will again be treated as order-preserving transofrmations on $Z^n = \{z_0, \dots, z_{n-1}\}$.

PROPOSITION 1. $(C_{z_0}^n)^S$ is the semigroup of $F_R(X_n)$ consisting of all of its order-preserving transformations.

Proof. (a) As with $(C_{z_0}')^S$, all of the transformations corresponding to unit length input strings are order-preserving, due to the nature of the model, and so $(C_{z_0}^n)^S$ is a subsemigroup of $F_R(X_n)$ and consists only of order-preserving transformations. This requires the same argument as in part (a) of the proof of Proposition 6.

(b) $(C_{z_0}^n)^S$ contains $(123\dots(n-1)0)$, since a stimulus sends each state z_i to the next state z_{i+1}, with the exception of z_{n-1}, which goes to z_0. $(123\dots(n-1)0)$ generates all other order-preserving transformations of rank n, the collection of which is cyclic group isomorphic to Z_n. Now at least one rank-$n - 1$ element exists since any stimulus of unit length is representable by the transformation $(01\dots(i-1)(i+1)\dots(n-1)0)$. Multiplying any rank-$n - 1$ element on the right by each of the elements of rank n gives a rank-$n - 1$ transformation of any desired range. Similarly, by multiplying a rank-$n - 1$ element on the left by all of the rank-n elements, all possible orderpreserving partitions of X_n of order $n - 1$ may be obtained. In order to get a rank-$n - 1$ transformation of range Y and partition π, choose one of the already existing rank-$n - 1$ elements with partition π and multiply it on the right by an appropriate rank-n transformation. Thus all order-preserving elements of $F_R(X_n)$ of rank n and $n - 1$ are included in $(C_{z0}^n)^S$.

Now all order-preserving elements of $F_R(X_n)$ of rank $1, \ldots, n - 2$ are obtained in like manner from the elements of higher rank.

PROPOSITION 2. $\#_G[(C_{z0}^n)^S] \le n - 1$.

Proof. There are again two methods available:

(a) $\#_G[(C_{z0}^n)^S] \le |\operatorname{spec}[(C_{z0}^n)^S]|$

$= |\{r > 1 : r = \operatorname{rank}(t) \text{ for some } t \in (C_{z0}^n)^S\}|$

$|\{2, 3, \ldots, n\}| = n - 1.$

(b) $\#_G[(C_{z0}^n)^S] = \theta(C_{z0}^n)^S \le |Z^n| - 1 = n - 1.$

By Proposition 2 it is possible to go directly to the "eggbox picture" of each of the "reduced" $\mathscr{J}$ classes of $(C_{z0}^n)^S$.

Since all of these $\mathscr{J}$ classes are regular, each J_i is isomorphic to a regular Rees matrix semigroup (Proposition 4, Section 4), and so it is possible to compute their structure matrices C_i.

PROPOSITION 3. $\#_G[(C_{z0}^n)^S] = n - 1$.

Proof. Notice that $C_2, \ldots, C_{n-1}$ are not normalizable to zeros and ones. Furthermore, $G'_i = G_i$ in each of these cases, since a generator of G_i is obtainable as a product of idempotents as described in the proof of Proposition 8 (Section 5), with the following modification:

$$e_{(1, n+2-i)} \cdot e_{(n+2-i, n+1-i)} \cdot e_{(n+1-i, n-1)} \cdots e_{(3,2)} \cdot e_{(2,1)}$$

$$e_{(1, n+2-i)} \cdot \prod_{j=n-2}^{-i-2} e_{(-i-j, -i-j-1)}$$

$$= g_{n+1-i}^{-1},$$

where g_{n+1-i} is the non-normalizable element of C_i.

Hence $\langle g_{n+1-i}^{-1} \rangle = G'_i = G_i$, since G_i is cyclic. Thus G'_i is essential for $i = 2, \ldots, n - 1$, and

$$Z_n \cong G_1 > G'_2 = G_2 > G'_3 = G_3 > \cdots > G'_{n-1} = G_{n-1}$$

is a chain of essential groups with length $k = n - 1$. Therefore $n - 1 \leq$ $\leq \#_G[(C_{z_0}^n)^S]$ and by Proposition 2, $\#_G[(C_{z_0}^n)^S] \leq n - 1$. Thus $n - 1 \leq$ $\leq \#_G[(C_{z_0}^n)^S] \leq n - 1$ and $\#_G[(C_{z_0}^n)^S] = n - 1$.

By Proposition 3, the complexity of $C_{z_0}^n$ is maximal regardless of the number of states n. This is significant in that it implies that the action potential is inherently complex, independently of the finite-state machine by which it is simulated. This result supports a theory of evolving organisms outlined by John Rhodes [9]. He states that "an evolving organism transforms itself in such a manner so as to maximize the contact with the complete environment subject to reasonable control and understanding of the contacted environment". Interpreting this statement in terms of automata theory, an "evolving" finite-state machine transforms itself in such a manner so as to maximize its number of states while maintaining its complexity at a near-maximal level. Evolved organisms, on the other hand, must be evolutionarily stable (i.e. complexity must be within approximately 5% of the contact). In this case, the fact that the action potential has absolutely maximal complexity regardless of the cardinality of the set of internal states $|Z'|$ indicates that it is indeed stable under the forces of evolution.

REFERENCES

[1] Arbib, M.A. (ed.), *Algebraic Theory of Machines, Languages, and Semigroups*, Academic Press, New York, 1968.

[2] Arbib, M.A., *Brains, Machines and Mathematics*, McGraw Hill, New York, 1964.

[3] Clifford, A.H., and G.B. Preston, *The Algebraic Theory of Semigroups*, Vol. 1, Amer. Math Soc., Providence, R.I. 1961.

[4] Eilenberg, S., *Automata, Languages and Machines*, Vol. B, Academic Press, New York 1976.

[5] Krohn, K., R. Mateosian and J. Rhodes, 'Complexity of Ideals in Finite Semigroups and Finite-State Machines', *Mathematical Systems Theory* 1 (1967), 59–66, and erratum, 1 (1967), 373.

[6] Minsky, M.I. and S. Papert, *Perceptrons: An Introduction to Computational Geometry*, M.I.T. Press, Cambridge (Mass.), 1971.

[7] Minsky, M.I., *Computation: Finite and Infinite Machines*, Prentice-Hall, Englewood Cliffs, 1967.

[8] Rhodes, J.L. and B.R. Tilson, 'Improved Lower Bounds for Complexity of Finite Semigroups', *Journ. Pure and Applied Algebra* 2 (1972), 13–71.

[9] Rhodes, J.L., *Application of Automata Theory and Algebra*, Lecture Notes, Dept. of Math., Univ. of California, Berkeley, 1971.

[10] Tilson, B., 'Decomposition and Complexity of Finite Semigroups', *Semigroup Forum* 2 (1971), 189–250.

CHAPTER 3

COMPLEXITY AND DYNAMICS

3.1 INTRODUCTION AND MOTIVATION

In this chapter we will be concerned with the common properties of various dynamic systems, including those occurring in biology and ecology as well as in the social sciences. We consider some broad characteristics before turning to analyses.

Although a dynamic system can be represented by a set of difference or differential equations specifying the direction and speed of points (objects) in some space, we find it more natural to emphasize the organizational aspects of dynamic systems as adopted by cyberneticians or system theorists: that is, in a dynamic analysis we meet the sequential machine in its most general form. In the case of living systems, organisms interact with the environment and change steadily or abruptly as impulses, stimuli, and messages are exchanged with the environment.[1] We assume that at any given instant of time, as the system proceeds, the state of the system can be observed, that the system is state – determined and that the *state* space is finite. It is also assumed that the system strives for "survival".

Survival may arise from competitiveness. To some extent the renewed interest in patterns of growth and survival elaborates on a well-known theme familiar to ecologists, as discussed by Gause [6], e.g. the "battle of life or the struggle for existence". Ecologists have both worked theoretically and experimentally on related aspects of the *Darwin – Wallace* theory of evolution, based on the problem whether plants or animals can grow without limit while striving for their existence given their environment.

Mathematically, the process of "struggle for existence" has been treated by ordinary or partial differential equations, possibly displaying the *Verhulst-Pearl* logistic curve given as $dN/dt = b \ N(K - N)/K$, where N denotes the actual population, K the maximal population, and b the potential increase of population, a parameter.

The general conclusion of these investigations is that environmental factors severely limit the growth rate and finally stop it – and this is supported by various experiments (see *Gause* [6], and also *Rapoport*

76

[10]). It is obvious that these systems belong to the class of competitive systems. We are interested in knowing whether such systems possess a stable equilibrium (in some appropriate sense), or whether the equilibrium is unstable and the system is bound to break down. What is a stable equilibrium? There exist various definitions by various authors, and it is good to find some agreement at the outset. Intuitively, an equilibrium could be called *stable* if any perturbation of the system in the neighborhood of a state will bring the system back to a stable state. A stable state in a stochastic sense is even weaker than this statement and additional qualifications have to be used. Adaptation and learning could be real sources for 'stability', some systems to be discussed may show a stronger tendency to adapt than not to adapt. However, adaptation certainly has some limits. Often it is less interesting to know whether systems are 'adaptive' or 'non-adaptive', but if they are, how fast adaptation is going to be. It is imaginable that even adaptive systems will break down if the rate of adaptation is too slow given the complexity of the system.

A more appropriate notion of stability for systems to survive is proposed by that of a *steady state* system. According to A. Rapoport [10] we may speak in the case of higher-order organizations not just primitive organisms, qualifying as living systems of *identity-preserving activities*. Those are usually governed by *homeostatic mechanisms* to keep the system in a relatively "steady state". A system is conceived to be in a steady state if all the variables of interest governing the transition of the system appear to be *constant* in time. Furthermore, the system remains in a steady state if it could preserve its identity over time, if it reproduces itself but does not do more than that. What could be meant by that? If we acknowledge the fact that a complex living organism develops from a single cell into an organized aggregate of differentiated cells, passing through periods of growth, maturation, and deterioration to death, preservation of identity should mean that in this *birth-growth-death* process a substitution rule takes place in which dying cells are replaced by growing cells so that the organism regenerates itself, a balance is kept over time and continuity of life is ensured.

In advancing the main conclusions to be attained we state that in the context of economic systems a steady state cannot be reached unless there is a potential of permanent change in the system resulting from *adaptation, goal-seeking, learning,* or *development of technology and resources,* otherwise a catastrophe may be unavoidable and can well be predicted for a foreseeable future.

There have been several approaches to dealing with these types of dynamic (competitive) systems, and we will discuss briefly one main line of thought bearing the name of catastrophe theory in a later section. Suffice it to make some principal remarks.

Whereas *Ashby* [1] acknowledges that 'living things' are complex, in particular biological systems as well as social systems he makes the point that a study of such complex systems requires methods of topology. We do agree with the first statement, although obviously not the second. It is clear that complex systems represent a matter which we do not understand sufficiently well; and we are even less able to describe them precisely.

Hence there is more recent emphasis on the *qualitative*, global behavior of such systems, although the question still remains how much mathematical structure do we really need to describe such systems fairly well. It is our understanding that algebraic structures are most natural to begin with – rather than topological considerations. After all, the approach adopted here can be extended to include topological considerations.

In what follows, we are mainly concerned with elucidating two cardinal problems arising in the study of survival for dynamical systems: these problems are intimately wedded. I shall call them the *global* and the *structural* problem, respectively:

(1) How to determine the overall *global* behavior of the system given uniform patterns of behavior among subsystems, equal distributions of resources, technology and power? Does the global behavior of the system attain some point of stability or does it lead to a breakdown due to inherent contradictions of the system?

(2) Independent of the global view of a system, could such system be called structurally stable or do there exist inequalities among subsystems which promote inbalances, rifts and overall tensions and therefore create structurally unstable states?

In fact, we could argue that the second problem is embedded in the first one since structurally unstable systems could put restrictions on the global behavior of a system and therefore could cause global breakdowns (catastrophes).

In the next section we consider some situations which emphasize the distinction between the global and the structural point of view. In Section 3 we are directly concerned with the global problem. If solved this way the solution could be put as a restriction on the global problem, e.g. by an appropriate parameterization.

3.2 COMPETITIVE PROCESSES AND DYNAMICAL SYSTEMS

EXAMPLE 1. A dynamic competitive situation which shows unstable global behavior and therefore fits our first case is that of the 'tragedy of the commons' (see G. Hardin [7]). This situation could result in a catastrophic global outcome of the entire system even if it is rational for individuals to stick to their own personal goals. The inherent logic of the commons – on the basis of their competitive behavior – generates their own tragedy. Consider a certain area of land (finite space). Each herdsman will try to keep as many cattle as possible and assume that this is equivalent to maximizing his gain. Suppose the marginal utility of adding one more animal to the commons is positive, say $+1$, for every herdsman; however, suppose further that the social utility contributed to him is negative, but only a fraction of -1 due to the effects of overgrazing, or more generally, due to the gradual depletion of resources. The tragedy consists of the incompatibility of individual rationality and social necessity. Every member of the commons pursuing his own best interests brings ruin to all. This should be a familiar example for economists who would argue on the basis of the theory of externalities in order to bridge the gap in this paradoxical situation which appears to be a prisoner's dilemma situation.

The deeper problem lies in the fact that we need voluntary restriction – or if not possible, some kind of effective control system which is able to reconcile the paradoxical nature in the 'tragedy of the commons'. The treatment of pollution is just a dual aspect of the 'tragedy of the commons'. The rational man finds that his share of the cost of the wastes he discharges into the commons is less than the cost of purifying his wastes before releasing them.

EXAMPLE 2. Another situation, pertaining to the second problem, is that of development of spatial life patterns in primitive organisms or complex social organizations. Here *structural instability* could occur long before global instability of the system would arise. This is the situation of Conway's Game of Life [5]. This 'game' reveals a similar development pattern as the 'Birth-Life-Death-Process' in struggle for existence models. Since this game forms an analogy to formation rules of living organisms or cell structures it belongs to a class of games which are known as simulation games, e.g. games which resemble real life processes. Conway's game could prove useful for providing new concepts in the study of those life processes (such as the development of cells), but could also form a starting point for studying more complex systems (such as the formation of urban structures).

Now, what is the basic structure of this game, what initial conditions are set, and what rules or "genetic laws" do apply so that the game adopts a certain pattern of stable or unstable configurations?

First it seems meaningful to classify the main types of patterns among infinitely many configurations to satisfy certain boundary conditions.

P. 1. There should be no non-trivial initial pattern (configuration of cells) where it can always be proved that the population can grow without limit.

P. 2. There should be at least one simple initial pattern that grows without limit.

P. 3. There should be simple initial patterns that grow over time up to a certain state where either

(a) they fade away (from overcrowding or isolation);

(b) they settle into a stable configuration that keeps a steady state;

(c) they keep an endless cycle (flip-flop or stationarity).

Only P. 3 classifies a reasonable and interesting class of configurations giving rise to the specification of the rules of the game and, consequently, to the characterization of survival, death and birth.

(1) *Survival* Every cell with two or three neighbors survives in the next generation (move).

(2) *Death* (a) Every cell with one neighbor or none dies from isolation.

(b) Every cell with four or more neighbors dies from overpopulation.

(3) *Birth* One empty cell adjacent to exactly three neighbors is a birth cell and matures as full cell in the next generation.

We denote a full cell by ($\otimes$) and a birth cell by ($\circ$). The Table I demonstrates the consequences of the rules in terms of possible simple configurations.

Conway recommends playing the game by starting out with some initial pattern, searching for cells which are going to survive, die or are birth cells; then we should determine all kinds of configurations possible in this game, hence we should show the complete life history of cells according to the rules. Conway demonstrated that, given some initial configurations, most patterns show a stable configuration in a finite number of subsequent generations, and that some patterns show a flip-flop behavior.

Conway's conjecture that there is no non-trivial pattern where it

TABLE I

	Initial Pattern	Next Generation (1)	Next Generation (2) ...	
Survival {	⊗ ⊗ / ⊗	⊗ ⊗ Survival	Death	
	⊗ / ⊗ / ⊗	⊗ Survival	Death	
	⊗ ⊗ ⊗ (converging to) ⊗	⊗ ⊗ ⊗ ⊗ Survival	⊗ ⊗ Survival	Death
	⊗ ⊗ ⊗	⊗ ⊗ ⊗ Survival (cycling)	⊗ ⊗ ⊗ Survival (cycling)	
Death {	⊗ ⊗	Death (Isolation)		
	⊗ ⊗ ⊗ ⊗ (converging to) ⊗	Death (overpopulation)		
Birth {	⊗ ⊗ ⊗ ○	⊗ ⊗ ⊗ ⊗ (stable)		

can be proved that it grows without limit has, however, been disproved in some cases (by counter examples) stemming from cellular automata theory.

In general we can use a network of finite state machines to generate spatial dynamics. Consider an infinite array (in two dimensions) of identical simple finite state machines, which we shall call *cells*. Each cell communicates with other cells in its neighborhood. The finite state machines, or cells, are described by specifying a set of *transition rules*. These rules specify which state a cell will enter (during the next step) as a function of the cell's neighbors. Except as otherwise specified, we will consider only two-dimensional square cells with the four nearest neighbors comprising the five-neighbor neighborhood.

A *configuration* is a specification of the states of the cells in the array at any given time. When started in particular initial configurations, the cells can be made to perform interesting processes. There is a natural link between these processes, games, and spatial configurations and patterns of growth of figures as stated mathematically by S.M. Ulam [16].

In summary, we consider the possible behavior exhibited by vast numbers (usually infinite) of identical, very simple machines each interacting with its nearest neighbors.

A particular *cellular space* is characterized by the transition rules. We could use the form CNESWR say, to write the rules. The letters stand for Current state, state of the North neighbor, East, South, West, and the Result state *R*. A set of rules in this form defines a cellular space.

A close analogy between Conway's Game and cellular automata theory has been established. The latter theory can be used as a methodological device, notably as a model of machine self-reproduction, and more specifically as that of self-reproduction of complicated living mechanisms. Every cell could be considered as an automaton being an element in a cellular space. The automaton would essentially be a pattern creating machine which is governed by the rules of Conway's game (see Kemeny [8]).

It would be interesting now, after accepting Conway's rules, to view this game as a competitive process acting over time. In particular, it would be interesting to know under what conditions competitive processes would be compatible with his results and what does "stable configuration" mean in this context.

We apply these ideas to urban and city formation constituting a complex social system.

One of the interesting questions to ask about social life is what kind of social processes have created urban structures. Unlike in earlier times, in particular in the middle-ages, where urban life predominantly has adopted a stationary pattern due to technological stationarity and social immobility, modern industrialization has brought some strong dynamic elements into force among which are those we today consider undesirable for social, ecological and economic reasons. Urban sociologists talk about the organizational structure of the city making a distinction between membership groups (those representing certain commercial interests) and spatial groups (those representing a specific area which could coincide with those of common ethnicity or cultural background). It is a general dynamic process acting in a particular system (the urban system) creating social and economic structures. The groups involved may compete for the city's resources, space, technology and environmental conditions. The dynamics of the system is basically given by the behavior rules of the major groups, by their interactions with the environment, by the changing structure of the competitive process induced by changes of rules or the environment. The system could be conceived as a machine where, at the initial state, inputs are received from the environment, and after the machine has started, outputs are received by other agents and by the environment.

Dynamic competitive situations like that of urban formation might involve quite different bargaining positions due to the sequential nature of games. In case of urban processes, for instance, it is possible to assume at the outset that for a given fixed number of (urban) players there are no institutional bounds (e.g. zoning regulations, land allotments etc.) or even opportunities for cooperative social arrangements. This corresponds to a laissez-faire spirit in urban formation! However, when the game proceeds, some players may form coalitions or anti-coalitions according to specific interests, thus reducing the number of players and possibly restricting the competitive situation (see Example 3). In the context of a game played sequentially the problem of realizing stable configurations poses interesting questions concerning the existence of Pareto optimal points. It should be clear that the realization of Pareto optimal points at each stage of the game itself in not sufficient for this game to obtain a stable configuration. The reason is that any Pareto optimal point realized in some distant future may be worse than any one realized in the near future. Thus more concretely, ghetto-type parts of the city, slums and blights, unequal employment opportunities etc. are well compatible with Pareto optimality given the rules of the game.

Hence, for achieving a stable configuration in a dynamic competitive process, the assumption of weak dominance of Pareto optimal points realized in the more distant future over points realized in the near future seems to be a satisfactory and reasonable condition.[2]

We may construct an analogy between urban formation as a dynamic process in an open system and the evolution of organisms where the formation of cells is modelled by finite state sequential machines and the concepts of "stability", "perfect balance" or "perfect harmony" have a precise meaning in this context.

EXAMPLE 3. (Schelling's Game)
The problem of structural stability in dynamic systems is intrinsically related to the concept of growth, form and competition. There are many indications that ecosystems organize themselves according to competition, for example, competition for moisture affects spatial positioning of desert plants (see Cody [3]), and, furthermore, specific living patterns have been found for birds and other species which are the result of competitive behavior.

In the dynamic context of social situations we observe an inherent relationship, between competitive, cooperative and controlling forces. Any of these forces may play dominant roles at some stages of development of the game. The formation of urban structures may present one good example among others where the starting conditions in the presence of a 'healthy' environment, with ample resources and unspoiled ecological conditions, tend to favor strong competitive forces, whereas at a later stage competitiveness may turn toward cooperativeness if environmental conditions worsen or if new players enter the game as countervailing powers or other participants alter their strategies. But if this procedure fails, controlling forces may take over which may limit competitiveness in some sectors and totally discourage it in others, establishing a different allocation scheme.

There may be many motivations why people tend to be more cooperative in a different more adversary environment, where they start to realize that cooperation unlike competition might serve their interests better, at least for long run purposes.

Such situations have been described at length by Th. C. Schelling [11]. Schelling's game covers most of the ideas exposed in Conway's game. However, Schelling is primarily interested in some practical problems, e.g. in some segregation patterns observed in cities and in the major factors that cause these patterns. Like Conway's game, the game devised can be played on a checker board with checkers of different colors representing different races, groups of different linguistic or cultural background etc. It involves definite rules to generate certain spatial patterns, for example, that every red checker wants at least half of his neighbors to be "red checkers", and every blue checker wants at least a third of his neighbors to be "blue checkers". The initial configuration, in order to make it a non-trivial initial pattern, will be randomly mixed. Every checker who tends to be discontent with his neighborhood is allowed to move. Every move is going to change the initial configuration, and the question is: under a given finite number of moves (stages of the game) do the configurations adopt a stable pattern? Essentially here it does not matter who moves first and in what order, hence the moves are basically random. A stable pattern is reached when everybody settles in a satisfactory environment, that is when nobody sees any reason to move elsewhere. If nevertheless he does, others will be caused to move also which might end up in a new configuration which again could be altered etc. In some cases this will result in a flip-flop. We observe that adjustment processes of this kind, if they exist, being completely determined by the "rules of the game", act exclusively within the internal system. Some specific cases and even generalizations of this game can be discussed.

(a) One obvious generalization is by considering an open system rather than a closed system as in Schelling's case), in which people interact with their environment and the environment changes over time. In such a system actions will be continuously revised (for instance due to learning) or new rules will be set: the number of players could vary over time; some players will leave; others will enter the game; new coalitions might be found, others will be abolished.

(b) One interesting additional set of rules would specify the direction of moves (subject to conditions of neighborhood) rather than assume merely random moves. For example, if Whites tend to move into neighborhoods of white dominance rather than black dominance or vice versa: e.g. under a possible and strictly verifiable hypothesis, if Whites tend to move into suburbs whereas Blacks tend to move into downtown areas. Those Whites still living in downtown areas and becoming discontent with their neighborhood thus tend to move into suburbs rather than into other downtown areas although the latter ones might still satisfy the minimum requirement of a suitable proportion between Whites and Blacks. Thus assumptions on the direction of moves together with its group-dynamic aspects seem to imply a stronger segregationist pattern. Another tendency toward a more segregationist pattern would be implied by a broader concept of a neighborhood, for example white enclaves surrounded by black communities would provide such an example.

(c) The game may be further complicated by admitting the complexity of human behavior, the motivation for moving usually will not only result from racial considerations or prejudices. Moves could be motivated by a chain of conditions, for example, as they appear in a lexicographic preference ordering of the type (Race, Educational Background, Religion ...). Such orderings would give rise to patterns of small homogeneous groups in all components with very little contact and information between these groups. In case of a non-lexicographic but compensatory preference ordering, as in ordinary indifference analysis, the behavior pattern of groups in a city at least becomes hard to determine. This is even more so if residential choices are linked to a negative choice rule "where not to move".

Given the existence of certain preference patterns, I think, it is fair to say that most of them are of a mixed compensatory-lexicographic type. For example, a convinced *environmentalist* would act according to a lexicographic ordering w.r.t. ecological attributes but will adopt a compensatory preference pattern w.r.t. other components.

From a descriptive point of view, however, most behavior patterns may not uniquely lead to a final configuration. Suppose we know the initial configuration and the final configuration: what set of behavior rules may have generated the final configuration given the initial one? This question is hard to answer, if at all, since we could think of a large number of behavior patterns generating the same final configuration. This is a kind of identification problem. From a normative point of view the advantage of Conway-Schelling-type games consists of showing which rules will give us a better understanding of survival chances of metropolitan patterns than any descriptive analysis can reveal (see Lynch [9]).

3.3 DESCRIPTION OF A DYNAMIC SYSTEM

Now let us exhibit the relationship between complexity and dynamics in the framework of algebraic system theory. In general, a dynamic system (T, Z, X, Y, X, Y) is characterized by the following properties:

(1) $X = \{x : T \to X\}$
$Y = \{y : T \to Y\}$,

where X, Y are sets of input and output values and X, Y sets of input and output functions, respectively.

(2) T is an ordered subset of the reals or the integers.

(3) Definition of input segment: for every $x \in X$ let $x_{(t_1, t_2]}$ be the input segments restricted to time interval $(t_1, t_2] \in T$. For $x, x' \in X, t_1 < t_3. \exists x''$:
$x''_{(t_1 t_3]} = x'_{(t_2, t_3]} \cdot x_{(t_1, t_2]}$ (concatenation).

(4) $\lambda : T \times T \times Z \times X \to Z$ is the transition function given by $z(t) = \lambda(t, \tau, z, x) \in Z$ with $\tau \in T$ as initial time.

(5) An output function given by $\delta : T \times Z \to Y, y(t) = \delta(t, z(t))$.

Based on the results of Sec. 2.2, let us state the following.

GENERAL PROBLEM: *Let X be the entire phase space on which a right semigroup S is acting – corresponding to a machine $f : \sum A \to B$ which is realized by serial-parallel or cascade decomposition into component machines. Then is it possible to find decompositions of (X, S) into transformation subsemigroups $(X_k, S_k), k = 1, \ldots, n$ such that one gets the minimal solution of $(X, S)|(X_n, S_n) \circ \cdots \circ (X_1, S_1)$?*

EXAMPLE. Let an experiment E be applied to a phase space X, (the space of all trajectories or behavior lines of the system), i.e. $E(X) \equiv X$, with input set $E(A) \equiv A$, action $E(\lambda) \equiv \lambda : X \times A \to X$. $\lambda(x, a)$ is the experimentally observed "effect" of a perturbation or stimulus $a \in A$ upon the system being initially in state x. Let E be an experiment giving rise to (X, A, λ). Let $E(S) \equiv S$ be the *semigroup of the experiment* E that, by definition, equals $\{ \cdot a_1 \cdots a_n : n \geq 1$ and $a_j \in A \}$ where $\cdot a_1 \cdots a_n$ denotes the mapping of X into X given by $x \to x \cdot a_1 \cdots a_n$ with $x \cdot a_1 \cdots a_n$ defined by recursive relations

$$x_0 \cdot a_1 \cdots a_n = \lambda(x_0, a_1 \cdots a_n) = b_n$$

with

$$x_0 = y_0 \text{ and } y_t = \lambda(b_{t-1}, a_t).$$

Thus $x_0 \cdot a_1 \cdots a_n = b_n$ is the resulting state after inputs $a_1, a_2, \ldots, a_n$ have been applied to the system in that order which was initially in state x_0. Then a physical theory for E is a solution of $(X, S)|(X_n, S_n) \circ \cdots \circ (X_1, S_1)$. *In order to invoke some optimality property one wants to have a minimal solution.*

In classical physics most of the fundamental processes are time-reversible and we are dealing with *groups of transformations*, on the other hand, societal and economic processes are time-irreversible and therefore we are dealing with semigroups instead of groups.

The deeper algebraic idea of realizing a machine by component machines is provided by the Krohn–Rhodes Prime Decomposition Theory (see Chapter 2, Section 4, for a comprehensive account with many ramifications), and even more fundamentally by the Jordan–Hölder-Theory in which it is proved that each finite group can be built from a fixed set of simple group (called Jordan–Hölder factors). In machine-theoretic language the corresponding problem is to factor finite state machines into the smallest (possible) component machines to obtain a prime decomposition theorem for finite state machines. A solution of this problem brings into play complexity as a natural tool.

(Let (X, S) be a right mapping semigroup. Then the (group) complexity $\#_G(X, S) = \#_G(S)$ is defined to be the smallest non-negative integer n such that

$$S \mid (Y_n, C_n)w(X_n, G_n)w \cdots w(Y_1, C_1)w(X_1, G_1)w(Y_0, C_0)$$

holds with $G_1, \ldots, G_n$ being finite groups and $C_0, \ldots, C_n$ finite combinatorial semigroups (flip-flops), i.e. the minimal number of alternations of blocks of simple groups and blocks of combinatorial semigroups necessary to obtain (X, S). Hence by making full use of decomposition results on sequential machines one could redefine complexity in terms of the phase space decomposition, i.e. optimal decomposition implies $\#_G(S) = \min \#_G\{X : X$ is a serial-parallel or cascade decomposition of $S\}$.

Therefore, *complexity finds its group-theoretic roots in the fact that the transformation semigroup can be simulated* (realized) *by the wreath product of all pairs of component machines whose semigroups are simple groups and those machines whose semigroups are finite combinatorial semigroups* (= flip-flop machines). Intuitively speaking, a *combinatorial semigroup corresponds to a machine that virtually does no computation but rather switches inputs and outputs among various input-output configurations.*

EXAMPLES. Take a three-element semigroup, say $U_3 = (\{a, b\}, \{S_a, S_b Id\})$, $a \neq b$, and every input $x \in \{a, b\}$ containing three transformations S_a, S_b, Id such that $x S_a = a$, $x S_b = b$, $x Id = x$. Then U_3, in machine-theoretical language, would be called a flip-flop or identity reset machine where S_a, S_b, Id respectively will correspond to the instructions "drop x and replace it by a", "drop x and replace it by b", and "do nothing". The flip-flop plays a prominent role in the Krohn–Rhodes Decomposition Theory in that it constitutes the combinatorial part of the irreducible subsemigroups that, composed together with simple groups, realize the given semigroup machine. The link between the Jordan–Hölder theory of decomposition of finite groups and the Krohn–Rhodes theory of decomposition is given by the statement that 'finite semigroup theory is finite group theory plus the "flip-flop"'. Another machine belonging to this class, generating a combinatorial semigroup is the *delay one* machine, D_1. A delay one machine over $\{a, b\}$ is by definition $D_1 : \sum \{a, b\} \to \{a, b, *\}$ with $D_1(a_1) = *$ and $D_1(a_1, \ldots, a_n) = a_{n-1}$. Likewise for all delay machines with higher order $1, 2, \ldots, U_3^f$ and D_1 have complexity zero. This property reminds us of information theory when selecting events which have information measure zero. These types of machine generate regular patterns to be expected, they do not yield any surprise. Therefore, their behavior does not produce information. Since everybody understands it, it cannot be complex. This result has some immediate impact on possible applications. It suggests that if we are able to detect subsystems that behave like flip-flops we could erase these subsystems without changing the structural complexity associated to other subsystems but, nevertheless, decreasing the computational complexity in terms of length of computations.

On the other hand, simple groups conform to machines that perform simple arithmetic operations (such as addition, multiplication, ...). A simple group constitutes the basic (irreducible) complexity element which increases the complexity of the machine by just one unit. Hence punching out groups of that kind in the decomposition lowers complexity at most by one. Now what is the significance of the Krohn-Rhodes theory? It shows us to which extent we can decompose a machine into components that are primitive and irreducible and that the solution depends on the structure of components and on the length of computation. Hence complexity does not depend only on how long a chain of components there are, but also on how complicated each component is. Therefore, complexity takes account of the total number of computations in a chain (the computational aspect) but also of the inherent complexity of the subsemigroups (submachines) hooked together via the wreath product (the structural aspect). The computational aspect can heuristically be represented by the amount of 'looping' in a computer program that computes S on X. This has been proposed by C. Futia [4] for computing sequential decision or search rules. These are the key features of an algebraic theory of complexity. It opens some interesting questions about which applications can be given to an algebraic complexity theory. Such questions will be taken up in a later discussion.

3.4 AXIOMS OF COMPLEXITY

Let $F_R(X)$ be the transformation semigroup of all functions on X. A function $\#_G : F_R(X) \to N$ (non-negative integers) is called a complexity function. One aspect of such a complexity function is to exhibit various properties of groups or semigroups which play a role in the decomposition theory. Instead we are interested in more general conditions to show that group complexity is virtually equivalent to machine complexity.

This gives us another clue for translating or transforming algebraic complexity into complexity of real systems. In general, there are two ways in which transformation semigroups are useful: (i) representing different machines or systems by semigroups for computing their complexity; (ii) representing one particular machine by different designs and each design having its own transformation semigroup.

Let M_F denote the collection of all machines (realizable by finite state circuits), let $\theta : M_F \to N$ and $f, g \in M_f$.

Let $f : \sum A \to B$ and $g : \sum A' \to B'$ be two machines. Then f is less than or equal in capability to g, e.g. $f \mid g$ iff there exists a homomorphism (trivial code) $H : \sum A \to A'$ and a function $j : B' \to B$ such that $f = gjH$.

The *parallel combination* of f and g, denoted by $f \oplus g$ is by definition $f \oplus g : \sum (A \times B) \to A' \times B'$ with $f \oplus g((a_1, b_1), \dots, (a_n, b_n)) = (f(a_1, \dots, a_n), g(b_1, \dots, b_n))$.

This definition can be easily generalized to an arbitrary number of machines in parallel combination.

Let $H : B \to B'$ be the trivial code depending on the number of inputs, denoted by H^Γ. Let f^σ be the extension of f if successively inputs $a_1, (a_1, a_2), \dots, (a_1, \dots, a_n)$ will be applied to f.

Then serial combination of f and g, denoted by $f \otimes g$, is by definition $gH^\Gamma f^\sigma = k = f \otimes g$. Thus $k(a_1, \dots, a_n) = g(h(f(a_1)), h(f(a_1, a_2)), \dots, h(f(a_1, \dots, a_n)))$.

Looking at the corresponding circuit construction, we consider serial parallel decomposition in terms of state and output representations. Therefore, let $M_1 = (A, B, Z_1, \lambda_1, \delta_1)$ and $M_2 = (C, D, Z_2, \lambda_2, \delta_2)$ be two state dependent output circuits. Let $H : \sum B \to \sum C$ be a homomorphism. Then a new machine $(A, D, Z_1 \times Z_2, \lambda, \delta)$ is the series composition of M_1 by M_2 with connecting homomorphism H, given in terms of $M_2 \otimes H \otimes M_1$, where

$$\lambda[(z_2, z_1), a] =$$
$$= (\lambda_2[H(\delta_1(\lambda_1(Z_1, a)), z_2), \lambda_1(z_1, a)], \delta(z_2, z_1)) =$$
$$= \delta_2(z_2).$$

Likewise, define the parallel composition of M_1 and M_2 by

$$M_1 \oplus M_2 = (A \times C, B \times D, Z_1 \times Z_2, \lambda_1 \oplus \lambda_2, \delta_1 \oplus \delta_2),$$

where

$$\lambda_1 \oplus \lambda_2((z_1, z_2)(a, c)) = (\lambda_1(z_1, a), \lambda_2(z_2, c)),$$
$$\delta_1 \oplus \delta_2((z_1, z_2)) = (\delta_1(z_1), \delta_2(z_2)).$$

The following result (which is easy to prove just by computation) demonstrates the interconnectedness of circuit and machine construction:

AXIOM 2. For all machines $f_1, f_2 \in M_F$

$$\theta(f_2 \otimes f_1) \leq \theta(f_2) + \theta(f_1).$$

If there is a feedback operation $\rightarrow$ from f_2 to f_1, then

$$\theta(f_2 \otimes f_1) \leq \theta(f_2) + \theta(f_1) + \theta(f_2 \rightarrow f_1).$$

AXIOM 3. $\theta(U_3^f) = 0$, $\theta(D_1) = 0$.
On the basis of Axioms 1–3 we have

$$\theta(f) = \#_G(f^S).$$

3.5 EVOLUTION COMPLEXITY

Up to now we have only dealt with design complexity of a particular machine or system. Under *design complexity* I understand that complexity (number) associated with the transformation process in which full use of the system potential is made. However, under design complexity, this transformation process need not result in stable configurations, for example, unstable configurations may result from a gap between computability requirements of the entire system and the computational capacities of the connected subsystems aiming at realizing the entire system. This situation occurs if there is no solution of $(X, S)|(X_n, S_n) \circ \cdots \circ (X_1, S_1)$, or, equivalently, if there is only a solution of $(X', S')|(X_n, S_n) \circ \cdots \circ (X_1, S_1)$ where (X', S') may represent some system with a lower performance than (X, S).
Let $(M_1)_1^z = f$, $(M_2)_{z_2} = g$. Then

$$(M_2 \otimes H \otimes M_1)_{(z_1, z_2)} = gHf^\delta \text{ and } (M_1 \oplus M_2)_{(z_1, z_2)} \equiv f \oplus g.$$

Let us rewrite the state transitions in the serial composition in a different form, making use of $z_i \cdot a = \lambda_i(z_i, a)$, $z_i \cdot t = \lambda_i(t, z_i)$, $t = (a_1, \ldots, a_n) \in \sum A$ when $i = 1$ and $t \in \sum C$ when $i = 2$ so that $(z_i \cdot t_1) \cdot t_2 = z_i \cdot t_1 t_2$. Then we have

$$(z_2, z_1) \cdot a = (z_2 \cdot H(\delta_1(z_1, a)), z_1 \cdot a) = (z_2', z_1'),$$
$$\delta(z_2, z_1) = \delta_2(z_2).$$

This reformulation provides us with more intuitive properties of triangularization and k-th component action lying in S_k used in the definition of the wreath product (Section 2.2).

We observe that z'_1 depends only on z_1 and a (and not on z_2). This is the meaning of *a acting in triangular form*. Also since $z_1 \to z_1 \cdot a$ is an element of M_1^S, the semigroup of M_1 associated to S_1 for each $a \in A$, so $z_2 \vdash$ $\vdash z_2 \cdot H(\delta(z_1, a))$ is an element of M_2^S (for each fixed $z_1 \in Z_1$ and fixed $a \in A$). We then say that a has *k-th component action in M_k^S*.

Let us now state the

Axioms of Complexity.

AXIOM 1. (a) $f \mid g$ implies $\theta(f) \le \theta(g)$;
        (b) $\theta(f_1 \oplus \cdots \oplus f_n) = \max\{\theta(f_i) : i = 1, \dots, n\}$.

Under *control complexity* we understand that specific complexity (number) that results from computations which keep the entire system or at least part of it under complete control.

Mathematically, represent the global input-output behavior by a semigroup $S \in F_R(X)$ associated to the system $f : \sum A \to B$. Then S is under *complete control* iff there exists an input sequence $t = (a_1, \dots, a_n)$ that applied to S_j, $j = 1, \dots, n$ leaves S_j in stable state $z_{f_{(j)}}$, i.e. that is invariant with respect to changes of t,

$$S_j \cdot t = S_{f_{(j)}} \quad \text{for all } j \text{ in the decomposition.}$$

Thus the control of S is complete iff all local states in the decomposition are invariant with respect to input sequences. In practice, we could adopt the above definition for all values of t in a sufficiently large interval. Otherwise the control of S is said to be not complete and no global stable configurations will result.

Unstable configuration may occur if some subsystems are unable to compute (adjust) fast enough in order to adopt changes of input sequences. This is behind the intuitive meaning of control complexity.

The relation between design and control complexity is called *evolution complexity*. A system is said to be in *perfect harmony* or *perfect balance* *whenever the utilization of its potentialities is complete, i.e. when design complexity and control complexity coincide.*

EXAMPLE. One problem is to define perfect harmony assuming the finite state machine modeling, and then to render in a precise form the evolution complexity relation. The cell is divided into two parts *Meta-*

bolism and *Genetic Control*, both are finite state machines interacting with each other. It is essentially the Jacob-Monod-model.

One way to consider the interaction within a cell is as follows: G is attempting to control M where G samples the output of M and then puts a correction input back into M (which is the usual setup in control theory). If G does it according to the design complexity and does not compute more or less than is required then stable configurations will result, and design and control complexity will coincide. Otherwise both will deviate and possibly a breakdown cannot be avoided.

Fortunately, in many cases of biological or ecological systems the principle of evolution works as follows: an evolving organism transforms itself in such a manner so as to maximize the contact with the complete environment subject to reasonable understanding and control of the contacted environment. This is why we consider most natural systems to be adaptive.

An intrinsic relation between complexity and catastrophe does exist. First, a system which develops beyond its complexity bound, e.g. that is required to perform more computations than is provided for in its design is not going to survive but to break down. This is intuitively quite acceptable but can be proved by determining upper complexity bounds along the alines as suggested in the previous section.

Next, the evolution complexity relation is crucial. The smaller this relationship the more balanced (stable) the system tends to be. We consider this situation as *qualitatively stable*. Such a system will survive if qualitative stability holds. On the other hand, the larger this relation the more unstable the system will become up to a point where a breakdown cannot be avoided. Such a breakdown will constitute a *catastrophe*. Recall that we want to model competitive systems, e.g. systems that strive for survival: in a biological context those which relate to the Darwin-Wallace theory of evolution.

EXAMPLE 1. In economic theory one is interested in what properties the competitive process invokes and the notions of competitive equilibrium and Pareto optimality apply in this context. It can be proved that every competitive process acting in a so-called classical environment is a Pareto satisfactory process. In the case where the environment is 'nice – i.e. where preferences and technology are convex and no indivisibilities and no externalities exist – one can prove that the competitive process will show a stable and optimal pattern. This situation corresponds to our case where design and control complexity coincide. On the other hand, if externalities are present we are able to show that the design complexity of the system increases whereas the control complexity remains unchanged. Therefore, in this case the competitive system acting under externalities does not produce an optimal pattern in terms of Pareto optimality. This can be demonstrated for very simple models of the tragedy-of-the-commons-type.

In the tragedy-of-the-commons-type situation it is obvious that the existence of externalities does lead to a non-optimal pattern of the competitive system. The same holds true for various environmental models of the competitive type where in general a breakdown, catastrophe, or chaos cannot be avoided unless there are significant changes in the level of contact or control by eliminating external effects.

EXAMPLE 2. Structural models of spatial distribution of cells of the Conway-Schelling type could be explored in terms of evolution complexity. These models aim at explaining optimal and non-optimal spatial configurations of cell development or more complex humanistic structures such as urban structures. Conway recommends playing the game by starting out with some initial pattern – searching for cells which are going to survive, or die, or are birth cells – then determining all the kinds of configurations possible in this game, hence showing the complete life-history of cells according to the rules. Conway demonstrated that, given some initial configurations, most patterns show a stable configuration in a finite number of subsequent generations. In our approach each cell could be modelled as a finite state machine interacting with other component machines governed by the rules of Conway's game. The interaction of all finite state (component) machines in simulating the entire system produces an overall pattern that according to its survival chances is judged on the basis of the evolution complexity relation. It would be quite natural to apply these ideas to more complex social systems as those pertaining to urban and city formation. In fact, this has been done by T.C. Schelling [12]. Schelling is primarily interested in certain practical problems, e.g. in segregation patterns observed in cities and in the major factor that cause the patterns. Like Conway's, the game devised can be played on a checker board with checkers of different colors representing different races, groups of different linguistic or cultural backgrounds, etc. It involves definite rules to generate certain spatial patterns, for example, that every black checker wants at least half of his neighbors to be 'black checkers', and every white checker wants at least a third of his neighbors to be 'white checkers'. Every checker who tends to be discontented with his neighborhood is allowed to move. Every move is going to change the initial configuration, and the question is: under a given finite number of moves (stages of the game) do the configurations adopt a stable pattern? A stable pattern is reached when everybody settles in a satisfactory environment, that is, when nobody sees any reason to move elsewhere.

Summarizing, therefore, the following applications of complexity to dynamic systems can be made:

1. Competitive economic models of resource allocation, models of the "tragedy-of-the-commons-type".

2. Specific models of resource depletion and environmental pollution.

3. Structural models of spatio-temporal development (Conway's game, Schelling's dynamic models of segregation).

3.6 DYNAMIC SYSTEMS OF RESOURCE DEPLETION

The idea is to consider the process of interaction between people, groups, that is decision-making units as components of a (big) machine embedded in some natural environment. In a rather natural way the decision-making units could be identified as "neurons" or "logical circuits" in a McCulloch-Pitts neural network since these neural networks are equivalent to the modelling of sequential machines. Consider a finite state machine working in serial-parallel connection with feedbacks. Every component machine at state $z = 0$ may receive a string of inputs from the environment, and, as the case may be, from other machines. It produces outputs (output strings) which partly go to other machines (or are fed back into the front machine) and partly are fed back into the environment. To every state we could associate an output table (or pay-off table) which describes the social and environmental conditions of the system at the given states.

The model of a *sequential machine* describes a competitive mechanism which strives for survival, that is to say, all machines compete for finite resources. Does there exist a "perfect balance" in the global behavior of this machine?

Next we consider several examples which constitute some specific cases of the more general model of serial-parallel decomposition. In the first example we emphasize the interaction process of two machines

(organisms, decision units, ... ,).[3] In the second model all component
machines receive external inputs from the environment which under the
sequential framework is going to be linearly depleted. Finally the third
example assumes in addition that the environment deteriorates over time
on the input and on the output side.

EXAMPLE 1

This situation can be illustrated as in Figure 1:

Let $C_1 = \langle X_1, Y_1, Z_1, \lambda_1, \delta_1 \rangle$, $C_2 = \langle X_2, Y_2, Z_2, \lambda_2, \delta_2 \rangle$, be *circuits*
associated to the machines $f_1 : \sum X \to Y$, $f_2 : \sum X \to Y$, respectively, all
sets X, Y, Z nonempty and finite.

Define $\lambda_1 : X_1 \times Z_1 \to Z_1, \delta_1 : X_1 \times Z_1 \to Y_1,$
$\lambda_2 : X_2 \times Z_2 \to Z_2, \delta_2 : X_2 \times Z_2 \to Y_2$
and let $Y_1 = Y_{10} + Y_{12}$, $Y_2 = Y_{20} + Y_{21}$ where '$+$' denotes algebraic
addition.

Both C_1 and C_2 receive inputs from outside (the environment) but
only once at some states z_1 and z_2, respectively. Both C_1 and C_2 start
operating successively, the interaction occurs via each machine splitting
its output, part of it, e.g. y_{12} and y_{21}, is fed into the other machine, constituting additional input in the next round.

Now assume C_1 and C_2 interacting, let $(z_1, z_2) \varepsilon Z_1 \times Z_2$. Then z_1
produces the output $\delta_1(x_1, z_1)$ in C_1 where the amount $\delta_{12}(x_1, z_1)$ from
$\delta_1(x_1, z_1) = \delta_{10}(x_1, z_1) + \delta_{12}(x_1, z_1)$ is fed into C_2. Correspondingly, z_2
produces the output $\delta_2(x_2, z_2)$ in C_2 where the amount $\delta_{21}(x_2, z_2)$ from
$\delta_2(x_2, z_2) = \delta_{20}(x_2, z_2) + \delta_{21}(x_2, z_2)$ is fed into C_1'.

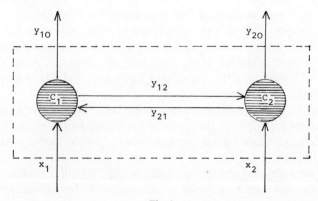

Fig. 1.

Consider the first round and see what happens if part of the output is fed into the other machine. For example, z_1 will change to z_1' under the interaction by $\lambda(x_1, z_1, \delta_{21}(x_2, z_2)) = z_1' \equiv x_1 \cdot z_1 \cdot \delta_{21}(x_2, z_2)$, where '$\cdot$' denotes multiplicative concatenation. More explicity, we could put this transition in the following form:

Define (the state assignments) $\eta : Z_1 \times Z_2 \longrightarrow$ subsets of $(Z_1 \times Z_2)$ and let η_1 denote the action acting only on Z_1 and η_2 acting on Z_2, respectively:

$$(z_1, z_2) \xrightarrow{\eta_2} (x_1 \cdot z_1 \cdot \delta_{21}(x_2, z_2), z_2).$$

Likewise, z_2 will change to z_2' (under the interaction) by

$$\lambda(x_2, z_2, \delta_{12}(x_1, z_1)) = z_2' = x_2 \cdot z_2 \cdot \delta_{12}(x_1, z_1)$$

so that

$$(z_1, z_2) \xrightarrow{\eta_1} (z_1, x_2 \cdot z_2 \cdot \delta_{12}(x_1, z_1)).$$

Thus under $\eta_1 \cdot \eta_2$ we get

$$(z_1, z_2) \xrightarrow{\eta_1 \cdot \eta_2} (x_1 \cdot z_1 \cdot \delta_{21}(x_2, z_2), x_2 \cdot z_2 \cdot \delta_{12}(x_1, z_1)).$$

Consider the second round, let

$$z_1' \equiv x_1 \cdot z_1 \cdot \delta_{21}(x_2, z_2) \text{ for } C_1 \text{ be given.}$$

Then z_1' will change to z_1'' by

$$\lambda'(z_1', \delta_{21}'(z_2')) \equiv \lambda'[x_1 \cdot z_1 \cdot \delta_{21}(x_2, z_2), \delta_{21}'(x_2 \cdot z_2 \cdot \delta_{12}(x_1, z_1))]$$
$$\equiv \lambda'\{\lambda(x_1, z_1, \delta_{21}(x_2, z_2)), \delta_{21}'[\lambda(x_2, z_2) \cdot \delta_{12}(x_1, z_1)]$$
$$\equiv z_1''.$$

Hence we have

$$(z_1', z_2') \xrightarrow{\eta_2'} (x_1 \cdot z_1 \cdot \delta_{21}(x_2, z_2) \cdot \delta_{21}'(x_2 \cdot z_2 \cdot \delta_{12}(x_1, z_1), z_2').$$

Likewise for z_2' which we do not write out because of complete symmetry. Thus we have under operations $\eta_1' \cdot \eta_2'$:

$$(z_1', z_2') \xrightarrow{\eta_1' \cdot \eta_2'} (x_1 \cdot z_1 \cdot \delta_{21}(x_2, z_2) \cdot \delta_{21}'(x_2, z_2 \cdot \delta_{12}(x_1, z_1)),$$
$$x_2 \cdot z_2' \delta_{12}(x_1, z_1) \cdot \delta_{12}'(x_1 \cdot z_1 \cdot \delta_{21}(x_2, z_2)).$$

Now under the assumption that the system only once, at the beginning, gets a big "push" from outside, by external inputs, and then feeds itself by partly exchanging outputs, we could have a finite chain of, say, n trans-

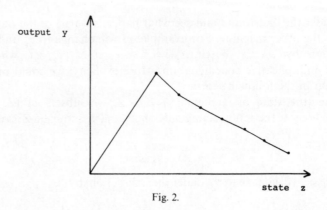

Fig. 2.

formations

$$(z_1, z_2) \xrightarrow{\eta_1^n \cdot \eta_2^n} (z_1^*, z_2^*) \text{ where } (z_1^*, z_2^*)$$
$$n = 1, \ldots, N$$

denotes the terminal state pair under n successive transformations $\eta_1^n \cdot \eta_2^n$.
Up to the number of transformations we could form concatenations of
the following sort:

$$x_1 \cdot z_1 \cdot \delta_{21}(x_2, z_2) \cdot \delta'_{21}(z'_2)) \cdot \delta''_{21}(z'_2 \cdot \delta'_{12}(z'_1)) \cdot \ldots \text{ and}$$
$$x_2 \cdot z_2 \cdot \delta_{12}(x_1, z_1) \cdot \delta'_{12}(z'_1) \cdot \delta''_{12}(z'_1 \cdot \delta'_{21}(z'_2)) \cdot \ldots, \text{ respectively.}$$

Notice that the transformations on the set of states characterize a *semi-group of transformations* (on the set of states) with respect to the operation of concatenation, representing the global behavior of the interacting system.

The geometric picture of the state transition would normally involve a sudden hike but then adopt relatively decreasing, discrete steps approaching slowly the z-axis before reaching it.

EXAMPLE 2. Let us consider the situation where the interacting system receives external inputs repeatedly over time, but in which its environment is depleted proportionally to each round. Let $r = \alpha n, \alpha > 0$ be the depletion rate. For two circuits, C_1 and C_2 in serial connection, we picture the situation as in Figure 3.

As in the previous case, let C_1 start the operation at state z_1. Then z_1 produces the output $\delta_1(x_1, z_1) = \delta_{10}(x_1, z_1) + \delta_{12}(x_1, z_1)$, where in this

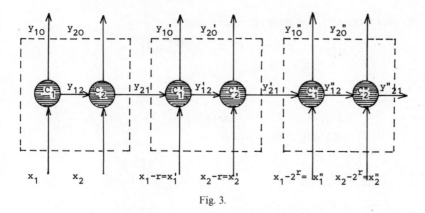

Fig. 3.

example we restrict ourselves to the case where $\delta_{10}(x_1, z_1)$, in general $\delta_{i0}(z_i)$, does not affect the environment from the output side.

We have $\delta_1(x_1, z_1) = y_1 = \delta_{10}(x_1, z_1) + \delta_{12}(x_1, z_1) = y_{10} + y_{12}$.

The state z_1 changes to z_1' under the operation $\lambda_1(x_1, z_1) = z_1' \equiv z_2$. Hence we let it always be the case that the next state of the "front" machine is identical to the state of the "tail" machine. Likewise, C_2 is characterized by output functions

$$\delta_2(x_2, z_2) = y_2 = \delta_{21}(x_2, z_2) + \delta_{20}(x_2, z_2) = y_{21} + y_{20}$$

and state representation

$$\lambda_2(x_2, y_{12}, z_2) = \lambda_2(x_2, \delta_{12}(x_1, z_1), \lambda_1(x_1, z_1))$$
$$= z_2' = z_1''.$$

This constitutes the first round, in the second two additional factors should be considered:

(1) the feedback from the machine acting second (C_2) into the machine having acted first (C_1).

(2) the environment undergoing changes by the depletion factor r after each round.

Thus for the modified machine C_1' in the second round, the output is given by

$$\delta_1' : Y_{21} \times X_1' \times Z_1'' \longrightarrow Y_1',$$

$\delta_1'(y_{21}, x_1', z_1'') = \delta_1'(\delta_{21}(x_2, z_2), x_1', \lambda_2(x_2, y_{12}, z_2)) \equiv$ (by complete substitution) $\delta_1'\{\delta_{21}(x_2, z_2), x_1', \lambda_2(x_2)\delta_{12}(x_1, z_1), \lambda_2(x_2, \delta_{12}(x_1, z_1)\lambda_1(x_1, z_1))\}$.

Correspondingly, the state representation is

$$\lambda'_1(x'_1, y_{21}, z'_1) = \lambda'_1(x'_1, \delta_{21}(x_2, z_2), \lambda_2(x_2, y_{12}, z_2))$$
$$= z''_2.$$

Analogously, for C'_2,

$$\delta'_2(y'_{12}, x'_2, z''_2) = \delta'_2(\delta'_{12}(y_{21}, x'_1, z''_1), x'_2, \lambda'_1(x'_1, y_{21}, z'_1))$$
$$\equiv \text{(by complete substitution)}$$
$$\equiv \delta'_2\{\delta'_{12}(\delta_{21}(x_2, z_2), x'_1, \lambda_2(x_2, \delta_{12}(x_1, z_1), \lambda_1(x_1, z_1)))\}$$

with state representation

$$\lambda'_2(x'_2, y'_{12}, z''_2) = \lambda'_2(x'_2, \delta'_{12}(y_{21}, x'_1, z''_1), \lambda'_1(x_1, y_{21}, z'_1))$$
$$= z'''_1.$$

For C''_1:

$$\delta''_1(y'_{21}, x''_1, z'''_1) = \delta''_1\{\delta'_{21}(\delta'_{12}(\cdots), x''_1, \lambda'_2(x'_2, \delta'_{12}(\delta_{21}(\cdots),$$
$$x'_1, \lambda_2(x_2, \delta_{12}(\cdots), \lambda_1(\cdots)),$$
$$\lambda'_1(x'_1, \delta_{21}(\cdots),$$
$$\lambda_2(x_2, \delta_{12}(\cdots), \lambda_1(\cdots)))\},$$

and $\lambda''_1(x''_1, y'_{21}, z'''_1) = \lambda''_1(x''_1, \delta'_{21}(\ldots), \lambda'_2(\ldots))$.
… etc.

We easily see that the complexity of computations increases substantially after a few steps. The question is whether the computations show a certain pattern with an increasing number of rounds (cycles). Notice so far that computations obey an 'embedding property', revealed by successive substitution, by this we mean that computations of output and state transition functions in later rounds can be traced recursively to computations in earlier rounds. Similar to example 1 we can show state transitions via concatenations.

First round: $x_1 \cdot z_1 = \lambda_1(x_1, z_1)$ for C_1,

$$(x_1 \cdot z_1) \cdot \delta_{12}(.) \cdot x_2 = \lambda_2(x_2, y_{12}, z_2) \text{ for } C_2.$$

Second round: $[(x_1 \cdot z_1) \cdot \delta_{12}(.) \cdot x_2] \cdot \delta_{21}(.) \cdot x'_1$

$$= \lambda'_1(x'_1, y_{21}, z''_1) \qquad \text{for } C'_1,$$
$$\{[(x_1 \cdot z_1) \cdot \delta_{12}(.) \cdot x_2] \cdot \delta_{21}(.) \cdot x'_1\} \cdot \delta'_{12}(.) \cdot x'_2$$
$$= \lambda'_2(x'_2, y'_{12}, z''_2) \qquad \text{for } C'_2.$$

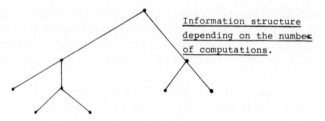

Information structure depending on the number of computations.

Fig. 4.

Third round: $\langle \{ [(x_1 \cdot z_1) \cdot \delta_{12}(.) \cdot x_2] \cdot \delta_{21}(.) \cdot x_1' \} \delta_{12}'(.) \cdot x_2' \rangle.$

$$\cdot \delta_{21}'(.) \cdot x_1''$$
$$= \lambda_1''(x_1'', y_{21}', z_1''').$$

etc.

The brackets $(.), [.], \{.\}, \langle . \rangle$ should demonstrate the embedding property of computations, if we consider the set of all expressions within a bracket as an information set we get a nested sequence of information sets in terms of inclusion corresponding to the number of computations.

This shows that reaching a certain state is the result of actions (computation) in past history.

Interpretations.

(1) Properties of the state transitions exhibit the fact that such sequential computations reveal a semigroup of transformations which could be solved by certain types of functional equations.

The semigroup theory of transformations is a most general vehicle for an algebraic theory of general dynamic processes. Let C be a circuit that by generating outputs occurs in various states $z, z', z'', \ldots$ according to certain actions of its subsystems interacting with each other. Suppose C is in some state z, then as a result of the aggregate actions of the subsystems it will be "transformed" to a new state z', say (which of course may coincide with the original z if the given state is not affected by the actions). Thus every action in C is simply a transformation on the set of states of the system, and a sequential machine forms such an appropriate system. Consider now that actions are sequentially produced by certain activities of the agents, then sequential actions could be concatenated to produce new actions. Obviously, the transformation produced by the last action (in a sequence) is, so to speak, conditioned on its past history, and forms the product of subsequent transformations corresponding to successive actions. In this way the totality of the actions fed into the system, being closed with respect to successive concatenations, is naturally a semigroup of transformations of the set of all states of the system under consideration.[4]

(2) If the global behavior of the functions δ, λ were known as well as environmental specifications there would be no problem in computing the global behavior of the system in finitely many states. As a first approach one could assume all functions to be linear, so the machines actually would be *linear* sequential machines. Given this knowledge one could use the sequential model for prediction purpose, no principal difficulty would arise to apply this process to more than two sequentially interacting units.

(3) The system breaks down, for instance, if the resources are completely depleted and if the internal inputs do not sufficiently feed the system. There could also be a breakdown on behavioral grounds (see Section 3.8). Under present assumptions the system *must* necessarily break down after finitely many rounds, if the depletion rate depends linearly on the number of computations. On the other hand, if the depletion rate is a concave, monotonically decreasing and bounded function then merely by this assumption the system could reach a *stationary state*.

Geometrically, we could picture the semigroup of transformations as a "kinematic graph" that according to previous discussions could assume different shapes.

The states represent vectors in the phase space. The semigroup of

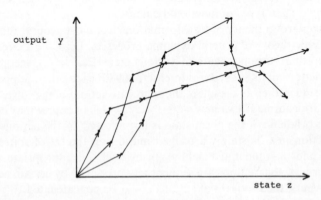

Fig. 5.

transformations could be identified as a *trajectory* or *line of behavior* (*Ashby* [2]).

EXAMPLE 3.

The third example starts out from the observation that in addition to changes of the environment from the input side (due to a natural depletion of resources) there could be disturbances of the environment induced from the output side. We could think of these changes as a deterioration of the environment to the extent that it would only adopt a finite amount of outputs sequentially produced: i.e., an upper bound beyond that there will be a break-down of the system. There are a number of plausible situations where this result could hold, those relating to pollution or "quality of life" affecting the inputs in subsequent rounds of the system. Pollution is a consequence of population, or better, of density of population. Discharge of pollutants into the air or water does not do any harm to the environment as long as the natural chemical and biological recycling process is kept intact, but to the extent that pollution becomes denser this is no longer true.

A simple hypothesis would be to let the state of the environment at the $k + 1$st round depend on the aggregate output, say on $\sum_{i=1}^{n_k} y_{io}$, of the systems acting in the immediately preceding, k-th round: $x_i^{k+1} = \phi^k(\sum_{i=1}^{n_k} y_{io})$, $k = 1, \dots, N$ rounds;

$$\sum_{i=1}^{n_k} y_{io} = \sum_{i=1}^{n_1} y_{io} + \cdots + \sum_{i=1}^{n_N} y_{io}$$

ϕ^k is a monotone decreasing function, i.e. if $\sum_{i=1}^{n_k} y_{io}$ increases x_i^{k+1} decreases.

In the case of linearity we write

$$x_i^{k+1} = \alpha \sum_{i=1}^{n_k} y_{io}, \alpha > 0.$$

We assume that there is an absolute upper bound K at the N-the-round so that $x_i^{N+1} = \phi^N(\sum_{i=1}^{n_N} y_{io}) = 0$ if $\sum_{i=1}^{n_N} y_{io} = K$, after which the system will break down.

Figure 6 shows the structure of this machine.

As in the second example we can immediately exhibit the transitional path of this system with the corresponding modification brought upon by the environmental changes.

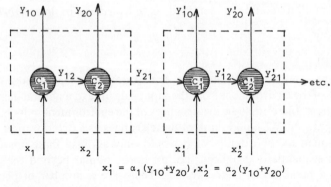

$$x_1' = \alpha_1(y_{10}+y_{20}) , x_2' = \alpha_2(y_{10}+y_{20})$$

Fig. 6.

The presentation of the semigroup of transformations is analogous to the second example and will therefore be omitted.

A few remarks concerning the behavior of the system is in order here. Among other factors mentioned in the previous example the behavior depends critically on the type of function ϕ^k, $k = 1, \ldots, N$ assumed at the beginning. The system develops up to the N-th stage where it reaches a major bottleneck constituted by the bound $\sum_{i=1}^{n_N} y_{io} = K$ at which point the external input from the environment drops to zero although the process is still kept alive by internal inputs until it breaks down completely. This course of events could happen even if the resources are not depleted; if the resources are depleted before this stage then this will constitute a breakdown of the system.

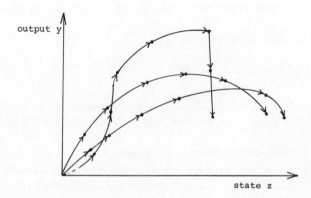

Fig. 7.

The behavior of the state transition is the same as that exhibited in Figure 4 and its description will be omitted.

Here we are only engaged in studying complexity relating it to the sequential machine framework. How does a theory of complexity relate to such dynamic systems of resource depletion? There is one major motivation to study complexity for these purposes. Complexity results from a possible gap between computability requirements of the entire system

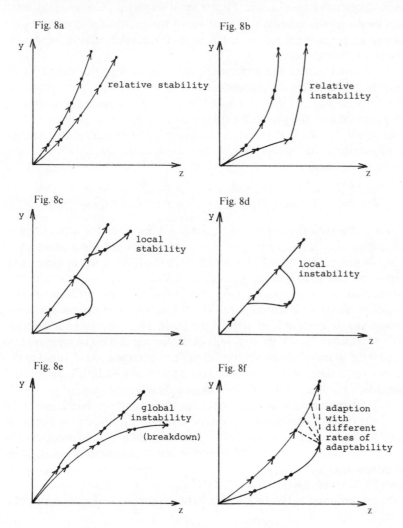

Fig. 8a — relative stability

Fig. 8b — relative instability

Fig. 8c — local stability

Fig. 8d — local instability

Fig. 8e — global instability (breakdown)

Fig. 8f — adaption with different rates of adaptability

106 CHAPTER 3

(machine) and the computational capacities of its interacting subsystems.[5] Complexity could then be viewed as a structural bound on the system to survive. The most important case of interest at least for complex societal systems is provided by the observation that the design complexity usually exceeds substantially the control complexity. This situation is of course a potential source for the breakdown of a system; here the question arises at which level of disparity between design and control complexity a collapse occurs. Figure 8a–d display a number of different, but by no means exhaustive situations of that particular case where the design complexity exceeds or shows at least the same relative increase as the control complexity.

As derived earlier the trajectories or lines of behavior could be represented by semigroups of transformations, its geometric shapes illustrate the dynamic system behavior (global input-output behavior of the system) as prescribed by the particular design independent of any man-machine interaction and by that particular design which yields all stable internal configurations. In the first case we can speak of the 'unrestricted design', in the second case of the 'restricted design'.

3.7 COMPLEXITY IN THOM'S PROGRAM

Some of the remarks in Chapter 1, Section 1.5, stating the advantages of allgebraic system theory may also be directed toward the evaluation of Thom's program (Thom [15]), which is in the framework of differential topology and global analysis, and therefore rooted in quite different mathematical considerations. One of the main technical problems here is to relate discrete descriptions of the 'form' (via transformation semigroups) to differentiable models of the form. Thom works with differentiable functions. Now if the topology of the form is carried or generated by a machine as a digitalized abstract simplicial complex, the changes in the form can be taken to be simplicial transformations. Take a machine and generate a configuration with this machine bearing topological properties or at least approximating such properties, then a study of the change of the form via transformation semigroups could replace a study of vector fields on manifolds as suggested by Thom. And this would lead to an algebraicization of Thom's theory and would make it amenable to large-scale computation. However, it is not clear *how to generate the topology of the form by algebraic tools.*

A second point is the connection between topological complexity of a form and information as discussed by Thom. This topological complexity assumes the form of a metric on the set of states (endowed with a suitable topology) that comprises the transformation process from one form to another. Thus topological complexity is related to the topology of the form and unless generated by a discrete model cannot be covered by algebraic complexity. This gives rise to questions whether one should have a total complexity measure comprising algebraic and topological complexity (see Futia [4]). One restriction of algebraic complexity is that it is *online*, e.g., computed when the system is running. We probably need a detailed theory of dynamical systems. Many dynamical phenomena (e.g. evolution, growth of form) should be modelled first descriptively, i.e. what a system is doing within finite time and not what it should be doing guided by a potential to optimize. The first aspect can be treated adequately by finite state machine theory whereas the latter aspect is more in the spirit of global analysis. These two aspects are complementary rather than substitutable, they cover both the descriptive and the normative aspect.

The problem of biological evolution is to explain the stability and the reproduction of the global spatio-temporal structure in terms of the organization of the structure itself. According to R. Thom [14] there exists an analogy between this problem of theoretical biology and the mathematics of topology. A similar idea has been put forward for generalizing classical mechanics, for making it more geometric, more global. The theory involved is that of *structural stability*, *qualitative dynamics* and *differential topology*, briefly summarized as the theory of *differentiable dynamical systems*. It attempts to study systems on a manifold.

Structural stability is a property of the dynamical system itself: it is a global property and not a local one. It asserts that nearby dynamical systems have the same structure, where the 'same structure' basically means that they have the same 'gross' behavior or the same *qualitative* behavior. For having the same 'qualitative behavior' one merely utilizes the information of topological isomorphism. Let (M, X) be a differential dynamical system with 'phase space' M endowed with a suitable topological structure and a vector field X (representing a set of differential equations) defined in M. (M, X) is then described as *structurally stable* if for some small perturbation δX on X the system $(M, X + \delta X)$ is topologically isomorphic to (M, X), i.e., if the perturbed system preserves the "gross" or "qualitative" behavior of the original system.

As a recently proved theorem we note that every compact manifold admits structurally stable systems, and almost all gradient dynamical systems are structurally stable. Investigation of such systems marks a different point of emphasis compared to quantitative ("classical") dynamics: one is not interested in quantitative aspects but in questions like 'will the system break down' 'achieve a steady state?'

For a survey of mathematical results of the theory of differentiable dynamical systems we advise the reader to consult Smale [13]; applications of the theory to the study of biological is mainly due to Thom. Also Thom provides a characterization of 'elementary catastrophes' which result from certain properties of such dynamic systems. Some of these catastrophies have a natural representation in the 'breaking' phenomena (e.g. the breaking of water-waves)–such as the Riemann–Hugoniot catastrophe which basically can be simulated by the machine model described in Example 1 of the previous section.

3.8 POLICY CONCLUSIONS

It is generally recognized that societal systems tend to be more complex than technological systems and this in turn has led to new ideas regarding the appropriate tools to be used for analyzing such systems.

Our analysis shows – roughly – that the global behavioral of complex dynamic societal systems embedded in the environment tends to a breakdown (catastrophe, chaos) after finitely many 'real-time computations' either because of changes in the environment or because of the 'evolution-complexity' character of the system which, if not sufficiently well understood, may lead to behavioral rules incompatible with survival.

These two basic, but different factors have both been considered as the major causes for a 'doomsday' situation but also as real sources for public policy recommendations about how to avoid the 'inevitable breakdown'.

The remedies suggested so far result from different philosophies: in one case it is believed that man is able to shape his environment to serve his needs for survival, mainly by means of technological changes, in the other case the real problem is seen in people's behavior rules as being the main source of creating a 'tragedy of the commons'. These two different points of view may be roughly referred to as the *technological* and the *behavioristic* view, respectively. Of course, neither are incompatible; and neither may be called 'pragmatic' in real situations, in particular if they degenerate to technocratic or ideological variants; however, they reveal a remarkably distinct attitude to handling things that is worth discussing.

In view of the remarks on complexity, one could argue that the disparity between a 'low level of contact' and a 'high level of (design) complexity' reflects the fact that – for reasons lying in human nature – social processes often do not match technological processes in terms of efficiency. The 'behaviorists' would therefore recommend us to put the emphasis on adjustments of the social process, whereas the 'technologists' would consider this as a fruitless enterprise in view of permanent human failure throughout its existence. Hence – according to this view – the only way out seems to be in realigning the technology to a socially satisfactory level.

Now how do these attitudes cope with our major world problems like those of population and its immediate subproblems such as pollution, energy, poverty, international peace, crime etc? Do some of these problems have technical solutions and if so how are they implemented? Of course the problems are only non-trivially posed if we admit that the world is finite, i.e. that space and resources are finite.

In general, technologists tend to adopt a more optimistic (non-catastrophic) point of view by applying a 'technological fix" to all social problems.

Examples of technological fixes applied to social problem include the following: recommendations of intra-uterine devices for birth-control problems instead of provision of pills whose failure because of neglect is evident in some developing countries; emphasizing nuclear desalination of water to supply sufficient water resources instead of attempting to change people's habits to consume less water for industrial and private uses or to produce safer cars instead of trying to educate people to reduce speed in order to have a more effective way to reduce traffic deaths.

The two views can be compared best as follows: the technologist believes that there will always be shortcomings in human society which cannot be overcome, not even by ideological indoctrination, and therefore, that technology should be applied to minimize the risk of possible outcomes resulting from these shortcomings. The behaviorist is much more pessimistic with regard to technological possibilities and believes that most problems are man-made and therefore should be solved by persistently changing habits, motivations, rules of behavior – on the basis of education or persuasion.

Hence in relation to our investigations this could mean that to the extent that people recognize the inherent complexity of a dynamic competitive system, they would adjust their level of contact (adaptation by learning) and therefore reorganize themselves by emphasizing cooperation rather than competition, or form countervailing powers to check and reduce social costs of competition. This could delay the occurrence of disaster at least for some time. Such reorganization, of course, could happen by voluntary actions in a democratic society but could also result in the course of a revolution where a new system was imposed.

NOTES

[1] The idea that living organisms are subject to the same laws and rules that govern man-made machines has been explicitly proposed by D.E. Wooldridge in *The Machinery of Life*, McGraw–Hill, 1966.

[2] This condition is fairly restrictive. It could be easily violated in any dynamic competitive system where the environment switches from a classical to a non-classical one, therefore permitting various kinds of externalities. If such a switch occurs, the system has to be immediately adapted to the new environment, possibly resulting in a restriction of the initial competitive situation. Otherwise the weak dominance condition is likely to be violated. (Of course, another possibility would be to substitute a competitive system by a non-competitive one that satisfies the w.d. condition, but we will not explore this situation in what follows.) With the help of new tools the degree of adaptiveness of a dynamic system can be described in terms of a comparison between 'design complexity' and 'control complexity' represented as the 'evolution complexity relation' .

[3] Incidentally, the first model could represent a good model of the cell, split into two parts: metabolism and genetic control. All inputs arrive once from outside the cell to the metabolism (e.g. sugar and oxygen via the bloodstream). Under the interaction process does there exist a 'perfect balance' in the sense of the evolution complexity relation?

[4] Sometimes it might occur that we know of a sequence of inputs and observe a sequence of outputs but that we don't know anything about the transformation process in the 'black-box' and therefore we have to conduct an experiment. If we are going to repeat experiments where certain inputs match certain outputs then we could identify a certain class of systems and see to which class a particular system is associated. These types of *system-identification* experiments are important for the specification of complex systems. One way to deal effectively with the problem how to bring light into the 'black-box' is to ask specific questions to the system in a 'questionnaire language' and then to construct its behavior according to specific responses provided by the system.

[5] What we have in mind here is known as the *evolution-complexity* relation (see Sec. 3.5) in the study of interacting processes in organisms. This relationship puts elements of an evolutionary system into 'perfect balance' or 'perfect harmony' and measures the complexity of contacts between the elements. The study of evolution-complexity relations evolves from considerations of stable configurations in cell development. Maximizing the complexity of contacts between elements leads to a maximal number of stable configurations. Small complexity means that relatively little potential use is made of the mechanism, high complexity means that the assignments or contacts at least guarantee a satisfactory performance. We note that increased complexity requires increased control. Hence low control and high complexity mean a low level of contact and are therefore a source of possible break-down of the system.

In this respect, the tragedy of commons results from a low complexity, since the 'rational individuals' do not sufficiently understand the mechanism; adaptation, learning and use of relevant information always induce higher complexity.

[6] Every subcomputation indicated by a point in the illustrations can be called a subprocess and its complexity can be measured in a third dimension on an integer scale (which has been omitted in the illustrations). Now for every subprocess of the (unrestricted) design there is associated its design complexity, and for every subprocess of the (restricted) design there is associated its control complexity. A comparison between the two for all concatenated subprocesses generating the global transformation would generally indicate the degree of stability in a dynamic system.

REFERENCES

[1] Ashby, W.R., *Introduction to Cybernetics*, Chapman and Hall, London, 1956.

[2] Ashby, W.R., *Design for a Brain*, J. Wiley, New York, 1960.

[3] Cody, M.L., 'Optimization in Ecology', *Science* (AAAS) **183** (1974), 1156–1164.

[4] Futia, C., 'The Complexity of Economic Decision Rules I and II', Bell Laboratories, Murray Hill, Jan. 1975.

[5] Gardner, M., 'The Fantastic Combinations of John Conway's New Solitaire Game "Life"', *Scientific American*, 221–223, 1970.

[6] Gause, G.F., *The Struggle for Existence*, Dover Publ., New York, 1971 (first published in English 1934).

[7] Hardin, G., 'The Tragedy of the Commons', *Science* (AAAS) **162** (1968), 158–165.

[8] Kemeny, G., 'Man Viewed as a Machine', *Scientific American* (1955) reprinted in *Computers and Computation* (R.P. Fenichel, J. Weizenbaum, eds.), W.H. Freeman and Comp., San Francisco, 1971.

[9] Lynch, K., 'The Pattern of the Metropolis', in *The Future Metropolis* (K. Lynch, ed.), George Braziller, New York, 1962.

[10] Rapoport, A., *Fights, Games and Debates*, University of Michigan Press, Ann Arbor, 1960.

[11] Schelling, Th. C., *Micromotives and Macrobehavior*, Norton, New York, 1978.

[12] Schelling, Th. C., 'Dynamic Models of Segregation', *Journal of Math. Sociology* **2** (1971), 143–186.

[13] Smale, S., 'Differentiable Dynamic Systems', *Bulletin Amer. Math. Soc.* **73** (1967), 747–817.

[14] Thom, R., 'Topological Models in Biology', *Topology* **8** (1969), 323–335.

[15] Thom, R., *Stabilité Structurelle et Morphogénèse*, W.A. Benjamin, Reading (Mass.), 1972.

[16] Ulam, St. M., 'On some Mathematical Problems connected with Patterns of Growth of Figures', in A.W. Burks (ed.) *Essays on Cellular Automata*, Univ. of Illinois Press, Urbana, Ill., 1970.

CHAPTER 4

STRUCTURAL CHARACTERISTICS
IN ECONOMIC MODELS

4.1 INTRODUCTION

In the past twenty years we have experienced a tremendous advancement of tools and techniques in analyzing, diagnosing, predicting and controlling economic processes. Sophisticated models have been built that claim to predict future economic trends of micro and macro-economic variables, largely facilitated by the availability of large-scale computational resources. These models also form the basis of policy recommendations such as the Brookings models or similar large-scale econometric models. There have been some major improvements in the design, estimation, statistical structure, and testability of economic model-building as also in decentralized decision-making, distributed computation and hierarchical control. Yet, there is still one major link missing which we consider as one of the most fundamental properties of any model-building in the large: namely, that one has not come to grips with the structural constraint of complexity, e.g. the information processing limits arising in the control of dynamic systems. Also in a recent survey on large-scale systems (N.R. Sandell et al. [11]) it is stated that an adequate measure of complexity is lacking for control systems and that a major task of constructing a unified theory of decentralized control is to include a formal measure of system complexity. We focus on this structural constraint of complexity by designing models that explicitly cope with this issue.

4.2 PRELIMINARY CONSIDERATIONS

From a methodological point of view there are two ways to understand and predict the behavior of (discrete-time) dynamic systems. The *first* is to evaluate changes in the future by past performance, to project realizations in the past into the future, what may be summed up as 'prediction by trends'. Intuitively, this is based on the idea that any system's behavior 'cannot escape the past to shape the future', that any evolving system develops its own memory which conditions it to past events. The more data are compiled from the past the more the memory activates its own self-organized dynamics. This appears to exclude purely random behavior in the past, exhibited by a random sequence, hence the occurrences of events do not seem to be statistically independent. The *second* is by constructing a model which is considered to be a representative mapping of the system under investigation. A model attempts to capture the basic technical, structural and behavior characteristics of the underlying system and on this ground estimates its potentialities for future development. This is referred to as 'prediction by models'. Now 'prediction by trends' assumes regularity of the process as if social and economic processes satisfy laws of statistical regularity. It comes very close to conceiving the world of being in a state of 'disorganized complexity' according to W. Weaver [13], meaning that we can view courses of events essentially as 'random sequences' and that the statistical law of large numbers is the basic concept to predict future behavior. Already F.A. Hayek [4] remarked that economic processes cannot be observed in a statistical fashion. The problem with a statistical assessment of complexity, or disorganized complexity, lies in the attempt to average over a large number of random variables, as represented by the mean or expected value, which, indeed, treats all phenomena of the system alike or as uniform whereas in reality there exist different structural relationships between elements that bear different characteristics and that may have a non-negligible impact on the behavior of the entire system. Hence, it is very doubtful that economic systems can be explained on the basis of pure random phenomena. We have shown (see Chapter 1) that this implies that economic systems would perform as if they were infinitely large systems. Instead, I have pointed out that economic systems are much more akin to finite complex systems' (FCS), i.e. systems that are much too complex to get explicit solutions for them, as is the case in 'simple' systems; neither is the number of parts large enough, nor the parts homogeneous enough, to be able to pass to the limit as in infinitely large systems. An FCS has some peculiar properties, not shared by its better worked-out counterparts, that make it difficult to analyze, understand and predict its behavior. It appears to be (1) highly sensitive in responding to changes or disturbances of its environment; (2) strongly interdependent with regard to actions of its components; (3) following a threshold discretionary type of behavior with qualitative jumps; (4) partially or locally controllable inducing global effects. In fact, these properties can be observed in modern economic systems that render them a higher degree of instability as similar behavior patterns are traced in ecosystems (R.M. May [8]). Hence behavior of an FCS is *not* of a purely random character. The reason for this is that it reveals certain imperfections like lagged responses, maladjustment, non-stochastic dependence between parts, discontinuity that appears not to be compatible with randomness.

4.3 DECOMPOSABLE SYSTEMS

We wish to explore the nature of the interdependence in economic systems, to show how these systems might be decomposed into their component parts for analytic purposes, and to relate the results to the choice of models in policy analysis and projection.

By the previous arguments and those provided by the algebraic theory of machines we are advised that there must be general principles of decomposition which arise in the design process of algebraic (computational) systems. From these general principles of decomposition we emerge with a natural theory and measure of complexity which is structural (intrinsically related to the parts, the basic building blocks) and computational, e.g. addressed to the computational links between these parts. We will see how this framework is useful for approaching more specific type questions in economic model building.

The core for the investigation in the present section is provided by the Ando-Fisher theorem [1] on the decomposability and independence in dynamic economic systems. The Ando-Fisher theorem and related results deal with general ways how to decompose a system into its component subsystems for purposes of analysis and prediction. They distinguish between (completely) *decomposable* and nearly (completely) *decomposable* systems. In the latter case, a nearly decomposable system consists of subsystems where each is causally dependent on the rest of the system but the rest of the system is only *weakly* dependent (or weakly coupled) on (with) each subsystem. In contrast, a decomposable system only allows for dependencies *within* systems but ignores intersystems dependencies altogether. The Ando-Fisher theorem asserts, for linear dynamic systems, that

(1) provided inter-systems dependencies are sufficiently weak (up to a negligible degree) relative to intrasystems dependencies, then, in the short run, the relative behavior of a nearly decomposable system becomes almost indistinguishable to that of a decomposable system.

(2) provided inter-systems dependencies are sufficiently weak relative to intra-system dependencies, then also, in the long run, the relative

behavior of the nearly decomposable system and of the decomposable system is approximately the same even though their behavior in terms of absolute levels and rates of change may be very different. In other words, if we give a nearly decomposable system enough running time, and that even when influences having been neglected have had time to make themselves fully felt, the relative behavior of the variables within any subsystem will be approximately the same as would have been the case had those influences never existed.

Now there are obviously two critical factors in the validity of the last result:

(a) *the degree of approximation depends on the number of computational cycles* (e.g. running time) *and is certainly a result in the limit;*

(b) *the degree of approximation depends on a prepostulated sufficiently weak linkage among the subsystems, below a certain threshold value, where the system moves continuously in an orderly manner.* This, however, presupposes a very large number of subsystems, acting uniformly on an equal power base, as in the classical model of economic equilibrium.

Both assumptions (a) and (b) are hard to defend in the context of analyzing real-life social and economic systems. For these systems, as real-time systems, we simply haven't got enough running time to force this approximation upon the system's behavior. Time is a scarce and valuable resource.

Second, there are only a few, relatively large subsystems, the relative behavior of which have a great potential impact on the entire system, and where the intra-system behavior is not limited to the subsystem itself.

In fact, we would very much argue in the opposite direction. The characteristics of large-scale complex systems are such that they are very sensitive to discretionary behavior of their subsystems and that actions, outcomes and consequences of these subsystems very often induce snowball-effects that pervade other subsystems and enforce actions, perturbations, maladjustments, and all sorts of reactions that deeply affect smoothness, regularity, stability, and control lability which are highly unpredictable because of the non-linearities involved.

4.4 SYSTEMS MODELLING AND COMPLEXITY

Let us start by describing a dynamic system very much like an automaton. The ingredients are given by:

an *internal state vector* $z_t = \left[z_{1,t}, z_{2,t}, \ldots, z_{n,t} \right]$;

an *external state vector* $x_t = [x_{1,t}, x_{2,t}, \dots, x_{n,t}]$;
representing exogeneous factors, driving the system from 'outside', and are not incorporated in the decomposition.

An *output* function δ that maps strings of inputs, say $(a_1, \dots, a_n)$ into single outputs $b_1, b_2, \dots, b_n$ which enter as inputs into other parts (components) of the system;

the *state transition* function λ with

$$z_t = \lambda(z_t, z_{t-1}, \dots, x_t),$$

given in difference equation form. The function λ, without any specification yet, represents the hypothesis about the process, inferred form the observations of real world systems.

The external state vector x_t can be conceived as a *primary* input factor (stimulus) which sets the system into motion, but which itself may be suitably partitioned as to which component is primarily affecting the process.

The behavior of the system is generated by the set of time series of the z_{it} which are produced as the model generates successive state descriptions plus the external states given exogeneously.

Now in the chartist approach to studying the future of systems it is assumed that the connections between different components either do not exist or are sufficiently weak that they can be safely ignored. The value of any component z_{it} depends only on its previous values and possibly random disturbances u: thus predicting a future course of actions or events means extrapolating past performance.

In a comprehensive modelling approach, as suggested here, at least some of the possible interdependencies among components exist in general. The behavior of each component may depend on its past behavior as well as on other variables in the system, the corresponding exogeneous factors x_{it}, $i = 1, \dots, n$, respectively, and possibly the random disturbances u, i.e.,

$$z_{it} = \lambda(z_{i,t-1}, z_{i,t-2}, \dots, z_{k,t}, z_{k,t-1}, \dots, x_{it}, u)\ k \neq i.$$

Three immediate problems in the model procedure arise from the Decomposition Scheme exhibited in Figure 1

(1) As the number of components and sufficiently strong connections among components increase, the behavior of the system becomes increasingly obscure by complex interactions which resemble very much nonlinearities in the total system's behavior in correspondence with size.

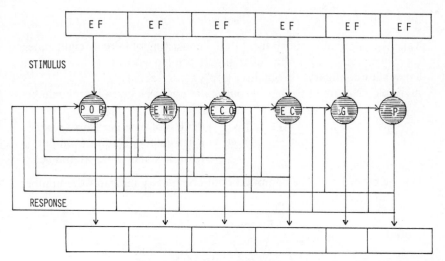

Fig. 1. Cascade form of decomposition.

(2) The structure and size of the components themselves present a potential source of complexity depending on whether and to which extent the component system is sensitive to disturbances, errors, threshold phenomena, etc.

(3) As the number of components and interdependencies in the system enhances, increasingly longer sequences of calculations are required to deduce the behavior of the system which results in computational complexity.

The solutions of these three problems would enable us to determine the complexity of the system on-line, as it is running from some initial time to some target time in the future. But knowing the complexity would permit us to design control strategies which are effective in guiding the system toward relative stability or harmony.

Therefore to understand the complexity of such systems we should be able to understand the strongly connected, coupled nature of its subsystems. For this purpose we need a measure of complexity that reflects the structural performance of each of the connected subsystems in terms of state space configurations *plus* the number of computational links that are established among the various subsystems and that reflect the richness of state representations in the global trajectory space of the entire system.

Illustration

Take the population subsystem [POP] consisting of initially eight states, e.g. $z = (z_1, z_2, \ldots, z_8)$, then after inputs are fed into the [POP] system a new state configuration obtains e.g., $z'_1, z'_2, \ldots, z'_8$, say.
A simple measure of *structural complexity* could be given by the number

$$\#_s(z) = \sum_{i=1}^{8} \overline{\#}_s(z_i) = \sum_{i=1}^{8} \text{(length of time needed to reach a satisfactory state)} \; x \; \text{(number of feasible states to be attainable)}.$$

On the other hand, the computational complexity indicates the number

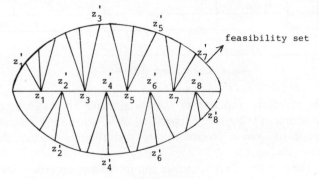

Fig. 2. [POP] – Subsystem

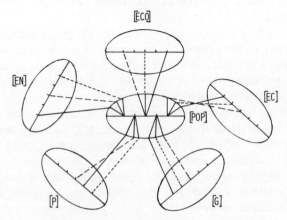

Fig. 3. Satellite system: links indicate computational complexity.

of links between various subsystems times the number of interactions that ensue until the computational cycle (in real-time) is completed, as roughly indicated only for one specific subsystem, say [POP], (for all other subsystems likewise) in the following illustration.

In the satellite system, connecting all neighboring subsystems, the *computational complexity* related to the [POP] subsystem amounts to

$$\#_c([\text{POP}]) = (\# \text{ links to } [\text{EN}] + \# \text{ links to } [\text{ECO}] + \cdots +$$

$$+ \# \text{ links to } [\text{P}]) = \sum_{i=1}^{n} \#_i(\text{links to } i).$$

Then the total computational complexity comprising all links among all subsystems within the satellite system is given by

$$\#_c([\text{POP}], [\text{EN}], [\text{ECO}], [\text{EC}], [\text{G}], [\text{P}]) =$$

$$= \#_c(Z_F, F) = \sum_{k=1}^{6} \#_k(Z_{Fk}, F_k).$$

Using the notation, let Z_F be the state space over which the entire finite state system is running; let F be all feasible semigroups of transformations acting on this space; then in accordance with decomposition results of algebraic finite state systems we establish a comprehensive complexity measure comprising structural and computational complexity, e.g.

$$C(Z_F, F) = \prod_{k=1}^{m} \#_s(Z) \#_c(Z_F, F),$$

and this is the measure we use in analyzing the structure of a particular economic model.

4.5 STRUCTURE OF THE MODEL

We wish to explore the nature of interdependencies in societal systems to show how systems might be decomposed into their component parts for analytical purposes and to relate the results to the choice of models in policy analysis and projection. According to what has been illustrated in Figure 1 we choose a kind of partition of the overall system into parts that comprise the main activities of complex societal systems – this is very much in the spirit of earlier attempts at modelling complex political systems for purposes of simulating their behavior, see R.D. Brunner and

G.D. Brewer [3]. The components of this model consist of the set of variables and parameters listed under the detailed description later.

[POP] – the population subsystem is relatively specialized to the growth and distribution (density) of the population N_t, being composed of the urban and rural population.

[EN] – the energy subsystem is singled out as the major resource sector which could be of mixed private-public activities, and where the energy basket consists of the output E_t of primary and secondary energy resources generated.

[ECO] – the environmental system puts environmental restrictions (water and air pollution) on growth of production in urban and industrial areas.

[EC] – the economic subsystem is relatively specialized to the production and distribution of economic goods and services within the private sector.

[G] – the government subsystem comprises all activities of the public sector which are directed at providing goods and services demanded by the market place or generated by political considerations.

[P] – the political subsystem is specialized to the production of changes in the size and distribution of mass support for the government MV_t to permit majority rule and conservation of power, furthermore, determines the consumptive and distributive characteristics of government expenditures G_t. The relationships in the model are grouped according to subsystems, these relationships are hypotheses about the way in which each variable changes as a function of the others, with the magnitudes of the changes being determined in part by the parameters.

The degree of connectedness or interdependence implied in the relationships can be explored by noting the presence or absence of causal links among the variables. Call this the *structural connectedness* of the model. In fact, there are *direct* causal and *indirect* causal connections (links) between the output and input variables, depending on whether they occur within the components blocks or are cross-connected among different blocks. The static description of the structural connectedness underestimates the degree of connectedness among variables as the model operates through time. For example, since government revenue R_t is merely a function of gross output Y_{t-1}, variation in G_t within one real-time cycle is limited to the variation in this variable. However, if the model is operated through time, the number of variables causally connected to R_t increases. Thus while R_t is a direct function of Y_{t-1} (or some aggregates thereof), it is also an indirect function through this variable of

C_{t-1}, I_{t-1}, G_{t-1}, and through these variables R_t is an indirect function of several other variables, etc. Obviously, the power of the connectedness matrix increases in correspondence with an increase in the number of real-time cycles of the model. The analysis of structural connectedness has obvious limitations for the chartist approach to prediction. If the analysis suggests that even in a system that is loosely connected in its static description every variable in the system may ultimately depend upon every other variable as the system runs on-line through time, then a simple extrapolation of trends which ignores these dependencies may indeed be highly misleading. In a situation where the number of outside factors tend to be increasing to infinity, we would well expect some statistical regularity in offsetting influences among the factors, and, indeed, a chartist approach may be a good thing to follow by neglecting these dependencies. This would correspond to viewing the real situation as a state of 'disorganized complexity'. However, in the course of previous arguments, the case of an FCS would not support this point. Then a serious modelling and prediction effort would have to take into account indirect effects that may have a highly nonlinear character. Of course, there is the possibility that in a particular system or in a particular application of the model, certain of these dependencies may be sufficiently weak that they can be safely ignored. If this were the case, the chartist's approach which ignores these dependencies and the comprehensive modelling approach taking them more fully into account may lead approximately to the same conclusions.

4.6 THE MODEL'S BASIC SET OF RELATIONSHIPS

(a) [POP] – Subsystem
Rate of population change

$\rho(N) = \alpha_1$ (average number of children per family)
$+ \beta_1$ (number of women of child-bearing age) $\Big\}$ exogeneous factors [EF]
$+ \lambda_1$ (availability of birth control devices and liberal abortion policies)

$+ \delta_1$ (expected average family income, given some current level of family income) $\Big\}$ [EC]

$+ \varepsilon_1$ (population supporting energy consumption level) $\Big\}$ [EN]

$+ \eta_1$ (population density index level)   [ECO]

$+ \xi_1$ (provision of public goods and services relevant to child rearing activities) $\Big\}$ [G]

$+ \theta_1$ (level of wide-spread political satisfaction and trust in political institutions) $\Big\}$ [P]

(b) [EN] – Subsystem
Supply of Energy

$S(E_t) = \alpha_2$ (availability of domestic energy resources)
$+ \beta_2$ (energy provision through imports)
$+ \lambda_2$ (potential of mobilizing new energy sources via technology) $\Big\}$ [EF]

$+ \delta_2$ (price expectations and market prices) $\Big\}$ [EC]

$+ \varepsilon_2$ level of manpower directed toward energy production) $\Big\}$ [POP]

$+ \eta_2$ (upper limits of energy provision by environmental factors, i.e. stripmining, health and environmental hazards, pollution) $\Big\}$ [ECO]

$+ \xi_2$ (degree of government intervention in terms of price or quantity regulation) $\Big\}$ [G]

$+ \theta_2$ (political interference in the industrial organization of the energy industry) $\Big\}$ [P]

$D(E_t) = \mu N_t + \lambda Y_t$, energy consumption is proportional to total population and to the level of G.N.P.

$\Delta(D(E_t) - D(E_{t-1})) = \mu(N_t - N_{t-1})$, the rate of energy consumption is proportional to the rate of population change.

(c) [ECO] – Subsystem

Abatement Performance (measured in terms of level of exhaust emission)

$AP = \alpha_3$ (index of industrial distribution)

    $+ \beta_3$ (environmental immersion factors)

    $+ \lambda_3$ (level of environmental technology) $\Big\} [EF]$

    $+ \delta_3$ (G.N.P. as related to regional and sectoral industrial activity)

    $+ \dot{\varepsilon}_3$ (rate of population change and structural population shifts from rural to urban sectors) $\Big\} [POP]$

    $+ \xi_3$ (government regulation and industrial incentive structure in terms of emission limits, waste disposal, land use zoning regulations, noise restrictions) $\Big\} [G]$

    $+ \eta_3$ (energy supply and mixture of energy sources) $\Big\} [EN]$

    $+ \theta_3$ (effectiveness of government control, efficiency/inefficieny ratio of supervision) $\Big\} [P]$

(d) $[EC]$ – Subsystem

Links of G.N.P. aggregates are by definition:

$$Y_t = C_t + I_t + G_t + F_t \ (F_t = \text{foreign trade, given exogeneously}).$$
$$C_t = m_t(1 - \tau)Y_{t-1}\dot{N},$$
$$I_t = I_{t-1}\dot{N} + r(\dot{C}\dot{N})^{+f(G_t)}, \dot{C} = dC/dt$$

where f represents the extent of government expenditure restricting private investment, to take care of welfare-state limits on private investment activity.

Growth of G.N.P.

$\dot{Y} = \alpha_4$ (resource endowment)

    $+ \beta_4$ (R & D level) $\Big\} [EF]$

    $+ \lambda_4$ (level of technology used)

$+ \delta_4$ (minimal level of energy supply needed to support growth) $\Big\}$ [EN]

$+ \varepsilon_4$ (minimal abatement performance AP = maximal pollution, noise, waste disposal limit) $\Big\}$ [ECO]

$+ \eta_4$ (size of government investment activities) $\Big\}$ [G]

$+ \zeta_4$ (rate of population change related to productive employment) $\Big\}$ [POP]

$+ \theta_4$ (government guidance and organizational support) $\Big\}$ [P]

(e) [G] – Subsystem

Government revenue is proportional to G.N.P. Y_t via the proportionality factor τ (tax rate).

$$R_t = \tau \, Y_t.$$

Government expenditure

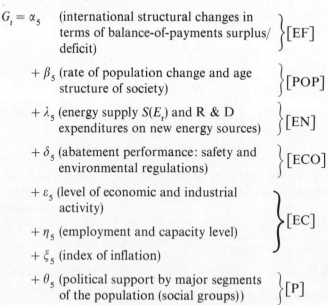

$G_t = \alpha_5$ (international structural changes in terms of balance-of-payments surplus/deficit) $\Big\}$ [EF]

$+ \beta_5$ (rate of population change and age structure of society) $\Big\}$ [POP]

$+ \lambda_5$ (energy supply $S(E_t)$ and R & D expenditures on new energy sources) $\Big\}$ [EN]

$+ \delta_5$ (abatement performance: safety and environmental regulations) $\Big\}$ [ECO]

$+ \varepsilon_5$ (level of economic and industrial activity)

$+ \eta_5$ (employment and capacity level) $\Big\}$ [EC]

$+ \zeta_5$ (index of inflation)

$+ \theta_5$ (political support by major segments of the population (social groups)) $\Big\}$ [P]

(f) [P] – Subsystem

Majority of votes from all or some segments of the population to achieve majority rule in Parliament.

$$MV_t = \alpha_6 \quad \text{(psychological conditions of trust, honesty and stability in society)} \quad \Big\}\, [EF]$$

$$+ \beta_6 \text{ (rate of population change)}$$

$$+ \lambda_6 \text{ (change of migration patterns from rural to urban areas)} \quad \Bigg\}\, [POP]$$

$$+ \delta_6 \text{ (occupational shifts)}$$

$$+ \varepsilon_6 \text{ (energy supply and distribution of energy resources)} \quad \Big\}\, [EN]$$

$$+ \eta_6 \text{ (level of pollution affecting major social groups and key industrial areas)} \quad \Big\}\, [ECO]$$

$$+ \xi_6 \text{ (composition of rate of G.N.P. in relation to political goals agreeing with major interests of the population)} \quad \Bigg\}\, [EC]$$

$$+ \theta_6 \text{ (provision of government services and collective goods)} \quad \Big\}\, [P]$$

4.7 EVALUATION OF COMPLEXITY

Now the static description of the structural connectedness underestimates the degree of interaction among subsystems as the interaction operates through time, this is true since the various feedback- and feedforward mechanisms reinforce the interaction in a nonlinear way. We consider the connected system as a real-time type, on-line dynamic system, see Martin [7], that starts operating at a specific initial state for which sufficient information is available, and which operates on an equal length time interval of one year. The selection of one year (in a real-time computational cycle) is arbitrary and used only for illustration purposes although parameter changes in this model appear to have only longer term impacts. Then the number of links to be estimated (pertaining to *computational complexity*) amounts to the following set-up. The entire system consists

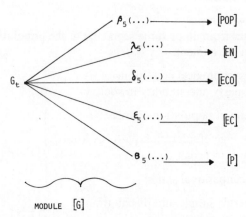

Fig. 4. Determination of G_t in module $[G]$ by direct links to other modules.

of altogether six 'modules', [POP], [EN], [ECO], [EC], [G], [P], plus the external environment, exogeneous factors [EF]. Each module consists of at least five linking factors to other modules, neglecting the exogeneous factors [RF] which are considered to be predetermined, the information of which is only directly accessible by the module concerned. Each of these five linking factors or parameters depend upon at most eight factors in some other module, therefore indirectly involving [EF]. In the first case we refer to *direct links*, in the second to *indirect links* of each of the modules involved.

For illustration look at the determination of G_t in Module [G] (Figure 4).

With six active decision-making modules operating, the total number of structural parameters to be computed amounts to at least 240 structural parameters, e.g. five direct links given by the parameters of each module times eight indirect links for each such parameter in some other module times six, the number of interactive modules.

Now granting that at least 240 structural parameters be estimated, and suppose a response cycle of yearly data for a period of a ten year planning model is used, then in view of the non-linearities of the system interactions as the system operates through time and extends the length of indirect links, we can show, by complete enumeration, that we arrive at a total number of 240^{10} structural links which is a dramatic increase. In other words, the same number of structural parameters would have to be estimated in order to reach a control complexity that fits the design complexity of the entire system – a formidable task. (Still, it would be even more dramatic if we relate the response cycle to quarterly or even monthly data.) Now this holds for a problem solving mechanism acting as a brute-force search, as built into large-scale computer programs, in which

(i) the modules do not provide any structural complexity, i.e. no intrinsic problem-solving power as given by a special heuristic,

(ii) there is complete ignorance on the controller's side concerning the parameter variations in the dynamic process.

In other words, this corresponds to a centralized controller who perceives the modules simply as 'black boxes' with no self-steering capability and who at each real-time response cycle is ignorant about (or does not learn about) parameter variations that ensue.

In the alternative case the controller may activate the problem-solving power, heuristic search capabilities of the modules where each module, as a decentralized unit, by itself intrinsically computes all indirect links, there-by decreasing the computational burden of the controller. Hence the computational process reduces to direct links only, at least five for each module, so that for each response cycle $5 \times 6 = 30$ structural parameters have to be estimated as compared to 240. This amounts to 30^{10} structural links in a ten years period. In fact, the reduction of the number 240^{10} to 30^{10} could be assigned to the 'smartness' or 'structural complexity' of the modules; to be precise the structural complexity amounts to $240^{10}-30^{10}$, the residual in the reduction of computational complexity. Therefore, we see how a tradeoff between structural complexity and computational complexity evolves in such an interactive model.[1]

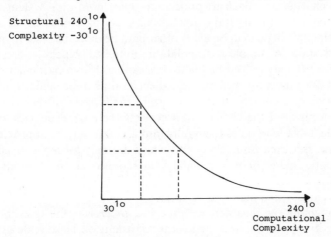

Fig. 5 Complexity Tradeoff.

4.8 DISCUSSION

The most interesting aspect of this analysis for problem-solving methodologies pertains to the distinction between design and control complexity. If the design complexity of the system amounts to 240^{10} structural links, the only way to cope successfully with the control of such systems is to use a decomposition that makes most out of the intrinsic computational capabilities of the modules, their smartness or sophistication, much in the same way as chess playing programs become smarter to match master chess players by building into the programs some sophisticated heuristics. This sheds new light on the question of centralization vs decentralization of decision-making in organizations: in particular, in view of these results, one could hardly hope to achieve rational centralized economic planning against market-type decentralized mechanisms (see F.A. Hayek [5]). At least the need for decentralization is now widely acknowledged in Soviet work on program-planning. As N.N. Moiseev and A.G. Schmidt [9] put it: 'it is not difficult to see that no matter how advanced the level of the techniques for data processing and data transmission may be, a certain level of decentralization in management will always be necessary'.

Furthermore, in general mixed-type economies, one can conclude that government regulation will easily find its limit of workability because of the computational burden that ensues. Another point worth considering is that the analysis of structural connectedness had obvious implications for the chartist approach to projection. Since even in a system that is loosely connected in its static description, every parameter in the system may ultimately depend upon every other parameter as the system operates through time. A simple extrapolation of trends which ignores these dependencies may indeed be highly misleading. If in a particular system it turns out that most of these dependencies (links) are sufficiently weak so that they can be safely ignored (according to the Ando–Fisher Theorem), the projections of the chartist who neglects these dependencies and the fundamentalist who takes them fully into account may be approximately the same. But even 'simple' systems which are only loosely connected in their static description are highly interconnected in their dynamic behavior.

Let's close with a methodological note.

Throughout this chapter *we attempted to answer* the question how complexity appearing as a structural constraint on large scale dynamic economic systems can be successfully handled from a controller's point of view. For answering this question it appears necessary to know what units of decomposition are most appropriate for designing and understanding complex systems. The sheer amount of computation, reflected by a measure of computational complexity, prohibits the decision-making or information-processing power of any human or artificial controller yet to be designed. This indicates that by proper decomposition we should strive to mobilize the problem-solving potentiality of systems components, which will help to reduce the computational burden of the controller. These systems components are supposed to activate useful heuristics at a local or decentralized level that involves sophistication, creativity, non-routine problem-solving vs standard operating programs under repetitive situations as required in purely arithmetical tasks. It is reasonable to assume that market-type processes, e.g. market clearing functions, taking place in well-defined subunits, provide such a useful heuristic: they substitute structural for computational complexity. This is an issue that drives at the core of discussion of human problem-solving and the principles of bounded rationality as applied to organizational mechanisms.

A case in point, where our complexity measures could be applied, is an unpublished study by P.L. Schmidbauer [12], which is an analysis of the heuristics of market decision-making applied to the wheat market. The key elements of the study will be summarized in what follows:

– Decision rules are assumed to be represented by computer programs, and their operating characteristics investigated in simulation runs.

– A descriptive analysis of the information handling and decision-making activities, by a market of the competitive type, is developed.

– The quantity of information resources (memory, computation time, and communication capacity) needed to carry out the activity corresponds to the computational complexity of the market mechanism.

– For practical purposes, in this study, computational complexity can be estimated either

(i)   by counting the messages that must be sent to dispatch the results of decision-making activity, or,

(ii)   by the amount of the time needed to send or receive information through the computer's model simulating the market process.

Estimation of information processing requirements for the wheat market's allocation mechanism requires computation, storage, and, communication estimates for the following class of agents (subsystems, modules):

(i) producers (farmers), (ii) country elevators, (iii) receivers and brokers,

(iv) terminal elevators, (v) consumers, (vi) minor agents, including some speculators, market inspectors, and floor buyers.

Computational complexity is given for each of the major agents as well as for the entire market process.

The gist of Schmidbauer's results is the statement ([12], pp. 28/29).

The total for the market comes to somewhat more than 6500 (IBM) 7090 – hours per year, or about 0.8 7090-years. When one considers that some 121,000 decision-makers participate in the market process, this number seems quite small.

Columns two and three of Table I indicate the decision-making computational load. The second column lists times for parameter adjustment, including both α-and β-adjustments. These activities, together with occasional revision of value standards, take up more than twelve 7090-years annually. ... How much time is actually used will depend upon the complexity of the adjustment and the algorithms or heuristics used in making the changes. ... Column three of the table shows the time used to interpret incoming messages and to decide where to file the information.

TABLE I

Computation time: 7090-hours/year, total market (Schmidbauer [12])

Agent	Decision Making	Parameter Adjustment	Data Input Processing	Total
Farmer	22	5.55×10^4	7.64×10^4	13.19×10^4
Country Elevator	3220	2.05×10^4	2.86×10^4	5.21×10^4
Receiver	1050	—	70	0.11×10^4
Terminal Elevator	1070	0.56×10^4	0.78×10^4	1.44×10^4
Consumer˙	1094	0.51×10^4	0.72×10^4	1.34×10^4
Misc.	63	1.18×10^4	1.55×10^4	2.73×10^4
IBM	6519	9.85×10^4	13.55×10^4	24.1×10^4
7090-Years/Yr.	0.8	12.5	17.2	30.5

TABLE II

Computation Time, 7090-hours/year, per firm

Agent	Decision Making	Parameter Adjustment	Data Input Processing	Total
Farmer	2.6×10^{-4}	0.66	0.91	1.57
Country Elevator	0.108	0.68	0.96	1.75
Receiver	0.53	—	0.04	0.57
Terminal Elevator	2.68	13.75	19.5	25.93
Consumer	1.04	5.1	7.2	13.34

As a major conclusion, Schmidbauer states (p. 38):

The tabled statistics indicate that centralized operations of the market would lead to considerable savings of information resources, ... one of the major reasons for decentralized decision making activity is the need to provide adequate monitoring of a complex and changing process.

One of the major drawbacks of Schmidbauer's analysis is that he provides only a descriptive analysis of computational complexity, hence, does not explore heuristics of decentralized units that cut short on computational routines, i.e., as intelligent units substitute structural complexity for computational complexity. Schmidbauer himself seems fully aware of this aspect (p. 40):

It is worth reasserting that the present study is concerned with the use of a computer to develop a descriptive estimate of market information processes under somewhat idealized conditions, it cannot be interpreted as a proposal for a system design.

Here we are concerned with the problem what is the minimum complexity, e.g., the design complexity, of the market operation in question.

4.9 COMPARISON WITH SOME STUDIES ON THE ECONOMICS OF ORGANIZATION

The results of this chapter seem to contradict claims such as that price systems require essentially the same calculations as command systems or that command and price systems are informationally equivalent. According to S.A. Marglin [6] the information aspect is essential for the distinction between price and command systems. Neglecting the incentive aspect, our analysis shows, on the other hand, that except for relatively small systems, in general, decentralized systems are more likely to cope with complex tasks than centralized systems. The reason appears to be that the market is a heuristic device, capable of searching for a 'good solution', whereas the centralized unit has to activate an algorithm that completely relies on an enumeration technique. A more differentiated view point has been taken by H. Oniki [10] who argues that centralized economic systems may perform better, e.g., with lower cost of communication, if only a low degree of accuracy is required (measured by the 'allocation error' as a departure from the efficient allocation), and if the system is relatively small in the number of interacting units, variables, etc. However, this applies only to tiny but not real economies so that – for all practical purposes – command and price mechanisms appear not to be informationally equivalent, agreeing with our lines reasoning. But we suggest even a stronger statement: not merely 'costs of communication' will be higher in a centralized system but beyond a certain threshold of complexity, centralized systems will not be able to control physically the economy without *simultaneously* achieving the same performance as a comparable decentralized system (of the same size). K.J. Arrow [2] reemphasizes the information economizing effect of decentralized systems, in his words:

But what was left obscure is a more definite measure of information and its costs, in terms of which it would be possible of affect superiority of the price system over a centralized alternative.

NOTE

[1] A complexity tradeoff between structure and computational complexity, pertaining to certain types of artificial intelligence programs, is the subject of a recent study by J. Pearl et al. [14]: 'When (the algorithm) employs a perfectly informal heuristic ($h = h^*$) it is propelled directly toward the goal without ever getting sidetracked, spending only N computational steps where N is available ($h = 0$), the search becomes exhaustive, yielding an exponentially growing complexity. Between these two extremes there lies an unknown relationship between the accuracy of the heuristic estimates and the complexity of the search which they help control'.

REFERENCES

[1] Ando, A. and Fisher, F. M., 'Near-Decomposability, Partition and Aggregation, and the Relevance of Stability Discussions', *International Economic Review* **4** (1963), 53–57.

[2] Arrow, K.L., 'Limited Knowledge and Economic Analysis', *American Economic Review* **64** (1974), 1–10.

[3] Brunner, R.D. and Brewer, G.D., *Organized Complexity*, The Free Press, New York, 1971.

[4] Hayek, F.A., 'The Theory of Complex Phenomena', in Hayek (ed.), *Studies of Philosophy, Politics and Economics*, Routledge, London, 1967.

[5] Hayek, F.A., 'The Use of Knowledge in Society', in Hayek (ed.): *Individualism and Economic Order*, Univ. of Chicago Press, Chicago, 1948.

[6] Marglin, S.A., 'Information in Price and Command Systems of Planning', in J. Margolis and H. Guitton (eds.), *Public Economics*, Macmillan, New York, 1969, chap. 3, pp. 54–77.

[7] Martin, J., *Design of Real Time Computer Systems*, Prentice-Hall, Englewood Cliffs, 1967.

[8] May, R.M., *Stability and Complexity in Model Ecosystems*, Princeton Univ. Press, Princeton, N.Y., 1973.

[9] Moiseev, N.N. and Schmidt, A.G., 'Some Problems of Centralized Economy', *Cowles Foundation Discussion Paper* No. 358, Yale Univ., 1973.

[10] Oniki, H., 'The Cost of Communication in Economic Organization', *Quarterly Journal of Economics* **86** (1974), 529–550.

[11] Sandell, N.R. et al., 'Survey of Decentralized Control Methods for Large-Scale Systems, *IEEE Transactions* AC-**23** (1978), 108–128.

[12] Schmidbauer, P.L., 'Information and Communications Requirements of the Wheat Market. An Example of a Competitive System', TR 21, Center for Research in Management Science, Univ. of California, Berkeley, Ca., Jan. 1966.

[13] Weaver W., 'Science and Complexity', *American Scientist* **36** (1948), 536–544.

[14] Pearl, J. et al., 'Probabilistic Analysis of the Complexity of A*, *Artificial Intelligence* **15** (1980), 241–254.

CHAPTER 5

COMPLEXITY, BOUNDED RATIONALITY AND
PROBLEM-SOLVING

5.1 INTRODUCTION

We claim that the three notions 'complexity', 'bounded rationality', and 'problem-solving' are intrinsically related.

(i) *Complexity* appears to be a structural property of any observable system (social, biological, mechanical), decision-making mechanism, organization, bureaucracy that imposes constraints upon the computability, selectivity, control, and decision-making power: hence it limits its proper functioning, *limits rationality*.

(ii) Structural constraints such as complexity modify the handling, manipulation, and controllability of the system and its solution requires heuristics, search, and step-by-step procedures leading to *problem-solving* in a task environment.

Let us see how we can establish the links in a meaningful way.

5.2 BOUNDED RATIONALITY

In the traditional theory of decision-making it is generally acknowledged that at least two definitions of rationality are conceivable, depending on whether the approach is abstract (normative) – based on non-contradictory reasoning, or pragmatic (descriptive) – based on experience. We hold that these two concepts are not necessarily mutually exclusive, if we add one important aspect to the description of rationality, e.g. *computability*. Rationality in the normative sense is too restrictive by granting the decision-maker *unlimited computational resources* which obviously fail to hold in view of complex (ill-structured) situations. On the other hand, rationality in the descriptive sense is too elusive and diffuse to be of any analytical or even predictive value since it violates the unique links to the consistency and coherence standards of normative postulates.

Reasons for using strategies of 'bounded rationality' could be itemized as follows:

(1) *limited computational resources* of the decision-maker;

134

(2) *thresholds of complexity* beyond which individuals are unable to discriminate, choose and reveal cognitive limits;

(3) many choice processes represent essentially *ill-structured* problems.

Let us take a moment to discuss the last point.

An ill-structured problem (ISP) fails to satisfy at least one, or more likely several, of the listed conditions:

DSC (Definite Single Criterion): there is a definite single criterion for testing any proposed solution;

RPS (Representation in Problem Space): there is at least one problem space in which can be represented the initial problem state, the goal state, and all other states that may be reached;

TPS (Transformation in Problem Space): attainable state changes (legal moves) can be represented via transitions in a problem space;

APPS (Accurate Prediction in Problem Space): if the actual problems involve acting upon the external world (environment), then changes of the state by applying operators can be predicted, controlled and directed toward the goal state with any desirable degree of accuracy, conditional on the knowledge of the environmental states;

PAC (Practical Amount of Computation): all basic processes underlying the step-by-step procedure of problem-solving search involve only a 'practicable amount of computation' so that only a practicable amount of search is needed for terminating the problem solving process.

Starting with characteristic DSC we note that ISPs usually involve a representation of *multiple criteria*, requiring *complex trade-off statements* which in fact would enhance the number of computational steps.

In the set-up of a decision problem the trade-offs may pertain to either of the following different situations:

(a) Two or more values are affected by the decision, but they are known to the decision-maker.

(b) At least one of the outcomes is subject to uncertainty, e.g. involves a lottery that has to be traded against a sure prospect. What is the *certainty equivalent*?

(c) The power to make a decision is dispersed over a number of individual actors or organizational units representing different values, goals.

These trade-off problems have been treated, one way or the other, in recent contributions to decision theory, see J. Marschak and R. Radner [6], J. Steinbruner, [16], R.L. Keeney and H. Raiffa [5]. They are exclusively confined to static problems which are not sufficient to exhaust ISPs.

Conditions RPS and TPS refer to the dynamic nature of the problem space and require that the problem to be solved is well-defined and well-structured per se so that the goal structure is clearly determined a priori.

APPS is the condition that alludes to the possible stochastic nature of the problem, in which the nature of uncertainty plays a definite role, and which reflects itself in the random character of environmental states.

Finally, PAC is the crucial condition here in which the computational aspect is of major importance. We have to look for effective heuristic procedures that at least partly compensate for excessive computational routines going far beyond the information processing capabilities of human decision-makers. Hence, what is needed is to make an ISP well-structured by using procedures that apply PAC to an ISP.

As H. Simon [13] argues, 'practicable amounts of computation' are only defined relatively to the computational power and there is a continuum of degrees of definiteness between the well-structured and ill-structured ends of the problem spectrum.

EXAMPLE. Limited Rationality in Chess-Playing Programs.

A good paradigm of limited rationality is provided by designing chess-playing programs. There are various reasons for studying outcomes and strategies in games in connection with the problem of complexity and problem-solving programs.

(1) First, people are involved in complex games and attempt to find good strategies. Does there exist a computer program that matches the best human play? Furthermore, if it exists, is there anything in the structure of the program that would be beneficial to be learnt by the human problem-solver? According to Newell, Shaw and Simon [9]:

We do assert that complexity of behavior is essential to an intelligent performance – that the complexity of a successful chess program will approach the complexity of the thought processes of a successful human chess player.

(2) So far computer programs as applied to a general class of problems did rather poorly, as compared to humans, although recently there have been some fascinating improvements as evidenced by chess-playing programs such as 'chess 5.0' (David Slate, Northwestern University). In a state-of-the-art survey Newell, Shaw and Simon [9] have pointed out that there are just too many alternatives for a computer to examine each move, so an adequate chess-playing program must contain heuristics which restrict it to the examination of reasonable moves. Also to win a game you need not select the best moves, just the satisfactory ones.

(3) Studying game playing sheds a crucial light on the concept of learning the games which is not well understood. To teach an intelligent person the rules of chess, by itself, does not make him an expert player. One must have experience. If we could define effective game playing programs which profit from experience we have at least some clue how to practice problem-solving in real life situations that require strategic planning.

(4) How a computer program should acquire chess knowledge is an interesting and difficult point. One way, of course, is for certain records to be built into the original program. To an extent this is done. Most recent chess-playing programs contain the sequence of moves and counter-moves for standard defenses. The situation at mid-game is more difficult, since so many positions might arise.

How is it possible that good chess-players still outperform computer programs of chess which are much more powerful in computing strategies? The answer is that they evidently activate useful heuristics that more than offset their lack of computational power.

We claim that activating successful heuristics is intrinsically connected to the notion of structural complexity in dynamic algebraic systems. Chess belongs to the class of two person games with complete information and no chance moves. It is known that there exists for each board position (or more generally for each state of the game) one (or several) optimal moves. A tabulation of the optimal moves is a tremendous task. Chess has on the average over 10^{120} board positions, hence the table would have to have the same number of entries. Such a complete search for the optimal move is so enormous that it transcends the capabilities of any physical computer, in other words 'brute force computing' is not likely to be the solution.

By designing the first chess playing program Shannon [12] proposed two principles on which an algorithm for playing chess could be formulated.

(1) Scan all the possibilities (moves) and construct a search tree with branches of equal length. Hence, all the variants of the moves to be searched for are computed to the same depth. At the end of each variation (at the end of the branch) the position is evaluated by means of a numerical evaluation function. By comparing the numerical values, one can choose the best move in any given starting position, simply by the minimaxing procedure, i.e. averaging strategies by the evaluation function.

(2) Not all possibilities are scanned, some are excluded from consideration by a special rule, e.g. by a special search. Some special search methods

have been proposed and proved to be successful, see B. Raphael [11, Chapter 3] In this method, with the same computational resources, the depth of computation can be greater.

In the first case, information of high value will be treated equally with information of low value, or collecting information is uniformly assigned equal cost to each node. A substantial part of the work will be useless, i.e. not leading to a desirable goal (checkmate). This is a modified breadth first search with a numerical evaluation function and minimaxing procedure.

In fact, in option (2) it appears that highly selective search, the drastic pruning of the tree or *in depth search* is likely to be more successful to treat highly complex decision problems. For this purpose one needs a heuristic, as a rule of thumb, strategy or trick which drastically limits search for solutions. All of these do not guarantee any solution at all, but a useful heuristic offers solutions which are good enough most of the time.

The pay-off in using heuristics is greately reduced search and, therefore, involves a 'practicable amount of computation'.

In fact, summarizing the experience of various chess-playing programs, we observe that some programs have put more emphasis on computing power along tree search in the direction of option (1) whereas others have traded off computing speed against sophistication or selectivity as sources of improvement in complex programs. Selectivity is a very powerful device and speed a very weak device for improving the performance of complex programs. By comparing two major chess-playing programs, the Los Alamos and the Bernstein program, we see that they achieve roughly the same quality of performance by pursuing different routes, the computational vs. the heuristic approach: the first by using no selectivity and being very fast, the second by using a large amount of selectivity but not relying on computational speed. So, in a way, Bernstein's program introduces more sophistication to the chess program. Most of the major game-playing programs are based upon (local) look ahead and minimax techniques. As might be expected such programs have been most successful in games that have challenged the memory ability of human players, but not in games that require experience, thinking, creativity, and sophistication, such as chess.

Quoting J. McCarthy [7]:

I think there is much to be learned from chess, because master level play will require more than just improving the present methods of searching trees. Namely, it will require the ability to identify, represent, and recognize the patterns of position and play that correspond to chess ideas ... .

5.3 PROBLEM-SOLVING

Let us start with a definition of a problem according to Newell, Shaw and Simon [8]: 'A problem exists whenever a problem-solver desires some outcome or state of affairs that he does not immediately know how to attain'. To generate all kinds of task-related information that pertains to 'problem-solving' is to involve heuristics that reflect practical knowledge, experience, but also logical consistency, smartness, sophistication.

A theory of problem-solving is concerned with discovering and understanding systems of heuristics. A particular, interesting method is provided by GPS, consisting of means-ends analysis and planning, a subject matter we will briefly describe in Sections 5.5 and 5.6.

Problem-solving has developed into a challenging subdiscipline of artificial intelligence, but the methods and techniques used are of sufficient general interest for dealing with decision-making situations of politicians, bureaucrats or managers. It is likely that these decision-makers could improve their decisions if they make use of a formal theory of problem-solving. The state-space approach is a very appropriate problem-solving representation, since it has a natural association to dynamic algebraic systems and complexity.

Assume the existence of a finite or countable set Z of states, and a set $\mathscr{S}$ of operators consisting of semigroups S acting upon Z. The problem-solver is seen as moving through space defined by the states, in an attempt to reach one of a desired set of goal states. A problem is solved when a sequence of semigroup operators $S = S_1, S_2, \ldots, S_n$ could be found for some decomposition of the state-space such that a nested relationship holds for some initial state z_0 to generate the goal state

$$z_n = S_n(S_{n-1}, (\ldots S_2(S_1(z_0)) \ldots)).$$

One could establish a one-to-one correspondence between the problem of finding S and the problem of finding a path through a graph. Let Z be defining the nodes of a graph, with arcs between nodes i and j if and only if there is an operation $S \in \mathscr{S}$ connecting z_i with z_j. The graphic representation of state-space problem solving has three advantages. It is intuitively easy to grasp, it leads to a natural extension in which we associate a cost with the application of each operation S_i. Finally, in many cases the next step to be explored can be made a function of a comparison between a goal state and a final state.

How does a theory of problem-solving relate to decision theory?

The ingredients of the conventional decision problem under uncertainty consist of

(i) a set of actions available to the decision-maker and subject to control by himself;

(ii) a set of mutually exclusive states of nature, one and only one of them can occur;

(iii) a set of consequences that obtain if the decision-maker chooses particular actions and a certain state of nature turns out to be true.

If the decision-maker is rational and satisfies certain consistency criteria for the choice of actions, he will attempt to maximize expected utility or expected pay-off. In this problem it appears that uncertainty about which event obtains is his most severe restriction in following an optimal course of actions. On the other hand, apparently, the decision-maker need not cope with computational constraints, either there are no physical or psychological limits on his ability to handle an immense amount of data, facilitating his choice problem, or else costs of computation are virtually known, so that the decision-maker need only determine his net pay-off making allowance for the computational costs.

A problem-solving situation, requiring decision-making in contrast reveals special features that could be circumscribed by *degree of difficulty*, *limited decision-making capabilities* or resources, and intrinsic complexity in finding *acceptable or satisfying strategies* (solutions). These characteristics, require adequate methods such as complexity-bounded search, heuristics etc.

EXAMPLE. Consider the description of a genuine problem in this framework. In the 'missionaries and cannibals' problem, three missionaries and three cannibals wish to cross a river from the left bank to the right. They have available a boat which can take only two people on a trip. All can row. The problem is to get all six safely to the right bank subject to the constraint that at no time the number of missionaries on either side of the river may be exceeded by the number of cannibals on that side. To translate the puzzle into a formal problem, let a state be defined by the number of missionaries and cannibals on the left bank and the position of the boat. The starting position is (3, 3, L) and the goal (terminal) state (3, 3, R). The permissible moves of the boat define the operators. The problem is solved in a number of steps, whereby the minimal number, if it exists, constitutes the optimal solution.[1]

Problem-solving is certainly linked to 'survivability': given a chess position, change it into a position in which the oponent's king is checkmated. En route to this position, avoid any position in which your own king is checkmated or in which a stalemate occurs. The board positions define the states, and the piece moves the operator.

In this example the terminal state need not be fixed, but in the process problem-solving may be subsequently redefined and modified subject only to the restriction that at no point 'survivability' is endangered (endogenous value generation).

Among the tools for a comprehensive assessment of complex public and private decision problems, decision analysis appears to be the most comprehensive one. But comprehensive methods of decision analysis, as proposed by H. Raiffa [10], for instance, are restricted in several ways:

(1) they are basically *off-line* procedures, i.e. limit choices to the 'givens' once stated;

(2) they limit complexity to the *determination of uncertainty* via probability;

(3) they address only to '*well-structured*' decision problems, where the whole set of alternatives is laid out before the decision-maker and where he knows how to achieve a particular course of action;

(4) they apply only to situations where the *goal structure has been fixed in advance* or no change of goals is anticipated in the process of taking a course of actions;

(5) they pertain to the *computational part* of decision-making using expected utility as the unique performance index, but making no use whatsoever of the strength of heuristics, sophistication, creativity, innovation etc., that is the unique feature of complex decision processes.

There have been recent criticisms on the major defects of contemporaneous decision analysis. They can be loosely summarized as follows:

(a) Complexity is an outcome of physical constraints on information processing and therefore a matter of design.

(b) Complexity is a matter of economic constraints imposed by costs of making decisions.

(a) and (b) could be considered as being of independent significance. The first point has been emphasized here from the point of view of systems complexity, the second point, not less important, has been more related to costs of economic decision-making. As Th.S. Ferguson [2] remarks,

one of the drawbacks of decision theory in general and of the Bayesian approach in particular, is the difficulty of putting the cost of the computation into the model. There are no doubt examples in which quick and easy rules are preferable to optimal rules for a Bayesian simply because it costs less to perform the computations.[2]

An example of a physical constraint of a problem-solving mechanism, as in chess-playing programs, is given by the well-known *travelling salesman problem.*

EXAMPLE. A salesman wants to visit all cities $C_1, C_2, \ldots, C_n$, pass through each city exactly once (starting from and returning to his home base city C) while minimizing his total mileage. The set of objects in the travelling salesman problem is the set of all acyclic permutations of the cities, i.e. the set of feasible tours. The number of these turn our to be bounded by $(n-1)!/2$ which is an extremely large number for moderate n. By stirling's formula $n! \cong (n/e)^n$, hence $n!$ increases very rapidly. For instance, for $n = 10$ the number is about 180,000 and for $n = 11$ it is nearly 2 million. Several exact mathematical solutions of this problem have been proposed, but they amount to sensible complete enumeration of the alternatives, that is, enumeration of the more likely cities. Such methods seem to work up to about $n = 20$ and then break down because of excessive demand upon computer time. For some promising heuristic solutions see G.L. Thompson [17].

The travelling salesman problem is closely related to many other problems that are considered to be NP-hard (M.R. Garey and D.S., Johnson [3]), the letters NP standing for 'nondeterministic polynomial'. These problems have recently received even more prominence by the invention of Khachiyan's algorithm (B. Aspvall and R.E. Stone [1]). Any problem for which an algorithm can be devised can be solved but no practical general solution may be feasible, because the solution requires an impractical amount of computational time and effort. This can be referred to as 'intractability'. It is now generally agreed by computer scientists that algorithms whose computational time increases exponentially as a function of the size of input are 'intractable' or simply inefficient: The only algorithms to be considered efficient are 'polynomial time' algorithms. Relating program size n to algorithmic complexity, $f(n)$, we see that for any f and for 'large' n the exponential f is always larger than the polynomial f. For the travelling salesman problem *exhaustive search* would constitute an exponential f, hence, be inefficient, whereas some shortcut heuristic procedure would let computational time increase as a polynomial function, constituting an efficient algorithm. Now, even among efficient algorithms some are faster than others, thus, it is important only to distinguish polynomial-time algorithms as a class from exponential-time algorithms. The speed of the algorithm is almost machine independent, thus, for large n, a polynomial-time algorithm will find a faster solution on a slow machine than an exponential-time algorithm on a powerful machine. This is another hard fact to support the thesis of complexity tradeoffs between computational and structural complexity (see, e.g., Chapter. 4)

A way to identify and classify *algorithmic complexity* i.e., the complexity assigned to the most efficient algorithm required to solve a problem provided it exists, is to count the number of arithmetic operations (additions, subtractions, multiplications, divisions) that are required in order to carry out an algorithm.

Sometimes it is possible to show that a certain algorithm is optimal. Here are some examples of optimal algorithms:

(1) To compute $\sqrt{2}$, Newton's approximation method may be applied to $x^2 - 2 = 0$, giving the iteration

$$x_{n+1} = x_n/2 + 1/x_n$$

The algorithm doubles the number of significant digits at each iteration, and, it is optimal in the sense that any algorithm can do at most this much per two arithmetic operations per iteration (Strassen [15]).

(2) Evaluate a polynomial

$$P(x) = a_n x^n + a_{n-1} x^{n-1} + \cdots a_1 x + a_0$$

Here it can be shown that Horner's method is optimal (Karp [4]). In this method a_n is multiplied with x, then a_{n-1} is added, the sum multiplied with x, a_{n-2} added, etc. Thus,

$$P(x) = (\cdots ((a_n x + a_{n-1})x + a_{n-2})x + \cdots a_1) + a_0$$

(3) Systems of linear equations $Ax = b$ may be solved by various methods, most well known are Cramer's rule and Gaussian elimination. Gaussian elimination requires $n^3 + \cdots$ arithmetic operations for an nxn system. Cramer's rule requires much more if determinants are computed by the method of developing them by the elements of a row or column (an nxn determinant in this way requires of the order of $n!$ operations). For a long time it was believed that Gaussian elimination is the best possible algorithm for solving linear equations. But Strassen [14] defined inductively an algorithm which requires only $c \cdot n^{2.72}$ arithmetic operations. Because of c, this algorithm is more efficient than Gaussian elimination for large n. However, it is not known whether this algorithm is optimal. On the other hand, it is not difficult to prove that any algorithm

requires at least n^2 arithmetic operations, hence, there is at least a lower bound.

We call arithmetic complexity the minimum number of *arithmetic* operations required to carry out a given task – in the context of our comprehensive algebraic complexity measure it is equivalent to sorting out the 'wreath connection' of irreducible units of a decomposed machine (system).

A universal notion of complexity should extend beyond arithmetic complexity – arithmetic operations constitute a subclass and thus arithmetic complexity would be an upper bound for a more general complexity measure.

5.4 AN OVERVIEW OF ALGORITHMIC COMPLEXITY AND PROBLEM SOLVING

A major purpose of the theory of algorithmic complexity is to characterize the intrinsic complexity of specific computational problems. This is typically done by fixing some idealized model of computation and establishing upper and lower bounds on the amount of time or space, or other resources needed to solve a giving problem. An upper bound on complexity is obtained by analyzing the resource requirements of known algorithms which solve the problem. Establishing lower bounds on complexity is usually a much more difficult process, since it involves demonstrating that no possible algorithm can surpass a given level of efficiency.

A frequent choice for the model of computation is a Turing machine, and the problems studied are often posed in the form of recognition problems. By a 'recognition problem' we mean any problem in which some string is initially placed on the tape of the Turing machine, and the Turing machine must decide whether or not the input string belong to some predefined set of strings. For example, the input string may be a formula in some logical theory, the truth of which is to be decided.

It is convenient to classify recognition problems into complexity classes defined in terms of worst-case time and space bounds, which are expressed as a function of the length of the input string if, for example, the class of problems known as polynomial space consists of all problems which can be decided by a Turing machine using an amount of tape that never exceeds some polynomial function of the input length. Similarly, the class 'polynomial time' consists of all problems which are decided with the polynomial bounded number of machine steps.

The complexity theory of specific problems, along the lines just described, have emerged in the past decade as an active and fruitful area of research. At higher levels of complexity (that is, where the time and space bounds are very rapidly-growing functions of the input length), this work shares much with the classical theory of undecidability. The objects of study are often formalogical theories, and the work has served to extend the negative results of undecidability theory by showing that many problems that are formally decidable are nevertheless not decidable in any practical sense because they have a very large (e.g. super-exponential) time complexity.

At lower levels of complexity, however, the problems studied often concern combinatorial objects such as graphs and other finite structures rather than logical theories. At this level, polynomial space contains many problems of great practical interest such as the travelling salesman problem, combinatorial assignment problems and network problems etc. which seem to be computationally unfeasible, in that all known algorithms have a time requirement which increases exponentially with the size of the input. Although the question of whether this exponential growth is unavoidable is one of utmost practical interest, the present state of the theory gives little aid for resolving this question.

In the absence of provable lower bounds on the complexity of these problems, relative measures of complexity have come to play an important role. It is in many cases possible to reduce one problem to another, that is, to find a way of mapping one problem into another, so that if an efficient solution were available for the latter problem, then this would also give a way of solving the formal problem efficiently. Thus, the latter problem can be thought of as being at least as hard as the former. Various definitions of reducibility have been given which formalized this intuitive notion of reducing one problem to another. Each of these reducibility relations is a partial ordering of the class of all recognition problems.

A key notion which arises in studying the problem of reducibility is that of a 'complete' problem. A problem is *complete in a complexity class if it lies in the class and every problem in the class is reducible to it.* Such a problem can be thought of as a hardest problem for the class, relative to the particular reducibility relation which is being used.

Complete problems are of interest for two main reasons. First, depending on the complexity class, completeness may constitute evidence of computational difficulty. For example, if a problem is complete in polynomial space or complete in NP (see Section 6.3), then it seems likely that the polynomial-time algorithm for the problem does not exist. This has practical value in that the decision-maker or researcher, knowing the problem is complete, can avoid wasting time looking for an efficient general algorithm and instead may look for some good approximation algorithm.

Second, complete problems provide reference measures of complexity, in relation to which the complexity of other problems and even the relations between complexity classes can be explored. For example, a problem that is complete in polynomial space serves as a kind of test case for the open question of whether polynomial time equals polynomial space. This question has an affirmative answer if and only if there exists a polynomial-time algorithm for the problem. Complete problems have been found in a number of different complexity classes, both within and outside polynomial space.

The completeness results which have attracted the greatest attention are those involving complete problems in non-deterministic polynomial-time (or NP). These are usually called NP-complete problems. NP-complete problems aroused particular interest because they included some very practical problems, for which efficient algorithms had been intensely (sought). As a result of linking these problems to each other and to the open question of whether 'polynomial' equals 'non-deterministic polynomial', the hope for finding efficient algorithms for these problems was greatly diminished. Since then hundreds of new NP-complete problems have appeared: a comprehensive list to-date is found in Garey and Johnson [3] and NP-completeness has come to be regarded as virtually certain evidence that a problem does not have an efficient solution.

Combinatorial games and decision problems arising in assignment and allocations problems of great public interest provide an obvious target for complexity theory, because it is easy to give examples of game positions which can be described very definitely, but would seem to require a vast amount of computation to analyze. The game of chess is a familiar example. A typical chess position may involve twenty pieces, with sixty or more possible moves for the player who is about to move. To determine whether that player can win within the next k moves, by means of a straightforward look-ahead rule, would thus require examining about 60^k different positions, representing all possible ways of playing the next k moves. Such an analysis becomes prohibitive for a computer, even for rather small values of k.

The difficulty of analyzing chess positions, while attested to by much empirical evidence, has not been rigorously proved. Moreover, since chess is a finite game, the complexity-theoretic tools we have discussed are not suitable for characterizing its complexity: it would in principle be possible to incorporate all possible chess positions into a huge look-up table which could be build into the internal control logic of a Turing machine. This would enable chess (and any other finite game) to be decided in trivial time and space bounds according to the complexity measures we have adopted. However, by our theory of algebraic complexity we have more refined and comprehensive algebraic measures available in which chess would have non-trivial complexity.

There are, however, certain games for which the techniques of complexity theory, no matter how comprehensive, are bound to yield compelling evidence of intractability. These games all have the property that a game position may be arbitrarily large, so that the total number of game positions that can arise is infinite. Such games tend to fall more in the realm of recreational mathematics than of games which are commonly played and decisions which seek practical solutions. For some of these games, as in the game Nim, theories have been developed which allow winning strategies to be computed with relative ease. Yet a great many remain 'unsolved', in the sense that there is not any known computationally feasible algorithm for recognising winning positions.

5.5 A CASE IN HEURISTICS: GENERAL PROBLEM SOLVING (GPS)

In the framework of subjective probability assessment Tversky and Kahnemann [18] found

that people rely on a limited number of heuristic principles which reduce the complex task of assessing probabilities and predicting values to simpler judgmental operations. In general, these heuristics are quite useful, but sometimes they lead to severe and systematic errors.

Now GPS is one of the major problem-solving programs that may also be useful as a normative program for human problem-solving.

From a purely computer science view, GPS, is a logical generalization of computer programs that have been written to solve problems in specific areas such as propositional calculus, integral calculus and plane geometry. In the view of psychology, GPS is considered as a model of information-processing characteristics of the mind, based on the idea that human heuristics could be made explicit in computer programs.

Another root of GPS lies in the work on the logic theorist (LT) program that was designed for solving sentential calculus problems in Whitehead and Russell's *Principia Mathematica*. It discovered proofs that are beyond the grasp of most college students, and the technique reveals sophistication rather than brute force search.

Two basic principles are intertwined in GPS: *means-ends analysis* and *planning* (or *recursive problem solving*).

Means-ends analysis (MEA) is a general purpose heuristic for making sure that an operator is only applied to the problem if there is some purpose to the application. In more economic type problem situations means-end analysis can be extended to an appropriate cost-benefit analysis where instead of 'difference operators' other suitable types of operators can be used. However, the general structure of MEA remains unchanged. Let us first address this set-up. It involves:

(a) A set of 'objects' that are relevant for the *problem definition*, $O_1, \dots, O_n$.

(b) A set of attributes $X_1, \dots, X_k$ attached to the objects, $k \geq n$, describing their problem-relevant location, characteristics, specifics, sometimes represented by proxies, defining the problem situation at each state of the problem-solving process.

(c) A set of operators acting on the set of attributes in terms of

$$
\left.
\begin{array}{ll}
\text{additivity operators:} & A_1, \dots, A_k \\
\text{difference operators:} & D_1, \dots, D_k \\
\text{multiplicative operators:} & M_1, \dots, M_k
\end{array}
\right\} Q_1, \dots, Q_k \text{ operators}
$$

such that they satisfy *algebraic operations* of finite simple groups.

(d) A terminal goal structure containing the desirable attributes $X_1^*, \dots, X_k^*$ such that the operations applied to $X_1, \dots, X_k$ generate the desirable set $\{X_1^*, \dots, X_k^*\}$ after a finite number of steps.
The goal structure may be either imposed *externally* as part of the task environment or *successively generated endogenously* in the problem-solving process.

(e) A problem solution exists after a finite number of steps.

For purposes of illustration, let us identify the various elements involved with chess-playing. In chess, a set of objects embraces all pieces on the board, pawns, bishops, rooks, king and queen etc., interacting with each other (a). Attributes of these objects apply to their location on the board, of course, in relation to the location of all other objects, whether they are attacked, defended, or attacking, or in retreat and relatively safe. Hence, attributes of the same piece change frequently with each move (b).

Operators correspond generally to the rules of the game or move: specifically they are identified with the allowable moves of each piece, a bishop, a rook etc. These moves satisfy a certain algebraic structure, which is obvious since chess is a discrete game (c).

A definite goal structure is clearly imposed on chess prescribing a configuration of attributes such that the opponent's king is checkmated. However, a goal structure may be endogenously formed, by missing subgoals such as king safety, material balance, center control etc. and therefore adapted to the terminal goal to 'avoid being checkmated' (d).

(e) Finally, a problem solution exists by reaching 'checkmate' or 'remis'! Consider, for illustration, a much more simplified problem, the so-called Monkey Problem:

A monkey is in a cage. Suspended over the center of his cage, out of reach, is a bunch of bananas. There is a box in the corner. What should the monkey do to get the bananas?

Here the objects are three: the monkey, the box and the bunch of bananas. The situation can be described by stating: the altitude of the monkey, the location of the monkey in the cage, the location of the box, and the location and altitude of the bananas.

The operators are the things that the monkey can do: walk, climb, reach for bananas, and push the box. The goal structure is simply related to 'reaching the bananas'. In this example, MEA uses the difference between attributes of objects to guide the problem-solving process. The steps for an analysis of the abstract problem transfer attribute X into attribute X' such that X' is closer to $X^{*\prime}$ could proceed as follows:

(1) The first step is to find that a difference D exists between the attributes X and X'' (if no differences are found you consider the subproblem solved and move ahead). This is represented in the flow chart:

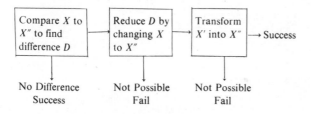

(2) Once differences have been evaluated, difference reduction is achieved by subsequent application of an operator sequence. Starting with given D and X, a list of operators is to be determined which, if applicable to X, will alter the characteristic D on X. Let Q_i be the first such operator. A check is made whether the form of X is compatible with the application of Q_i. If feasibility is guaranteed the subgoal of applying the operator Q_i to X is established. If this succeeds the transformation $X' = Q_i(X)$ is made, and the result constitutes an intermediate success in the problem-solving program.

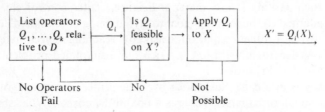

In many cases steps (1) and (2) will do, but in some cases the situation is more complicated.

(3) Then, one more step must be explained, how do we solve the subproblem of applying Q to X? This involves a test whether the assignment of attributes to a particular object is unique. Think of a car. Are there attributes or characteristics uniquely assigned to a car or do they also apply to other transportation modes? Suppose the set Y gives an exhaustive and unique representation of the object 'car', then X is matched to Y to determine if there are any differences in form. If there are not, i.e. if X and Y are identical, then Q_i is applied directly to form $X' = Q_i(X)$. Suppose, however, that difference D' between Y and X is found. Then proceed according to (1), i.e. establish a subgoal of transforming X into a special case Y' of Y. The solution to this subproblem may require further difference reduction and operator application. If Y' is finally established, Q_i is applied to construct X'.

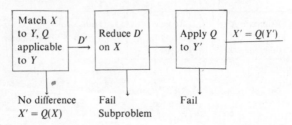

These steps require that GPS be a recursive program, i.e. that it be capable of calling itself as a subroutine. This leads to a discussion of recursive problem-solving and change of context in solving subproblems.

5.6 PLANNING

Thus far MEA, as being a part of GPS, is only an evaluation device confined to making balances (trade-offs) in local situations, such as relating benefits to costs at each step of the problem-solving process, or at each move in a chess game. Now it is clear that a successful problem-solver, as evidenced in chess-playing, evidently pays more attention to global guide-lines of progress and then fits local improvement into this global framework.

For example, in planning an itinerary one first decides what cities one wishes to visit. Then in a 'boxes-within-boxes' procedure, air-line, taxi and limousine schedules are then fitted into the global plan. Human problem-solvers rely very much on intuition, organization of mind and fixing a planning horizon to achieve problem-solving on a global scale. It appears that global planning and local look-ahead rules are intertwined by subtle, complicated trade-off evaluations in the sense 'does the local step contribute to the global plan?', or by feed-backs from locally feasible steps toward global goals that might modify the global framework.

For example, in chess-playing and likewise strategic systems, from a global perspective it may pay-off to lose some valuable pieces, e.g., a rook or a bishop, to achieve global success (checkmate), but from a local perspective it appears to be the wrong thing to do. All this could cast some doubt on the question: Can some provision for global planning be introduced into computer-aided problem-solving? In principle, yes, as Newell and Simon [9] have proposed. The general approach is that of successive approximation. If this proves successful, we could go back to the human problem-solver and provide him with analytical guide-lines or skills that he might apply instead of purely intuitive, ad-hoc methods to achieve global success. These skills may be taught or communicated to other persons so that problem-solving becomes a professional activity. We will see how this approach fits neatly into MEA, which in fact completes the previous analysis so that a measure of structural complexity can be applied to enlarged problem spaces. Starting with the observation that complex problems require more time for its solution, the fixing of the time horizon is of essential importance for problem-solving. The larger the time horizon, however, the more difficult it becomes to set up a *tight* problem-solving framework. In other words, with the length of the time horizon one must become increasingly flexible. The global conceptual framework containing the global objectives must take care of encompassing as many options as there are available. This amounts to first solving the global program in a simplified planning space and then to adjusting the solution to the more detailed, more definite problem space as one approaches closer to the situation 'what to do next'. This is the essential of *recursive* problem-solving. Newell's and Simon's method consists of simplifying a problem by considering only 'important' differences between states, then solving the problem in the simplified problem as a way of setting subgoals. A difficult GPS problem is (hopefully) made simpler by solving a simpler but related GPS problem.

5.7 CONCLUSIONS

Structural complexity is a measure of an algebraic structure ('module') that pertains to a class of heuristics and cuts drastically on the computational dimension of the problem-solving process.

We have argued that in large-scale decision problems there is necessarily a complexity-trade-off between structural and computational complexity.

The complexity theory of the algebraic theory of machines points to the fact that any non-purely-routine type oprating system carries 'modules' of a simple problem-solving power as well as computational steps that can be identified with routine-type operations. This seems to explain the major strengths and weaknesses of human and computer problem-solving capabilities. The human decision-maker is comparatively strong in activating heuristic principles pertaining to structural complexity, but is restricted to depth-tree search, whereas the computer is comparatively strong in searching for many different types of solution in a breadth-type search, emphasizing computational routines by computational power and speed. The construction of useful heuristics built into computer programs, aimed at solving major tasks of a problem-solving variety, becomes a tremendous challenge to artificial intelligence, amounting to substituting computational complexity by structural complexity.

Useful heuristics with high structural complexity must include:
(i) *long-run 'look ahead' rules*, fixing the planning horizon,
(ii) *reasoning by analogy*, e.g. evaluating subtle patterns of change,

(iii) *depth-tree search*, e.g. exploiting more relevant information affecting the goal or payoff-structure in the search process,

(iv) *experience* entering problem recognition,

(v) *endogenous value generation*, striking a delicate balance between local and strategic behavior.

A successful heuristic, revealing high structural complexity, should adapt these components repeatedly to the changing problem structure.

The tradeoff balance between structural and computational complexity can hardly be determined in advance, but in the history of chess-playing programs there are indications that such a balance exists. By comparing two differently designed chess-playing programs, the Los Alamos Program {1956} and the Bernstein Program {1958}, Newell Shaw and Simon [9] definitely make a statement on the complexity tradeoffs in terms of overall global performance of the two programs:

> To a rough approximation, then, we have two programs that achieve the same *quality of performance* with the same total effort by two different routes: the Los Alamos program by using no selectivity and being very fast, and the Bernstein program by using a large amount of selectivity and taking much more effort per position examined in order to make the selection. ... For instance, suppose both the Los Alamos and the Bernstein programs were to explore three moves deep instead of two as they now do. Then the Los Alamos program would take about 1000 times (30^2) as long as now to make a move, whereas Bernstein's program would take about 50 times as long (7^2), the latter gaining a factor of 20 in the total computing effort required per move.

From this we may conclude that as the depth of the moves increases it becomes correspondingly more difficult, at some point even practically impossible, to trade off computing speed and power, as represented by computational complexity, for sophisticated heuristic search procedures given by structural complexity.

APPENDIX

PROBLEM SOLVING FOR ENERGY TECHNOLOGY ASSESSMENT

Using various elements of *energy technology assessment*, such as proceeding along a taxonomy of technical, economic, and environmental options within a hierarchically organized mobile, and applying multi-criteria decision analysis successively on each level of the mobile, we can set up a GPS-type program that amounts to a balancing procedure, a tradeoff or an on-line benefit cost analysis along the mobile path, from the bottom up. The problem solving procedure consists of *means-end analysis* and *planning* (or recursive problem solving). It involves:

(i) a set of 'objects', here to be identified by feasible options on some level of the assessment mobile;

(ii) a set of attributes $x_1, \ldots, x_k$, represented by measures of effectiveness $x_1, \ldots, x_k$, associated to the objects, $k \geq n$ and structured along the levels of the mobile;

(iii) a set of operators acting generally on the class of attributes in terms of algebraic operations (additivity, multiplication, difference etc.), in particular, *successive reduction* as indicated below;

(iv) a terminal goal structure, covering the desirable attributes $X_1^*, \ldots, X_k^*$, yielding the highest benefits. By invoking successive application of algebraic operations on the class of attributes, the decision maker's balancing effort to trade-off several criteria will be continuously improved to a level where further improvement is infeasible or impractical;

(v) a problem solution exists after a finite number of steps. This condition assures that the process stops at one point in time.

The goal structure may be either imposed externally, this being the case if the decision maker is given certain policy directives as imposed on him by political program decisions; or it may be generated endogenously, as generated on-line in the problem-solving process.

The steps for an analysis of the abstract problem weigh attribute x against y such that by *successive reduction*. The decision-maker identifies an attribute being indifferent to preset y^*.

(1) The first step is to find that a difference D exists to match x and y (if no differences are found you consider the subproblem solved and move ahead). This is represented in the flow chart:

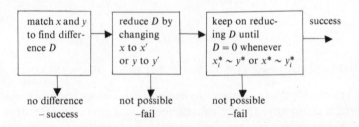

(2) Once differences (e.g. 'preference gaps') have been evaluated, difference reduction is achieved by subsequent application of an operator sequence, such as by 'successive reduction'.

Starting with given D and $X = \{x_1, \ldots, x_k\}$, a list of operators is to be determined which, if applicable to X, will alter the characteristic D on X. Let Q_i be the first such operator. If feasibility is guaranteed the subgoal of applying the operator Q_i to X is established. If this succeeds the transformation $X' = Q_i(X)$ is made and the result constitutes an intermediate success in the problem-solving program.

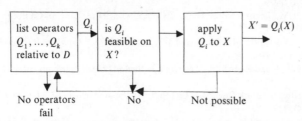

By proceeding along these two steps one can devise a tradeoff-analysis that balances benefit/costs in local situations at each step of the problem-solving process.

This problem solving process can be looked at as *interactive guided soul-searching* between the decision-maker and the decision analyst (consultant), in which the decision maker repeatedly reveals his value judgements on a number of conflicting objectives and organizes his choice process in an adaptive fashion.

The foregoing analysis, being comprised of a

(i)   Taxonomic analysis of technology assessment,

(ii) Multi-criteria benefit cost analysis,

(iii) GPS-type problem solving,

lends itself to a comprehensive assessment of energy options.

NOTES

[1] For a complete treatment of the 'missionairies and cannibals' problem and its solution by
   (i) complete enumeration
   (ii) trial-and-error search
   (iii) analytical methods such as dynamic programming see R. Bellman et. al., *Algorithms Graphs and Computers*, Academic Press, New York 1970.
[2] An attempt to combine the strength of the Bayesian decision analysis and problem solving procedures for the purpose of making cost-benefit decisions on large-scale technologies has been suggested; an outline of it is presented in the appendix.

REFERENCES

[1] Aspvall, C.B. and Stone, R.E., 'Khachiyan's Linear Programming Algorithm', Stan-CS-79-776, Dept. of Computer Science, Stanford Univ., Nov. 1979.

[2] Ferguson, Th.S., 'Prior Distributions on Spaces of Probability Measures', *Ann. Statist.* **2** (1974), 615–629.

[3] Garey, M.R. and Johnson, D.S., *Computers and Intractability*, W.H. Freeman, San Franciso, 1979.

[4] Karp, R.M., Lecture Notes, Dept. of Computer Science, Univ. of California, Berkeley, Ca. 1972.

[5] Keeney and Raiffa, R., *Decision Analysis with Multiple Conflicting Objectives*, Wiley, New York, 1976.

[6] Marschak, J. and Radner, R., *Economic Theory of Teams*, Yale Univ. Press, New Haven, 1972.

[7] McCarthy, J., 'Book Review of Lighthill: Artificial Intelligence', *Artificial Intelligence* **5** (1974), 317–322.

[8] Newell, J., Shaw, P. and Simon, H., 'General Report on GPS', in R.D. Luce et al. (eds.), *Readings in Mathematical Psychology* II, Wiley, New York, 1963.

[9] Newell, J., Shaw, P. and Simon, H., 'Chess-Playing and the Problem of Complexity', in Feigenbaum (ed.) *Computers and Thought*, McGraw Hill, New York, 1967.

[10] Raiffa, H., *Decision Analysis*, Addison-Wesley, New York, 1968.

[11] Raphael, B., *Thinking Computers*, W.H. Freeman, San Francisco, 1976.

[12] Shannon, C.E., 'A Chess Program', *Scientific American*, 1950.

[13] Simon, H., 'The Structure of Ill-structured Problems', *Artificial Intelligence* **4** (1973), 181–201.

[14] Strassen, V., 'Gaussian Elimination is not Optimal', *Numerische Mathematik* **13** (1969), 324–356.

[15] Strassen, V., 'Evaluation of Rational Functions', in *Complexity of Computer Computations*, R.E. Miller et. al. (eds.), Plenum, New York, 1972, pp. 1–10.

[16] Steinbruner, J., *A Cybernetic Theory of Decision*, Princeton Univ. Press, Princeton, 1974.

[17] Thompson, G.L., 'Some Approaches to the Solution of Large-Scale Combinatorial Problems', in M. Shubik (ed.), *Essays in Honor of O. Morgenstern*, Princeton Univ. Press: Princeton.

[18] Tversky, A. and Kahneman, D., 'Judgement under Uncertainty', *Science* **185** (1974), 1124–1131.

CHAPTER 6

COMPLEXITY AND DECISION RULES

6.1 INTRODUCTION

This chapter attempts to show how the comprehensive algebraic measure
of complexity, as derived from automata theory (in Chapter 2), can be
meaningfully interpreted in a program of 'limited rationality' regarding
individual or social choices. It presents a continuation of the discussion
started in Chapter 5, though the emphasis is put more specifically on
the impacts of algebraic complexity concerning individual and collective
decision rules. Clearly, then, the results feed back into the framework of
a theory on individual and social choice. The complexity measure appears
to be a natural consequence of looking at a decision rule as a finite-state
machine that computes preferences bounded by computational constraints. By factoring the decision process into component processes it is
demonstrated how searching for improvement depends on 'structural'
and 'computational' limitations.

6.2 BACKGROUND AND MOTIVATION

The notion of 'global rationality' underlying the construction of 'economic
man' that is generally accepted, at least in normative economics, has come
increasingly under attack by those who care for more fruitful behavioral
assumptions in economic reasoning. This notion is intrinsically related
to various optimization programs that have been implemented in economics but that have been found to have only limited use in realistic, complex
situations. H.A. Simon [13] deserves credit having observed the limitation
of global rationality and suggesting a modification of this program by
introducing his concept of 'limited rationality.' To a great extent these
ideas were carried forward in studying human thought processes where it
was found that decision-makers, for purposes of problem-solving, go
through several stages of goal formation – a hierarchical representation
of goals, super- and subgoals – where at every stage goal attainment rather
than optimization is called for. Such programs are motivated by the
complexity of problem-solving tasks that are treated successfully by de-

157

composing problem-solving in a sequential way and by associating to every stage of the process the attainment of a subgoal. Goal-oriented behavior, therefore, is non-optimizing behavior and only improvement-related with respect to the attainment of the next goal in a sequence. (G.W. Ernst and A. Newell [4]).

Simon [13] relates a need for revision of the 'economic man' to the limitation of access of information and computational capacities available to human decision-makers. The computational dimension is probably the most important aspect of characterizing 'limited rationality', in fact, this point has been brought up in a similar connection by H. Leibenstein [7] where he interprets 'rationality' in terms of 'calculatedness' (computability) and tightness or looseness of calculatedness is supposed to cover the whole spectrum between rationality and limited rationality.

The computational dimension of limited rationality as applied to the social choice process is analyzed here in a more rigorous fashion than has been done before. It turns out that complexity is an essential tool for analyzing constraints on the decision process. Moreover, any axiomatic system of 'limited rationality' yet to be constructed must contain complexity as a primitive notion.

6.3 CHOICE PROCESSES AND COMPLEXITY

On the level of individual or social choice problems complexity relates to the ability or inability of human beings to make effective choices in a consistent or rational way. In this regarded complexity exhibits some kind of uncertainty that cannot be treated properly in terms of probabilities.

One clear indication when complexity enters individual decision-making is given by not being able to prove that a utility function representing preferences or choices does exist. If this proves to be a legitimate question on the level of individual decision-making, it is even more so on a social choice level.[1] F.S. Roberts [11, p. 127] proposes two ways out of this dilemma:

... one approach to decision making is to describe a procedure whereby we can modify or redefine or make explicit our preferences in the course of decision-making in order to become more 'rational' (i.e., that such a utility function will exist).

A second approach, somewhat less demanding, is to settle for a utility assignment which best approximates the utility function.

It is doubtful whether the first approach leads to a satisfactory solution: since, even if it is possible to teach individuals how to act more rationally than they used to behave, they will never be 'perfect computers', and there is a threshold of complexity beyond which they cannot effectively handle situations, for instance, when making choices among many alternatives. Put in a different way, you can try to teach subjects how to make optimal decisions in a simple course of actions, as J. Marschak [9] suggests on the basis of psychological studies on that matter. But still teaching optimality does not cope with the problem that people simply make mistakes because of complexity or 'embarras de richesse' in choosing among many alternatives – in the same way as people may understand simple arithmetical rules but cannot solve complicated arithmetical problems in the large because of time, resource and computational constraints.

The alternative then is that people adopt reasonable behavior strategies (in the sense of being within their 'computational budget') which cope with the intrinsic complexity of (social) choices, e.g. those rules exihibiting non-optimizing behavior.

Regarding the second approach, much of the contribution by measurement theory has been in the direction of weakening preference requirements (for example, Luce's semiorder theory, avoiding indifference, but admitting thresholds, see Luce [8]).

The weaker assumptions aim at reducing the computational burden of decision-makers, yet they fail to make explicit the complexity bounds in forming decision rules.

Many choice processes in the real world, in contrast to theoretical constructs used by choice theorists, represent essentially *ill-structured* problems to the extent that solutions of these problems are not readily available and they involve an excessive amount of computational power. In general, a problem is considered to be *well-structured* if it satisfies a number of criteria, the most important of which relate to the existence of at least *one* problem space that provides for solvability with the help of a practicable (reasonable) amount of computation or search. Apparently well-structured problems such as theorem-proving and chess playing in artificial intelligence turn out in many instances to be *ill-structured*, given the problem-solving power of contempory problem-solving methods. There seems to be an intrinsic relationship between well- or ill-structuredness of a problem and the threshold of complexity (in von Neumann's sense) below which a system shows a regular, stable and predictable behavior but beyond which often quite different, sometimes counterintuitive modes of behavior can occur. A problem can be well-structured in detail, but ill-structured in the large. According to H. Simon [15] 'the difficulty stems from the immense gap between computability *in principle* and *practical* computability in problem spaces as large as those of games like chess.' This generally applies to complicated choice processes.

Therefore, the problem of complexity is similar to the problem a chess player faces when searching for a 'satisfactory' strategy in chess. Individual and collective choice behavior resemble the choice of strategies in chess-playing to the extent that the decision-maker is involved in a choice problem of combinatorial dimension. To search for all game-theoretically possible alternatives goes far beyond the computational ability of the human being.

One conclusion, therefore appears to be obvious: we have to depart from behavioral hypotheses involving optimizing behavior, as convenient as it might be in mathematical terms, since it does not come to grips with non-trivial choice problems in complex situations. We do not have to leave the grounds of rationality – a rule-of-thumb method may be rational in a restrictive sense – thus we have to view it in terms of 'limited rationality.' Rule-of-thumb methods may be applied for various reasons: either because the individual faces expected costs of computation to be far beyond expected utility of further searches in choice-theoretic behavior or he (she) is faced with an immense mass of alternatives to the effect that he (she) is psychologically outstripped by the ensuing 'complexity of computation.' Chess players tend to choose simpler decision rules: they do not consider all possible strategies and pick up the best, but generate and examine a rather small number, making a choice as soon as they discover one that they regard as satisfactory. According to H. Simon [14],

limits of rationality in chess involve (a) uncertainity about the consequences that would follow from each alternative; (b) incomplete information about the set of alternatives; and (c) complexity preventing the necessary computations from being carried out.

All three properties may be subsumed under a more general concept of complexity in choice-theoretic situations. For example, uncertainty and lack of information may here assume different aspects to what is widely known in statistical decision theory and the economics of uncertainty, e.g. uncertainty resulting from computational incapability when faced with a large number of choice alternatives. These are essentially non-probabilistic situations. Thus, complexity is an important tool for evaluating decision rules, in fact, it may prove instrumental for an axiomatic analysis of 'bounded rationality' which is still lacking.

6.4 AN EXAMPLE OF A DECISION OR SEARCH RULE

The subsequent example has been adapted as an illustration from a similar search problem presented by Futia [5]. An individual, as a member of society (or voter) is subsequently confronted in a 'large' market of public goods to choose among different kinds of commodities or services (nuclear energy, missiles, health care, etc.) offered to him for sale by different government agencies at different prices (i.e. tax rates). Of course, according to highly paid, 'highly' qualified political representatives and bureaucrats, we all need more nuclear energy, missiles, more and better health care; but the well-informed voter knows that eventually society has to choose among alternatives and pay the bill. In order to receive a tax rate quotation (or possibly some other relevant information) from any given agency, the voter must incur some (not necessarily monetary) cost constituting his marginal search cost. The voter's goal is: given a certain bundle of public goods that satisfies his aspiration he wants to search for low tax rates such that his final taxes (plus total search costs) will be kept as low as possible. This problem can be formalized as follows:

Let t_i denote the tax rate quotation of agency i. Let $t = (t_1, \ldots, t_n)$ be the tax structure and suppose $t_i \in [0, 1] = I$. Denote by I^n the n-dimensional Cartesian product of I, and define a probability density F on I^n representing the voter's initial belief about which tax rates the agencies are likely to quote. The order of quotations presented to the voter is considered to be irrelevant, thus, for simplicity, it is assumed that F is symmetric, i.e. if p is a permutation of $\{1, 2, \ldots, n\}$ and if $t^p = (t_{p(1)}, \ldots, t_{p(n)})$, then $F(t) = F(t^p)$.

The set-up of this problem enables us to construct a decision rule which prescribes to the voter, for each i, whether to stop searching after receiving i quotations or whether to continue searching on the basis of the i quotations he has received. A decision rule is assumed to be a mapping from a set of observations into a set of actions. In this problem, for each i, let the set of actions be $A = \{\text{'accept', 'reject'}\}$, and the set of observations be $O_i = I^i$. Then a decision rule is a sequence of functions $D = (D_1, \ldots, D_{n-1})$, where $D_i : O_i \to A$ if $(t_1, \ldots, t_i) \in O_i$, then $D_i(t_1, \ldots, t_i)$ records the voter's decision to either accept the tax rates that have been quoted to him and choose (by vote) the given bundle of public goods presented to him, or to continue searching and reject tax rates $t_1, \ldots, t_i$.

Now it is perfectly legitimate to ask for this kind of problem what is the voter's optimal decision rule? This question could be answered by the machinery provided in statistical decision theory to find optimal solutions for search problems. Instead, here we are interested in the basic ill-structuredness of the problem given by the complexity of the decision rule. To this end, on the basis of the previous section, we proceed to associate with every decision rule D a (computer) program f_D which computes D. This permits us to define the complexity of the program by the amount of 'looping' between subprograms (computational complexity) and by the intrinsic complexity of the subprograms (structural complexity). The conceptual framework, as presented in Chapter 3, applies. Hence, a sequential machine is used as a metaphor for determining complexity of sequential decision rules. This can be further illustrated by elaborating on the problem above by using the sequential machine framework.

Let A = set of observable tax rates = finite subset of $[0, 1]$. Let $B = = \{$'stop', continue to $i + 1, i = 1, 2, \ldots, n\}$. Then the machine f_D is defined inductively on the length of the input sequence by

$$D_1(t_1) \text{ if } m = 1, \text{ or if}$$
$$f_D(t_1, \ldots, t_{m-1}) =$$
$$= \text{ 'stop' or } = D_i(t_{m-i}, \ldots, t_m) \text{ if } f_D(t_1, \ldots, t_{m-1}) =$$
$$= \text{ 'continue to } i + 1\text{'}$$

The computational length and the structural complexity of subsystems that are needed to compute f_D reflects a measure of complexity for f_D (equivalently for the decision rule D). Obviously, a rule is optimal if it is generally more sophisticated and more expensive but which may very well be beyond the computational power and sophistication of the voter. Hence the voter, facing an ill-structured problem wants to make it well-structured by seeking a decision rule which matches his computational ability and sophistication.

6.5 A SOCIAL CHOICE MACHINE

It is possible to construct a machine simulating strategies of each individual in society, one machine for each individual's preference structure. The *internal states* of this machine are strategies and strategic preferences, the inputs are possible actions of others in the society. The final strategy the individual will use in voting is the state reached when no further input messages occur. With no input at all from other members of the society, the strategy simulated by the machine with be the individual's true preferences.

A special case has been investigated by H. Varian [17], where he showed that a (generalized) social choice machine with n agents and acting according to the 'method of majority decision' has structural complexity zero.

Suppose an individual 1 with true preferences $a \succ b \succ c$ (read "a is preferred to b is preferred to c") is in a society with individuals 2 and 3 whose preference structures he perceives to be, respectively, $b \succ a \succ c$ and $c \succ b \succ a$. Suppose also that the society is voting by the 'method of majority decision' in which each member casts his vote for his most preferred alternative. Individual 1, knowing the others' preferences by communications from them or his own perception of their tastes, realizes that no alternative will win out since each alternative will receive only one vote. He does not know which voter will have a casting vote. If, however, he chooses to strategically represent his preferences as $b \succ a \succ c$ and votes according to those preferences, he will be able to block the choice of his least preferred alternative, c.

Let us consider the strategy machine for individual 1. It begins in the initial state "$a \succ b \succ c$, vote a" representing his sincere preference and strategy. The machine receives inputs of the perceived preferences of individual 2, "$b \succ a \succ c$", and individual 3, "$c \succ b \succ a$", and also input that he is chossing a strategy for voting under the 'method of majority decision'. The next state of this strategy machine for individual 1 is "$b \succ a \succ c$, vote b" representing his strategy and strategic preference, given the information he has on the decision situation. If, as an alternate case, he had no information or preferences of others in the society, the machine would never change state from his sincere strategy representing his true preferences. If, too, he revised his perceptions of the strategies of other individuals at any time before the actual voting, his strategy machine may move to a different strategy state in response to this changed input situation. A machine to simulate the actual social decision making can be constructed. This machine would use final strategies of all individuals as well as the legal voting procedure and method as input, calculate and move to a final decision state to simulate the social decision made at each stage in the voting.

For example, let us illustrate an actual voting machine. The machine

is in intial state, 'no decision yet made', receives input on the voting method
and procedure. It also receives input on the strategic preferences of the
members of the society, which may be $a \succ b \succ c$ for individual 1, $c \succ b \succ a$
for individual 2 and $b \succ c \succ a$ for individual 3. On this input, the next
state of the machine is "reject a", since a is only preferred over b and c
by individual 1. Again receiving the same input, the next state is "decide
b" since $b \succ c$ for individuals 1 and 3, a majority, and this is the final step
in this decision procedure. Thus the machine, given the necessary information on situation, procedures, voting method and strategies, gives
the results of the decision.

A test on whether society follows some sort of transitive social preference
rule can be made by checking if the social decisions of this society would
be accepted by any machine which recognizes a transitive preference
structure. If the decisions are recognized by some automaton like this,
social preferences are transitive. If no such machine recognizes the decisions, then social preferences are intransitive. If intransitive social preferences are undesirable, the society would change the social or legal
structure and try new social procedures or voting methods with the hope
of finding a transitive social decision process. Transitive social preferences are often called "rational" in the social choice literature.

The aggregation of individual preferences to form a social preference
structure, and the fairness criteria under which this is possible, form one
branch of the axiomatic development of social choice theory. Arrow's
result [2] showed that five seemingly innocuous ethical requirements
were inconsistent and thus the formulation of a social welfare function
satisfying them, a social preference ordering, was impossible. As a formulation of Arrow's fairness criteria in our system, the machine to test transitivity could be further restricted to only accept (recognize) procedures which
additionally satisfy all Arrow's conditions of fairness. This illustrates an
axiom system as the intersection of structures which satisfy each individual
axiom: that is, an acceptable voting procedure must satisfy all the axioms
in order to be accepted by this machine (see J.M. Blin [3]).

6.6 COMPLEXITY OF DECISION RULES

We suppose that the decision-maker identifies alternatives in his choice
space and expresses preferences between at least two alternatives by
simply computing, else he finds alternatives 'undecidable' or 'incomparable'
that cannot be computed. Preference statements are therefore translated

into computing devices, indifference statements are kept out because of possible vagueness. The decision-maker represented as a simple finite state machine, can be decomposed according to preforming these tasks.[2][3] In the first case the job to be done, e.g. computing preferences, is achieved by a simple group machine (that is a decision machine acting as a simple group in the mathematical sense), in the second case the activity consists of a combinatorial machine, acting as a 'flip-flop' which does not compute anything.[4] Realizing a decision-rule therefore means a decomposition of the decision process according to the decomposition of machines into component machines that 'hooked' together (via the wreath product) realize the overall machine. Of course, the complexity of decision rules may vary; a 'sophisticated' decision-maker may activate more simple groups, less flip-flops, or groups that compute faster, more accurately and more reliably. This type of decision-maker will carry more structural complexity in the sense given in the previous section.

A (social) decision rule is a sequential decision rule and as such is considered to be a finite state machine (associated to a finite semigroup), and according to complexity theory it has a finite decomposition. In this regard the results of Krohn-Rhodes complexity theory apply. The idea involved here is to factor a social choice process into parts (components) where the global process is modelled as a transformation semigroup associated to a social decision rule, and the local parts are represented by transformation subsemigroups. The new tools originate from decomposition results in automata theory.

Consider a choice set of finitely many alternatives $X = \{a, b, \ldots, x, y, z\}$ and let $D_i = 1$ iff i prefers x to y, $D_i = 0$ iff i is 'undecided' about x and y, $D_i = -1$ iff i prefers y to x. Let $\mathscr{D}$ be a nonempty set of decision rules D_i, $\mathscr{X}$ a nonempty collection of subsets of X, a social decision function (SDF) then is a function $F : \mathscr{X} \times \mathscr{D} \rightarrow P(X)$, $P(X)$ being the power set. ASDF for individual i is given by $F(\{x, y\}, D_i), x, y \in X$.

Social decision functions are in fact decision machines in the sense that they decide on propositions about accepting or rejecting social states, computing them by discrimination, (preference, non-preference). By doing this, they generate decision rules as outputs and induce next states representing changes in preference profiles or configurations. There is good reason to argue that we should leave out indifference statements since they cannot clearly be distinguished from the phenomenon of 'undecidability'. *Intransitive indifference* arises in situations where a chain of indifferences, each of which seems reasonable, adds up to a sufficiently large difference to yield a definite preference between the first and the last items in the chain. We would like to avoid intransitive indifference, therefore we require the decision machine only to accept preference rather than indifference statements.

In order to construct such a decision machine let us state the following

PROBLEM. Let $X^n = X_1 x \ldots x X_n$ be the social choice set when the DM is confronted with a sequence of finitely many social alternatives. Let $A_0 \subseteq A_1 \subseteq \ldots \subseteq A_n$ be those sets of alternatives in which the DM can actually find comparisons (in the sense that he prefers alternatives in these sets and finds himself in a position to compute preferences). Let $\mathscr{A}$ be a nonempty collection of all $A_0, A_1, \ldots, A_n$. Then he constructs selection functions $\rho_0, \rho_1, \ldots, \rho_n, \rho_i : X^n \to \mathscr{A}$ such that for all $x_i \in X_i$, $\rho(x_i) \in A_i$. In a way, ρ_i constitutes a reduction mechanism by reducing all possible alternatives with which the DM is confronted to those which are computed as actual choices.[5] It is said that the DM accepts the decision rule $D_i(x_0, \ldots, x_i)$ if $\rho(x_0, \ldots, x_i) \in A_i$, more explicitly, accept $D_0(x_0)$ if $\rho(x_0) \in A_0$, accept $D_1(x_0, x_1)$ if $\rho(x_0, x_1) \in A_1$, etc.

There is an upper bound, representing the complexity bound of the DM, beyond which he is unable to compute his preferences. The upper bound somewhat restricts him in selecting decision rules which are 'beyond his complexity.' Therefore, let $\mathscr{K}(D)$ be the largest integer satisfying the bound such that $A_{(D)-1} \nsubseteq A_{(D)}$. How is the bound to be determined?

In a different context, regarding the complexity of (dynamic) finite-state systems, we distinguish between *design* and *control* complexity.

To recall, under *design* complexity we understand that complexity (number) associated to the transformation semigroup in which full use of the system potential is made. Under *control* complexity we understand that specific complexity (number) that results from computations which keep the entire system or at least part of it under complete control. A *qualitatively* stable decision rule would be a rule for which design and control complexity coincide. However, in most practical cases design complexity will exceed control complexity. Since one cannot assume that the control complexity of an average (unsophisticated) DM can be increased by teaching him how to behave in a rational manner one should pick up designs of decision rules for which there is a reasonable understanding and control.[6]

EXAMPLE. In a game of chess the number of all possible strategies to achieve a chess-mate corresponds to the design complexity of a chess-playing program. The number of all actual strategies chosen by a particular chess player to achieve success corresponds to his control complixity. Given two chess players both initially endowed with the same knowledge of how to play chess, then if in a sufficiently long sequence of repetitive plays one does better than the other, he exhibits a better understanding of the game, e.g. a higher control complexity.

In a certain way both concepts are naturally associated to 'programs of optimization' and 'programs of satisficing or bounded rationality,' respectively. That is to say, design complexity pertains to that decision rule (which is best in some appropriate sense), in general an optimization principle is involved, which, however, cannot be realized given the limited computational resources of the DM (control complexity).

To which extent this bound can effectively be determined by experiments appears to be a problem of experimental psychology. However, it is possible, at least in principle, to give a set of criteria under which it can be determined whether a DM chooses decision rules violating his bound of complexity.[7] Whenever individuals in experiments violate a set of consistency postulates (such as transitivity), namely those which they have accepted at the very beginning, they will realize that they have committed computational errors. Thus commitment of errors or violating consistency postulates seem to be suitable criteria for determining complexity bounds of computation. In experimental situations, subjects then have to be confronted with various decision rules of a different complicated character and the class of decision rules in which no errors or almost no errors occur constitute those which satisfy the control complexity of the DM.

Those decision rules are called qualitatively stable. Only qualitatively stable decision rules gurantee that social, economic and political processes can be controlled in any effective way by social choice, otherwise the amount of error, misrepresentation of preferences, etc. could easily lead to a destabilization of the social system, and some degree of rationality can no longer be maintained.

6.7 A CONSTRUCTION OF COMPATIBLE DECISION RULES

Let $P_1, P_2, \ldots$ be sets of computable preference profiles for $i = 1, 2, \ldots$ individuals of the social group achieving a common social decision rule D (matching the preference profile of the social group). Let there be $D_1, D_2, \ldots$

decision rules acting as sequential machines such that D_k computes the preference profile P_k. Then we define the complexity of the social decision rule D, $\theta(D)$, to be equal to min $\{\theta(D_j) : j = 1, 2, \ldots\}$.

In short, the complexity of a social decision rule is bounded by the minimum complexity of any individual decision rule D_j which is able to generate any individual preference profile matching the preference profile of the social decision rule. We proceed to associate a social decision rule (SDR) D for the social choice problem with a finite semigroup $S(D)$. We could envisage the social choice process as a transformation semigroup $(X, S(D))$, where X is the set of social choice alternatives each individual (in the social group) is searching for, while elements of $S(D)$ will be finite sequences of preference quotations generating the preference profile.

We could define $X = \{*\} \cup A_0 \cup A_1 \cup \ldots \cup A_{n-1}$ with $\cup$ disjoint. This is the set of the DM's choice histories. Then $\rho(x_1, \ldots, x_i) \in A_i$ represents the history of the DM's preference statements who has completed i searches and has made choices over $x_1, \ldots, x_i$.

A DM will stop searching if further searching will violate reasonable consistency criteria. The stop rule of searching is imposed by the complexity bound of the social decision rule. By construction, the complexity of D, $\theta(D)$, is equal to the complexity of $S(D)$, $\theta(S(D))$. Again the complexity of the SDR D is bounded by the minimum complexity of the individual decision rules D_j (finite state machines) which by interacting realize a compatible social decision rule.

The procedure how to generate a compuatble SDR when all members of the society set up their own individual decision rules can be described as a *sequential game* among the members. If the game has a *von Neumann value* we agree to say that a compatible SDR has been realized.

For simplicity, let us assume that there are only two members of the society which after having computed their individual decision functions want to find a compatible SDR (which satisfies both).

Assume that the game starts in C_{z_0} with strategy ρ constituting the selection rule of the first member of society, then the circuit $C = (A, B, Z, \lambda, \delta)$ is the preference profile with $\lambda : A \times Z \to Z$ and $\delta : Z \times A \to B$. Let A be the set of social choices that have been made by Player I (and the configuration is revealed to Player II). Then B is the set of resulting social choices of Player II that adjust to the preference profile of Player I. Z is the set of adjusted social choice configurations of the game as they appear to Player I. $\lambda(z, a)$ and $\delta(z, a)$ are interpreted as follows: if z is the adjusted social choice configuration, as it appears to Player I, and a is the choice which enters as input to Player II, let $z \cdot a$ be the social choice configuration after the choice a is made on the configuration z. Let $D(z \cdot a) = b$ be the decision rule generated by C when the position presented to C is $z \cdot a$. Define $\delta(z, a) = b = D(z \cdot a)$ and furthermore define $\lambda(z, a) = (z \cdot a) \cdot b \equiv (z \cdot a) \cdot D(z \cdot a)$, where z_0 is the initial position. Suppose our SDR can be put in binary form, whenever the 'compute preferences' key is followed we assign 1, otherwise 0.

The latter case will be interpreted as meaning that no consistent preference statement can be made since the number of choices involved is too large and therefore we have to eliminate redundant choice alternatives. Then under these circumstances, we could consider for at least two players the construction of a compatible SDR to be equivalent to a game tree with with binary outcomes.

EXAMPLE. In this game each player plays zero or one successively – corresponding to the construction of the decision rule. Let us assume the circuit C is a player who responds to the action of the first player, and the

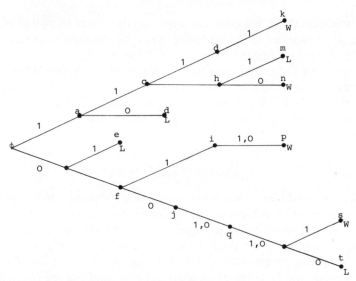

Fig. 1. Game tree with binary outcomes (winning strategies for C):
 (a) $(\phi, 1), (a, 1), (c, 1), (g, 1), (k, W)$,
 (b) $(\phi, 1), (a, 1), (c, 0), (h, 0), (n, W)$,
 (c) $(\phi, 0), (b, 0), (f, 1), (i, (1, 0)), (p, W)$,
 (d) $(\phi, 0), (b, 0), (f, 0), (j, (1, 0)), (q, (1, 0)), (v, 1), (s, W)$.

circuit C'. W denotes a win for the player, L denotes a loss for the player. The payoff is $+1$ for W, and -1 for L. Clearly, the von Neumann value for this game is $+1$ for the player who goes second. Assuming C goes second the strategies achieving the von Neumann value $+1$ can be listed as follows (and read out of the game tree):

Let $C = (A, B, Z, \lambda, \delta)$ be defined as follows:

$$A = \{0, 1(0, L), (0, W), (1, L), (1, W)\}, B = A,$$
$$Z = \{\phi, a, b, c, d, e, f, \dots r, s, t\}.$$

Then $C_{z_0} : A^* \rightarrow B$ induces a sequential social decision rule to which there is associated a complexity, the complexity of the transformation semigroup (X, S). The problem is to find a minimal complexity of the transformation semigroup that permits a construction of a social decision rule compatible with the choice behavior of individual members of the society. In view of (a) $-$ (d) we succeed in doing this by finding the string of minimal length, i.e. the decision rule with the minimal complexity. The upper bound for the complexity follows from the following result:

PROPOSITION (J. Rhodes). Let S be a semigroup of mappings on the finite set X (sequential choice space). Let r be the maximum range (or fixed points) of any idempotent $e = e^2 \in S$. Then $\#_G(S) \leq r - 1$.

Proof. Let I be the ideal generated by the idempotents of S. Then S/I is combinatorial and $I \leq \{f : X \rightarrow X : |f(x)| \leq r\} = I_r$. Further $I_k, k = 1, \dots, n$ are the ideals of $F_R(X)$, the semigroup of all mappings of X into X. Then by the results of Rhodes et al. [8] it can be shown that $\#_G(S) = \#_G(I)$ and $\#_G(I_r) \leq r - 1$.

6.8 SUMMARY AND EXTENSION

We have noticed how choice processes could be factored into component subprocesses and how these are associated to properties of transformation semigroups. A social choice process could be understood as a sequential game, as an interaction between individual choice processes in such a way that the interaction generates a SDR that is compatible with all individual choice processes. To achieve this, we use new tools of 'limited rationality', derived from automata theory, embodied in the system of social decision-making. Complexity as a crucial factor in the choice of decision rules is related to limitations of human decision-making in terms of their capacity to recall, memorize and compute only relatively few items among which consistent choices can be made. In contrast to conventional social choice theory we only consider preference profiles that are in a certain sense 'computable', thus restricting the social choice process to reasonable behavior rules. It is not clear so far to which extent the ideas expressed herein will have an impact on traditional social choice theory, namely relating to Arrow-type impossibility or possibility theorems. In actual human decision-making, alternatives are often examined sequentially, consequently we consider this approach to be basically of sequential type, whereas traditional theory is static, e.g. all alternatives are evaluated before a choice is made. Furthermore, in view of Arrow's assumptions on constructing a social welfare function (SWF) it appears that the assumption of 'unrestricted domain' of the choice set will no longer hold because of imposing strict computational requirements.

An obvious extension would consist of using complexity of decision rules as a primitive notion for an axiomatization of economic behavior that introduces explicitly behavioral assumptions related to limited computability. A set of structural constraints for such an axiomatization could be linked to assumptions DSC-PAC in Chapter 5. A DM is not only limited in his choice behavior by computational requirements; equally important, he is also restricted by acting as a member of a group or social class where in order to achieve some consensus (for example, a common group decision function) he has to adjust his behavior to past choices of other group members. This is illustrated by looking at the adjustment mechanism as a sequential game. The determinants of the game (environmental conditions, previous choice configurations) are themselves determined as outcomes of complicated cognitive processes, bounded by complexity. Complexity of this kind virtually covers two aspects: one is *structural*, the other *computational*. Structural complexity here relates to the 'sophistication' of the DM, how he can reason when confronted with difficult tasks, depending on his problem-solving capability (as discussed in the example of the missionaries and the cannibals, see Ernst and Newell [4]).

Computational complexity relates to experience, to the ability to learn doing things, organizing computations. Both factors are likely to be highly correlated, but to a certain degree there will be tradeoffs between both, thus they are comprised in one complexity measure. For a particular decision-making design both factors add up to yielding the control complexity which together with the given design complexity provides the fundamental *evolution* complexity relation. This again has a clear interpretation in defining *qualitatively stable* decision rules.

NOTES

[1] Likewise, a similar problem arises if you want to capture (probabilistic) uncertainty by the representation of finite subjective probability measures. Here it is by no means clear that the representation is unique. P. Suppes [16] reports, in referring to Scott's axioms of finite probability, derived from a qualitative probability structure:

'The more profound difficulty ... is the *combinatorial explosion* (my italics) that occurs in verifying the axioms when the number of events is large. To check connectedness, for example, we need only consider pairs of events, and to check transitivity, only tuples of events. But, it is fundamental for the kind of axiom schema required to express necessary and sufficient conditions in the finite case that n-tuples of events of arbitrary n must be studied as the number of events increases. As a possible empirical theory of belief, or as a rational one, this seems impractical, and even for fairly small experiments, the effort to determine whether there is a representing unique probability measure requires the use of a moderate size computer facility.'

P. Suppes then sets out to search for simpler axioms, which he terms 'inexact measurement', that attempts to reduce the implicit complexity of finding unique measures of belief.

[2] In a different context, such a problem-solving machine transforming 'tasks' into 'satisfactory actions' (controls) as a model for an adaptive mechanism has been described by B.R. Gaines [6].

[3] This decision-making process, organized in this way, is somewhat related to the heuristic conceptualization of the decision-making process as proposed by R. Selten in his 'Chain Store Paradox' [12]. The simple group machine pertains to his *level of reasoning* which is characterized by a conscious effort to analyse the situation in a rational way on the basis of explicit assumptions whose validity is examined in the light of past experience and logical thinking. On the other hand, the combinatorial group machine applies to his *routine level* where 'decisions are made without any conscious effort'. Now it seems evident that the higher level of reasoning brings 'sophistication' in the decision process, increases complexity (structurally) whereas routine decisions do not establish structural complexity by itself. This is not to say, in agreement with Selten, that the higher level always yields the better decision, but this is to say that decision problems of the problem-solving variety require the activation of computational devices with more rather than less structural complexity. But in general, again in agreement with Selten, it depends on the nature of the decision problem.

[4] According to C. Futia [5], since combinatorial semigroups ('flip-flops') generate no feedbacks, he argues that feedbacks are only provided by the basic complexity elements, the simple groups, in the Krohn–Rhodes decomposition. Since complexity of his sequential decision rule D, equivalent to the complexity of the associated semigroup $S(D)$, is considered to be proportional to the amount of 'feedback' or 'looping' in a computer program that executes D, it is obvious that he measures only a restrictive notion of complexity, what I call structural complexity. However, he neglects the number of wires or interconnections between *all* components within the Krohn–Rhodes decomposition, i.e. the length of computations,

what I call computational complexity. But only structural plus computational complexity provides a comprehensive measure of complexity for sequential processes. The distinction between both is important, particularly in view of possible tradeoffs between both in the design of decision rules and by comparing decision rules with different designs.

[5] Now this reduction mechanism induces the choice space to be partitioned into at least two parts, one part which is 'computable', generated by computable preference statements, the other part is 'non-computable', imposed by indecisiveness in choosing among alternatives. Therefore the actual choice space generated by the selection functions is derived from the following equivalence: computable choice space equals given choice space modulo non-computable choice subspace.

[6] Another way of looking at it utilizes H. Simon's [15] distinction between a well-structured and an ill-structured problem. A *stable decision rule* is equivalent to a well-structured problem. An unstable decision rule results from the possible 'computational gap' which may occur in the problem-solving process. As Simon [15, p. 186] puts it: '... definiteness of problem structure is largely an illusion when we systematically confound the idealized problem that is presented to an idealized (and unlimitedly powerful) problem-solver with the actual problem that is to be attacked by a problem-solver with limited (even if large) computational capacities'. So, in way, if the problem-solver's control complexity is below the design complexity of the decision rule, he himself encounters an ill-structured problem, or equivalently, his decision rule is unstable. Then, it is desirable to redesign the decision rule in such a way that ill-structured problem becomes well-structured to the extent that the new design coincides with the computational power of the problem-solver.

[7] H. Simon suggests a 'common sense' test based on the introspective knowledge of our own judgemental process.

REFERENCES

[1] Arbib, M.A. (ed.), *Algebraic Theory of Machines, Languages and Semigroups*, Academic Press, New York, 1968.

[2] Arrow, K.J., *Social Choice and Individual Values*, Cowles Foundation Monograph 12, 2nd. ed. Wiley, New York, 1963.

[3] Blin, J.M., *Patterns and Configuration in Economic Science*, Reidel, Dordrecht, 1973.

[4] Ernst, G.W. and Newell, A., *GPS: A Case Study in Generality and Problem Solving*, Academic Press, New York, 1969.

[5] Futia, C., 'The Complexity of Economic Decision Rules I', Bell Laboratories, Murray Hill, Jan. 1975.

[6] Gaines, B.R., 'Axioms for Adaptive Behavior', *Int. Jour. Man-Machine Studies* 4 (1972), 169–199.

[7] Leibenstein, H., *Beyond Economic Man: A New Foundation for Micro-Economics*, Harvard Univ. Press, Cambridge (Mass.), 1976.

[8] Luce, R.D., *Individual Choice Behavior*, J. Wiley, New York, 1957.

[9] Marschak, J., 'Guided Soul Searching for Multiple-Criterion Decisions', in *Multiple-Criteria Decision-Making*, M. Zeleny (ed.), Springer Verlag, New York, 1976, pp. 1–16.

[10] Rhodes, J., *Application of Automata Theory and Algebra*, Lecture Notes, Dept. of Mathematics, Univ. of Calif., Berkeley, Ca., 1979.

[11] Roberts, F.S., 'What if a Utility Function Does Not Exist?', *Theory and Decision* **2** (1972).

[12] Selten, R., 'The Chain Store Paradox', *Theory and Decision* **9** (1978), 127–159.

[13] Simon, H.A., 'A Behavioral Model of Rational Choice', Ch. 14 in H.A. Simon, *Models of Man*, J. Wiley, New York, 1957.

[14] Simon, H.A., 'Bounded Rationality', in C.B. McGuire and R. Radner (eds.), *Decision and Organization*, North Holland, Amsterdam, 1971.

[15] Simon, H.A., 'The Structure of Ill-Structured Problems', *Artificial Intelligence* **4** (1973), 181–201.

[16] Suppes, P., 'The Measurement of Belief', *Journ. Royal Statist. Soc.* **36** (1974), 160–175.

[17] Varian, H.R., 'Complexity of Social Decisions', unpubl. manuscript, Univ. of Calif., Berkeley, Ca. 1973.

CHAPTER 7

COMPLEXITY AND ORGANIZATIONAL
DECISION MAKING

7.1 INTRODUCTION

In this chapter we investigate certain types of organizational forms which are considered to be *sequentially* computable rather than *Turing* computable, i.e., we are considering those organizations which are subject to definite resource and time constraints and which can be split into elemantary computational operations.

It is argued that organizations could be effectively modelled in the sequential machine framework and that topics dealt within conventional organization theory could be treated more generally. Furthermore, problems concerning the structure of information technology, incentive compatibility and computational complexity fit naturally into this approach.

We also expose an algebraic theory of adjustment possesses based on semigroups of transformations which could be solved by certain types of functional equations. As a starting point we choose the well-developed economic theory of optimal organizations and we attempt to translate some of the key notions into the language of sequential machine theory. The former theory shows several shortcomings which we wish to avoid: First, it does not provide a theory on the design of an organization, hence, it does not show the 'architecture of complexity' and the 'economy of construction'. Second, it does not come to grips with the problem of information decentralization generated by an appropriate information technology. Third, it does not provide means to perform computations in organizations since the analytical framework used does not lend itself to computational experience. The practical aspects of sequential machine theory in the design of organizations would be two-fold.

First, given certain performance standards is the design of a particular organization compatible with meeting these standards? If so, does there exist a 'better' design in terms of being more efficient and/or less costly?

Second, given certain performance standards how would you design an organization which meets these standards in a most efficient and/or in a least costly way?

Although both aspects seem to be related, they represent different approaches to the problem. In the former case the 'organizer' is engaged in a check-up of the existing organizational structure and proposes changes if the feasibility requirement is not satisfied. In the latter case, the organizer is actively involved in the design of the organization and is left with considerable leeway to construct the organization subject only to meeting some performance standards.

7.2 ORGANIZATIONAL STRUCTURE AND PERFORMANCE

We suggest that an organization reveals very much of the structure of a sequential machine, and for that purpose, in this approach, the structure of the organization is very much determined by the capabilities and limitations of the organizations members which weakens the rigorous normative set-up of other organization theories.

We deal here with the major building blocks of the kind of organization which has been described as 'task-oriented'. The purpose of such organizations appears to be best modelled as a decision-making task, so we start with an extremely simple decision-making or 'computational' model.[1]

We assume that

(1) the organization receives an input drawn from a certain set of inputs and is required to respond to it with an output;

(ii) It is rewarded for such a response with a certain payoff which in general depends on the response, as well as the input;

(iii) the goal of the organization is to maximize the expected or 'average' payoff.

It will be useful to consider the inputs to come from 'sources' and the outputs to be delivered to 'destinations', both outside the organization. In information-theoretic terms we may speak of all inputs and outputs as being 'signals', the same term may also be applied to transmissions among organization members.

A *signal* will be understood to be a sequence of symbols: a symbol may be a single letter, a memo, a certain number of resource costs, a job specification, a price quotation, etc. The collection of different symbols that are used in a signal are its 'alphabet'. All alphabets are assumed here to be finite but possibly quite large.

The members of the organization will be assumed to operate in the same way as the organization as a whole. They will acquire symbols as inputs, either from outside sources or from other members, and will dispatch them after suitable processing to certain destinations inside or outside of the organization. The members can be thought of as persons or machines. For simplicity, we designate them with impersonal letters such as alpha, beta, gamma, etc. If the organization is of a centralized nature we will have to add a centralized unit.

Suppose now that x_j is an input symbol received by the organization at a certain point of time, either from one source or jointly from several. It is assumed that if x_j is dispatched the symbol will be received with a known 'symbol probability' P_j and that one such symbol is acquired per unit time. The incidence of symbols in different time units, as they subsequently come in, are assumed to be *statistically independent*.

The organization is required to respond to the input symbol x_j with an output symbol y_k. It need not do so within the same time interval as the acquisition of x_j. Thus delays are permitted provided they do not pile up. That is, the average delay between the receipt of an input symbol and the delivery of an output symbol must not exceed one time unit.

Under these general conditions, if the organization responds to x_j with y_k it receives a reward R_{jk}. Of course, it would be desirable as a normative postulate, to respond in such a way that the reward is maximized.

However, under the assumptions to be made here concerning the individual organization members, in situations in which they have difficulties in coping with the schedule, the optimal response will rarely be realized.

Rather, when the input symbol x_j is received, every output symbol v_k is a possible response, and in fact will be the response with a certain conditional probability $P(y_k|x_j)$. The performance of the organization will be given by the average payoff, i.e. the quantity

$$(*)ER = \sum_j P_j \sum_k R_{jk}P(y_k|x_j)$$

in which j and k range over the input and output alphabets, respectively.

Optimal performance is, of course, a special case of $(*)$, i.e. it is the largest expected pay-off that the organization can obtain if all messages will be responded properly, when $k = k(j)$.

This appears to be the case, if

$$(**)P(y_k|x_j) = 1, \text{ if } k = k(j)$$
$$= 0, \text{ otherwise.}$$

Completing the definition of the organizational goal we have a decision-making problem of a conventional type, with the restriction on the organizations to stay on schedule. The theory of teams [7] in particular uses a very similar set-up. The problem itself, as formulated, appears too simple; and if any claim to realism is to be made, some more restrictions have to be imposed.

7.3 ORGANIZATIONS AND ENVIRONMENTS

In recent years, particular research efforts have been directed toward explaining structure, behavior and performance of economic organizations. It has been increasingly recognized in most approaches that we should look upon organizations in a normative fashion – from a designer's point of view – e.g. how to construct organizations which will perform certain tasks we want them to do. To some extent we are interested in their existence and then ask the question how they would perform 'best', i.e. most efficiently or at least satisfactorily given their existence. A particular organizational form, the competitive economy, has received most attention. The question is essentially the following: Let an economy $\mathscr{E}$ consist of agents, involved in a competitive process, and so, that they act in response to their changing 'environments' and to actions by other agents resulting in 'messages' (prices). Now an adjustment process in this organization, more informally, is a kind of scheme or *process* which this organization reveals at each iteration and which would satisfy certain properties to the best of all members of this organization. In this context, an adjustment process can be viewed as a sequence of aggregate actions (behavior patterns) taken by each agent. A class of (economic) environments is the triple $X = (\Omega, \mathscr{R}, \mathscr{T})$ where Ω describes the set of resources, $\mathscr{R}$ a set of preference relations on Ω and $\mathscr{T}$ a set of feasible technologies. Any given environment can be represented as a parameter x of the class X.

For different classes of environments, L. Hurwicz [3] has studied adjustment processes in terms of difference equations in which agents respond to messages from other agents including themselves (memorizing). (Of course, the agent may be completely or only partially ignorant about the environment, in this case stochastic responses have to be considered). Hence, in technical language, an adjustment process is a triple $(\lambda, \delta, \mathscr{M})$, consisting of a response function λ (possibly a vector a finite number of agents), an outcome function δ, independent of the environment but depending on the amount of resource endowment, trade, production, etc. given the environment and a message space ('language') $\mathcal{M}$ whose elements ('messages') generate new messages (via the response function λ) for any given environment e. There is associated a message acting as a stimulus on every agent. If sufficient information has been collected by the agents (and the response resulting in different types of actions such as trading, producing, storing, etc. is uniquely determined such that additional information will not result in a different response), the process is said to be *in equilibrium* and the message received at that stage is *stationary*. To every informational equilibrium value of the process $\bar{m} = \lambda(\bar{m}, e)$ there may correspond a (Pareto-) satisfactory outcome level $\delta(\bar{m})$ which is not preferred to any other outcome level for any given environment. The behavior pattern of such an economic system can be studied in terms of a particular social welfare function satisfying an optimality criterion (Pareto optimality) given an environment of a particular kind (classical or non-classical environments). A class of environments is called 'classical' if externalities and indivisibilities are absent and if both technology and preferences are convex; otherwise it is called non-classical. On the basis of the adjustment process new states will be generated up to a point where the final state is compatible with the welfare criterion. Some important results in this area have been obtained, notably by Hurwicz [5], for a class of processes which may or may not be Pareto satisfactory for all conceivable environments. In particular, it has been shown that the competitive process acting in a classical environment is Pareto satisfactory. In principle, at least, a similar adjustment process could be established by a central agent having only partial information about the environment, constituting an algorithmic approach to the solution of the problem. On the other hand, in non-classical environments with externalities and indivisibilities present and technology not necessarily convex, other types of processes different from the competitive process have been studied w.r.t. optimality properties. It is well known that the evaluation of the process has to be based primarily on the informational requirements necessary to establish a Pareto satisfactory process, and secondarily on the incentive compatibility with the actions of the various agents. The first point has to do with the computability of the adjustment process, i.e. with the capacity of various agents to process and disseminate information. There are actually two aspects of the first point: one aspect concerns the purely 'technological' problem of selecting the appropriate or even the minimal 'information-handling equipment' capable to do the job. Since information-handling usually involves costs the other aspect relates to the problem of selecting those information-handling equipments which cause minimal costs. Both aspects deal with the question of informational efficiency in various organizations. (Both aspects will come up later in a different framework). As is known, the question of informational efficiency, in a more imprecise formulation, gave rise to controversies about the choice of economic systems many years ago.

The second point involves the question of goal-compatible behavior patterns of economic agents (incentive compatibility) which in a competitive system are satisfied, given the classical environment, by assuming profit – and utility maximization. We will not deal with the second point in this paper, although this point will come up at various instances.

Recent work on adjustment processes along Hurwicz' lines (see Reiter [12]) contains mainly some mathematical refinements of previous results which center around the question of information efficiency. It is assumed that the space of environment X, the message space $\mathcal{M}$ and the space of actions A are all topological spaces whereas the adjustment process starts from some subset of the message space defined by a correspondence $\mu : X \rightarrow \mathcal{M}$ and a response function $\lambda : \mathcal{M} \rightarrow A$. Hence the adjustment process (μ, λ) is induced by an initial message set $\mu_0(x)$. The outcome function $\delta : \mathcal{M} \rightarrow A$ may be introduced in the appropriate context. It is clear – technicalities apart – that the response function satisfies some 'nice' properties which could be derived from the topological structure of the underlying spaces. Contrary to this approach we consider it more natural that such a response function reveals its structure and behavior in the context of a device which is known as a *sequential machine*.

The perspective is to consider sequential machines as basic analogues for modelling complex 'humanistic' systems (organizations), and to treat adjustment processes in terms of transformations on the set of states of a machine. Later we will give some examples demonstrating the usefulness of this analogy. Not only would we be interested in translating the language of the economic theory of organizations into proper machine language but also we would like to answer some specific questions within the framework adopted. We list these questions now, somewhat informally, since we provide suitable definitions later.

(1) Given a machine M, what 'information technology' is necessary and sufficient to realize this machine by serial, parallel, serial-parallel or cascade decomposition into component machines? In other words, what kind of information technology is needed to accomplish the task of the original machine by an appropriate sequence of submachines?

(2) If several information technologies are compatible with the performance of the original machine, then does there exist a unique optimal one? If so, are the costs of information processing, induced by the information technology feasible in view of an initial resource endowment given to the machine.

(3) What corresponding type of adjustment process could be derived for an optimal information technology?

7.4 A REAL-TIME ORGANIZATION

As an example let us first consider some kind of control device where you (the designer) want to control someone's action according to the message received. Take such organization as an Airport Parking lot and look at it strictly from a designer's point of view: how should a parking lot be operated? The first thing to do is to announce an exhaustive list of instructions and to make it available to everyone entering the parking lot. There may be a set of instructions such as: 'Stop until 75 cents (in coins) are deposited (red light). Then go if light turns green.' Now everything is fine if this set of instructions is complied with. However, there are other possibilities to be taken care of by the organization constituting a penalty-reward system. Consider the following cases.

(1) the message is not received for whatever reasons (nothing happening).

TABLE I

		no message received	message incomplete	message violated
states	0	stop	stop, go to row 1	alarm, go to row 0
	1	stop	stop, go to row 2	alarm, go to row 0
	2	stop	go to row 3	alarm, go to row 0
	3	go	go	stop

next states

(2) the instructions are only complied with incompletely (only one quarter is deposited but not two, three, etc.).

(3) the instructions are flagrantly violated (no money is deposited). In all these cases appropriate actions have to be taken describing the response to the message given the state and they reflected in Table I.

We could look at this organization as a human automaton, but we could also look at it as an electrical device which simulates the human machine: in fact, it could be a device which transforms the state-message pair into an action-next state pair. Of course, this requires quite a bit of hardware construction, but what it mainly amounts to is to put stimulus, response or state as voltages on a bundle of lines (wires) and to encode them in proper form (for example in binary form). The organization we would like to describe as an electrical device would then be represented by Table II (here → denotes an instruction).

In the case of the states we have the following correspondences: 0–00, 1–01, 2–10, 3–11. There are similar assignments to stimuli and responses, as exhibited in Table II. Both devices, the human and the electrical one, obviously perform the same tasks: in terms of performance, one machine is as good as the other. It is hence natural to describe the second machine as a homomorphic image (or homomorphism) of the first, since it is supposed to transform all operations performed by the first machine into the same operations performed by the second machine.

Now, for this simple kind of example, which obviously is a crude one, all that we want to conclude is that, in principle, there is no difference between an engineering design and the design of a human organization. Other examples of control systems and organizational designs are discussed by T. Marschak and C.B. McGuire [8]. They describe different control systems in terms of car-driving. Consider a car driving along a windy road. The conditions of the road may constitute the stimuli to the car-

TABLE II
stimuli

		00	01	10
	00	00	00 → 00	10 → 00
states	01	00	00 → 10	10 → 00
	10	00	01 → 11	10 → 00
	11	01	01 → 11	00

next states

driver, e.g. left curb, right curb, going straight. The question is how to control a car in order to stay on the road, hence it concerns various steering actions given the stimuli. Although this might be obvious for execution-type operations as described above, we will face difficulties where managerial-type decision will come in to play or where problems of incentives, competence, cooperation competition etc. enter the picture of the organization's performance. In fact, it is this type of situation for which one might question the applicability of sequential machine theory to the design of organizations.

In view of suggestions due to Marschak and McGuire we consider first two kinds of organizations, a decision and a pay-off machine, hooked together, to make a new machine.

DEFINITION. Given an organization $M = (X, Y, Z, \lambda, \delta)$. Then it is possible to represent M by a *serial decomposition* into decision machine $M_1 = \langle X, A, Z_1, \lambda_1, \delta_1 \rangle$ and payoff machine $M_2 = \langle A, Y, Z_2, \lambda_2, \delta_2 \rangle$ to generate the machine $M_1 \oplus M_2 = \langle X, Y, Z_1 \times Z_2, \lambda, \delta \rangle$ with $\lambda[(z_1, z_2), x] = [\lambda_1(x, z_1), \lambda_2(a, z_2)] = [\lambda_1(x, z_1), \lambda_2(\delta_1(x, z_1), z_2)]$ and $\delta[(z_1, z_2), x] = \delta_2[z_2, \delta_1(x, z_1)]$.

For reasons of nontriviality, M_1 and M_2 have fewer states than M.

Fig. 1. Serial connection of decision machine M_1 and payoff machine M_2.

A slightly more general case is provided by a serial decomposition of M into three types of machines

$$M_0 = \langle X, M, Z_0, \lambda_0, \delta_0 \rangle \quad \text{(message machine)}$$
$$M_1 = \langle M, A, Z_1, \lambda_1, \delta_1 \rangle \quad \text{(decision machine)}$$
$$M_2 = \langle A, Y, Z_2, \lambda_2, \delta_2 \rangle \quad \text{(payoff machine)}$$

to generate a new machine

$$M_0 \oplus M_1 \oplus M_2 = M = \langle X, Y, Z_1 \times Z_2 \times Z_3, \lambda, \delta \rangle$$

with somewhat more complicated state and output functions than those given in the foregoing example.

Fig. 2. Serial connection of message machine, decision machine and payoff machine.

In an analogous way we could talk about *parallel decomposition*.

DEFINITION. A (decision) machine M can be realized by parallel decomposition into component machines to generate

$$M = M_1 \oplus M_2 = \langle X_1 \times X_2, A_1 \times A_2, Z_1 \times Z_2, \lambda, \delta \rangle;$$

with state representation

$$\lambda[(x_1, x_2), (z_1, z_2)] = (\lambda_1(x_1, z_1), \lambda_2(x_2, z_2));$$

and output representation

$$\delta[(x_1, x_2), (z_1, z_2)] = (\delta_1(x_1, z_1), \delta_2(x_2, z_2)).$$

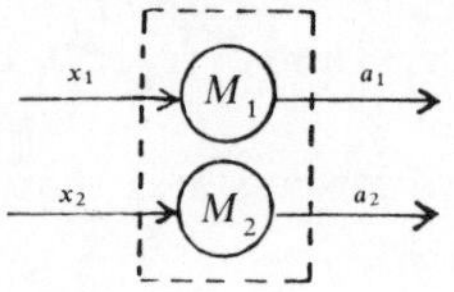

Fig. 3. Parallel connection 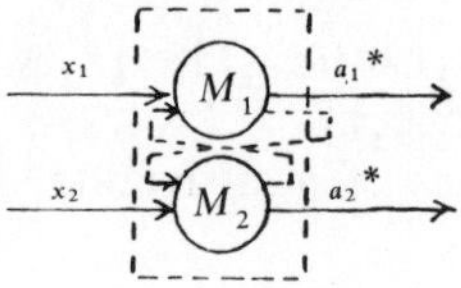   Fig. 4. Cross connection and parallel connection

Given these definitions we actually could consider a combination of both, e.g. serial-parallel decompositions, and in terms of applications these prove to be the most interesting ones. We neglect here some more complicated versions of decompositions, which are not loop-free, for example those known as cross decompositions as shown in Figure 6. These cross decompositions are usually handled in connection with abstract network systems. However, under some restrictive circumstances we could achieve the same effect by an appropriate serial-parallel decomposition without loops. We only need to consider an appropriate restructuring of the machine exhibited in Figure 6. This is illustrated in Figure 7.

Care must be taken of the operations $\oplus$ and $\otimes$, for example, distributivity does not hold for both, in particular, even commutativity does not hold for $\oplus$. One can easily check the validity of permissible operations by drawing machine diagrams and finding the corresponding state and

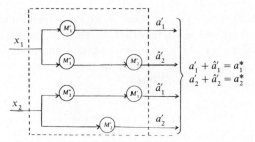

Fig. 5. Serial-parallel restructuring of two cross-connected parallel machines.

output representations.[2] A somewhat stronger form of decomposition which essentially could be treated within the same mathematical framework has become known as *cascade decomposition*.

A simple illustration of a *cascade machine* is this:

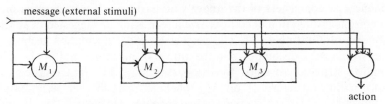

Fig. 8. Cascade machine.

There are messages (external stimuli) affecting all component machines however, every machine produces its own messages affecting all other machines on line. As one realizes, the information process in such cascade form tends to be increasingly complex, the highest degree of complexity is obtained by M_3. This will lead to a peculiar resolution principle with which we will deal later.

Which kind of decomposition one would like to choose for an organization depends on various factors, certainly on the economic environment it faces, on nature and extent of its performance, and last but not least there is some other important consideration. One could argue that decomposing an organization into information, decision and payoff machine is a rather artificial procedure since we all know that often parts of an organizational unit do all this simultaneously. However, besides emphasizing the point that we are not primarily interested in what actual organizations do, the crucial point in the attempt to construct an organizational unit is how much information the system as a whole needs in order to select the 'right' actions and to produce a 'desirable result'. The second question, equally important, is how to disseminate information among organizational units in order to achieve this result. A possible third question is that of cooperation or even competition between these units so that an optimal use is made in the allocation of 'informational resources' (incentive compatibility).

7.5 INFORMATION TECHNOLOGY

Now given a machine M we may consider a state partition of M, say π, which induces homomorphic π-images of M, say M_π. M_π could be thought as performing subcomputations for M depending on which block of π contains the state of M. Looking at the set of all partitions of a machine M' it can be verified that this set forms a lattice under the natural partition ordering. The partial order in this lattice is a comparative relation on the fineness or coarseness of the underlying partition. It also permits interpretation as a relation of comparitive information as suggested in another context by Gottinger [3]. The very essence of information technology lies in the state decomposition (partition) of machines and in the information structure revealed by the partitioning. The lattice reflects the information structure of all M_π machines, possibly in serial-parallel connection, which realize the original machine M. We call this the *information technology* of all M_π machines realizing M.

EXAMPLE. Let us give a simple example where π-images of a machine M perform subcomputations which in parallel connection completely realize M. Let $Z = \{1, 2, \ldots, 6\}$, let $\pi_1 = \{\langle 1, 2, 3 \rangle, \langle 4, 5, 6 \rangle\}$ and $\pi_2 = \{\langle 1, 6 \rangle, \langle 2, 5 \rangle, \langle 3, 4 \rangle\}$ be two partitions of Z, hence define the image

	input								
	a	b	output		a	b		a	b
1	4	3	0	s	t	s	p	r	r
2	6	3	0	t	s	t	q	p	r
3	⑤	2	0				r	q	q
states 4	2	5	1	$t = \langle 1, 2, 3 \rangle$			$p = \langle 1, 6 \rangle, q = \langle 2, 5 \rangle$		
5	1	4	0	$s = \langle 4, 5, 6 \rangle$			$r = \langle 3, 4 \rangle$		
6	3	4	0						

next
state

Fig. 7. Representation of M, $M_{\P 1}$ and $M_{\P 2}$. Circled number is a unique state given input b, realized uniquely by $M_{\P 1} \otimes M_{\P 2}$ in block s given b and block r given b, respectively.

machines by M_{π_1} and M_{π_2}. It is helpful to represent M, M_{π_1} and M_{π_2} by the flow table in Figure 7.

As can easily be seen every block of π_1 has exactly one state of M in common with every block of π_2. Hence the states of M_{π_1} and M_{π_2}, when being operated jointly, uniquely determine a state of M.

We observe that if π_1 and π_2 are partitions of (the states of) M, then also $\pi_1 \cdot \pi_2$ and $\pi_1 + \pi_2$ form partitions of M and the binary operations '.' and '+' determine the 'inf' (g.l.b.) and 'sup' (l.u.b.) respectively, hence satisfy the definition of a lattice. Let P be the set of all possible partitions of M, with $\{\langle Z \rangle\}$ being the *unit* partition and $\{\langle 1, 2, \ldots, n \rangle\}$ the *null* partition. Then P forms a partition lattice and the g.l.b. $\prod_1^n (\pi_i) =$ $= \pi_1 \cdot \pi_2 \cdots \pi_n$ forms the coarsest among all finest partitions in P, likewise the l.u.b. $\sum_1^n (\pi_i) = \pi_1 + \pi_2 + \cdots + \pi_n$ forms the finest among all coarsest partitions in P. Since P is a lattice it is perfectly legitimate to conceive the operations '.' and '+' or the generalized operations '$\prod$' and '$\sum$' as partial algebraic operations (see [3]). In this case the equivalence holds: $\pi_1 \leq \pi_2$ iff a l.u.b. (π_1, π_2) and a g.l.b. (π_1, π_2) exists in P for any $\pi_1, \pi_2 \in P$. Viewing the lattice of partitions as 'information technology' we would like to give '$\leq$' the meaning of 'not more informative than'. Then in the lattice of partitions, partitions are only partially ordered according to their information content (induced by the state behavior of machines).

DEFINITION. A partition π on the state Z of a machine M is *output consistent* iff $z \equiv z'$ given π implies $\delta(z, x) = \delta(z', x)$ for all $x \in X$.

Since sometimes the lattice of partitions of Z does not fulfill this requirement one would have to consider a sublattice of partitions if it exists. With regard to the associated machine one might find – as an interesting counterpart – that a possible lack of output consistent partitions reflects redundancy of state information, hence by performing computations for machine M it would be sufficient to confine the computational process to the realization of a reduced machine M_R. M_R can be constructed (or induced) by a homomorphism between the original machine M and M_R. Let then M_π and M_{π_R} be those machines that compute M and M_R respectively. Then M_π and M_{π_R} are trivially equivalent. This property certainly has a meaningful interpretation in organization theory. Output – consistency, in fact, is an immediate consequence of the substitution property (S.P.) of machines.

DEFINITION. A partition π on Z has the S.P. iff $z \equiv z'$ given $\pi \Rightarrow \lambda(z, x) =$ $= \lambda(z', x)$ given π.

This property actually ensures that if some M_π could perform sub-computations for M then for any given block B_π in π we could find a smaller block B'_π contained in B_π where for every input the state transition function acting on the smaller block generates only states in the larger block, i.e. there is a unique block to block transformation on π.

One technical problem might arise in the case of realizing a machine by a sequence of M_{π_i} machines, serially connected. For example, if M_{π_1} is the first machine in line doing subcomputations for M, then we would have to know about those remaining states which still have to be computed in order to realize M. This is necessary to know what kind of M_{π_2} machine, say, is required to do supplementary subcomputations. Now if we could think of an organization to achieve a certain performance standard within some time limit (in terms of computational, not historic time), one has a fairly accurate perception which states have to be computed at various instances of time. Hence this gives some hint on answering the question which information technology could be used for the realization of M by serially connected M_{π_i} machines. This problem is rather deep and we will deal with it next in a more general way.

Adopting the idea that we can effectively compute a machine by various kinds of compositions of its π_i-images M_{π_i}, we would be basically interested in the following.

PROBLEM. Given any π-partition of a machine, could be find another π-partition which fits π in an appropriate way.

We call such a pair (π, π') *complete*, if it exists and constitutes the entire information technology needed to realize M. This problem can be given different kinds of interpretation, but what it really amounts to is determining clearly what kind of complementary information π' is needed for machine $M_{\pi'}$, in order to compute jointly with M_π the states and possibly outputs of the original machine M. More generally, we could consider the minimal partition

$$\pi_* = \prod(\pi_i : (\pi, \pi_i) \text{ is complete w.r.t. } M)$$

and a maximal partition

$$\pi^* = \sum(\pi_i : (\pi, \pi_i) \text{ is complete w.r.t. } M).$$

In the first cast π_* describes the largest amount of information (given the partition $\prod$) necessary to compute the next state(s) of M for all π_i finer than π_*. In the latter case π^* represents the least amount of information (given π) to compute the next state(s) of M for all π_i coarser than π^*.

EXAMPLE. Given a partition $\pi_1 = \{\langle 1, 2 \rangle, \langle 3, 4 \rangle, \langle 5 \rangle\}$, then compute all possible states onto which all blocks of π_1 are mapped. Assume they are given by the sets $\{4, 5\}, \{1, 4\}, \{2, 3\}$, then $\pi_* = \{\langle 1, 4, 5, \rangle, \langle 2, 3 \rangle\}$.

We already know that the set of partitions forms a lattice L under the natural partition ordering, the set of partition pairs will be a subset $\mathscr{P} \subseteq L_1 \times L_2$. We call $\mathscr{P}$ are *pair algebra*[3] satisfying a closure, completeness and boundedness property e.g.

(a) (π_i, π_j) and (π_i', π_j') in $\mathscr{P}$ imply that

$$\prod_i \{(\pi_i, \pi_j), (\pi_i', \pi_j')\} \text{ and } \sum_i \{(\pi_i, \pi_j), (\pi_i', \pi_j')\} \text{ are in } \mathscr{P}.$$

(b) For any π in L_1 and π' in L_2, the trivial partitions $(0, \pi)$ and (π, I) are in $\mathscr{P}$.

(c) For some $\pi \in L$ there exists $\pi_* = (\pi, \pi')$ and $* = (\pi, \pi'')$ constituting g.l.b.'s and l.u.b.'s in $\mathscr{P}$, respectively.

Obviously, $\mathscr{P}$ is again a lattice under the natural partition ordering $\leq$ since $(\pi_1, \pi_2) \leq (\pi_1', \pi_2')$ in $L_1 \times L_2$ is equivalent to $\pi_1 \leq \pi_1'$ in L_1 and $\pi_2 \leq \pi_2'$, and $\mathscr{P}$ has the zero element $(0, 0)$ and the unit element $(1, 1)$.

In some sense the lattice L_1 describes the ordering of information about the machine (we have got) whereas L_2 describes the ordering of information to which the previous information can be transformed by M. Hence M is considered to be a transformation machine which already suggests that any adjustment process acts as a 'transformation walk' on the lattice of partition pairs.

In many cases it would be sufficient to start out with a subset (not necessarily sublattice) $\mathscr{P}_0$ of $\mathscr{P}$ containing all initial partition pairs. If additional information is needed to compute the next state(s) of M then this information can be obtained by modifying $\mathscr{P}_0$ in an algorithmic fashion, i.e. by refining the first component and/or coarsening the second component of the pair. In an organizational context this procedure is very much like the process of interchange of messages between various subunits.

Since the lattice of partition pairs is uniquely associated to the machine structure it is possible to reveal the informational skeleton of the machine in this way. In particular, given a machine M it is possible by an appropriate decomposition to compute the next-states and outputs by π-images of the machine obtained by partition analysis. One question then naturally arises which information obtained by partitioning the states of the original machine is *sufficient* to compute the future states of this machine? The following algorithm is not claimed to be unique or exhaustive but it provides the main steps to be checked:

ALGORITHM.

(a) Start with a certain partition based on present information and past history.

(b) Look for future states which have to be computed.

(c) Look for that π' that requires the minimal amount of information in terms of the partition ordering.

(d) If π' does not fit π, look for some π'' which is finer or coarser than π', or take concatenations $\pi_1 \cdot \pi_2 \cdot \ldots \cdot \pi_n$ (in case of serial decomposition) or $\pi_1 + \pi_2 + \cdots + \pi_n$ (in case of parallel decomposition).

(e) Compute the partition pair and determine its locus in the lattice of partition pairs (pair algebra).

(f) Determine (technological) informational efficiency by the minimal dimension of the sublattice in $\mathcal{P}$ given by the computed partition pair (π, π') as illustrated in Figure 8.

Fig. 8. Dimension of sublattice reflects highest informational efficiency or minimal information needed to realize M.

We could define a dimension function as a function $D: \mathcal{P} \to [0, 1]$ with the following properties:

(i) $0 \le D[(\pi, \pi')] \le 1$ for every $(\pi, \pi') \in \mathcal{P}$, in particular $D[(0, 0)] = 0$, $D[(I, I)] = 1$;

(ii)   if $(\pi, \pi') > (0, 0)$, then $D[(\pi, \pi')] > 0$;

(iii) Let $\perp$ denote an algebraic independence relation,

if $\perp \{(\pi_1, \pi'_1), \ldots, (\pi_n, \pi'_n)\}$, then $D\left(\bigcup_1^n (\pi_i, \pi'_i)\right) = \sum_1^n (D(\pi_i, \pi'_i))$;

(iv) $\quad D\big[(\pi_1, \pi_1') \cup (\pi_2, \pi_2')\big] + D\big[(\pi_1, \pi_1') \cap (\pi_2, \pi_2')\big] =$
$\quad = D\big[(\pi_1, \pi_1')\big] + D\big[(\pi_2, \pi_2')\big];$

(v) $\quad D$ is order-preserving on $\mathscr{P}$, D can be shown to be unique.[4]

The algorithm then contains the following instruction. Choose that (π, π') in $\mathscr{P}$ which has minimal dimension in terms of D. Of course, in case $\mathscr{P}$ represents a metric lattice D would be identical to a metric on $\mathscr{P}$. Again, the economic analogue of this procedure can be easily presented, it relates to the problem of how much and what kind of informational decentralization is necessary (and not whether it is necessary at all) to resolve the computational burden brought upon by a highly complex organization. On the other hand, given a set, say of parallel connected component machines $M_{\pi_1}, M_{\pi_2}, \ldots, M_{\pi_n}$ realizing M, could we find a simpler set of component machines which will do the job as well. This relates to the question of *information redundancy* and amounts to finding the smallest sublattice within the lattice of partition pairs, given the performance standard of the original machine, where informational efficiency could be measured by the dimension of the sublattice. The task to avoid information redundancy can be approached by an algorithmic search procedure substituting M_π by $M_{\pi'}$, in case both are equivalent machines (in the precise meaning defined above) but where π' is finer than π so that $M_{\pi'}$ requires less information than M_π. Such an algorithmic procedure finds its counterpart in a policy aiming at the change of the organizational design (organizational change).

We have to mention at least one technical difficulty arising in the case of redundant information. Suppose that partitions π_1 and π_2 are sufficient to realize M. Then the sum $\pi_1 + \pi_2$ represents a redundant computation which should be factored out, but in some instances it might occur that factoring out will cost additional memory. Thus, in general, when dealing with the problem of factoring out information redundancy one should only select partitions which do not enlarge the memory requirements. Here we have dealt only with the construction of the information technology involving the partitioning of the state set of a machine. We could, however, think about partitioning in a broader sense affecting the input, output and state set simultaneously. Given a machine M, we then say a $X-Z$ partition determines an 'input-state' set, accordingly, a $Z-Y$ partition determines a 'state-output' set, both sets form pair algebras. In general, $M = \langle X, Y, Z, \lambda, \delta \rangle$ could be replaced by the partition machine $M' = \langle X_\tau, Y_\omega, Z_\pi, \lambda_{\tau\pi}, \delta_{\tau\omega} \rangle$ τ, ω, π denote partitions, induced by a π-partition on Z of M. In fact, M' is a homomorphic image of M where $h_1 : X \to X_\tau$,

$h_2 : Y \to Y_\omega$ and $h_3 : Z \to Z_\pi$, and M may be realized by a serial-parallel decomposition of M'. In all discussions concerning performance of economic systems (Reiter [12]) the question of performance and size of message space arises. It is generally acknowledged that there exists some kind of trade-off between both, characterizing an efficiency frontier of allocating information. In particular, a legitimate question is what is the minimal size of the message space still able to sustain a certain performance standard. Nothing is known about the absolute size of a message space but something could be said about the ordering of message spaces given different economic environments where the competitive process is the most natural to start with because of its Pareto optimal property. The efficiency question can be translated appropriately in our framework. Now translated in the language of machine theory we are interested in finding the minimal information technology sustaining the realization of a machine. Whereas the traditional approach actually studies the size of a message space (or information-carrying capacity) in terms of topological properties we believe that this is rather unnatural from a machine-theory viewpoint where information technology (here message-transferring technology) really has an algebraic counterpart.

7.6 COSTS OF INFORMATION PROCESSING

Although principally, we could solve the technological aspect of informational efficiency we still have to take care of the economic problem of finding an information technology with minimal costs. Here machine theory doesn't provide tools for the direct solution of this problem. The reason is that engineers and computer scientists are not so much worried about monetary costs of operating components or pieces of hardware, all that they are worried about is the feasibility of the design with the performance standards set out in advance. However, they are much concerned about problems like computational complexity (measured in terms of number of diodes used in the realization), real-time computation, and algorithmic efficiency of a machine. These are important parameters of 'computational costs' and they have some relevance for economic considerations, too. Nevertheless, we wish to treat costs associated to the information technology in a more unified analytical way. If we could find some link between computational complexity and costs of information we will be able to speak intelligently in economic terms about the optimal size of a machine. Now it seems intuitively reasonable to argue that the cost of operating a machine is associated to the information technology necessary to realize the machine, or more explicitly, is associated to a certain partition pair satisfying this requirement. Hence, we would like to associate the cost function to the lattice of partition pairs mapping the state set generated by the partitions into an appropriately defined vector space, the cost space. Unfortunately, we do not know much about the properties of this function, except, perhaps, that it is monotone-increasing. Informally, this means that handling more information is more expensive, or that handling more complex messages causes higher information costs. However, this implicitly assumes that information handling equipment is completely divisible and equally effective for all kinds of computations, i.e. independent of the size and complexity of computations. On the other hand we know that more complex computations could be handled more efficiently by more advanced technology which, if introduced, might even decrease total unit costs of information-processing. Hence, there is no uniform pattern regarding cost function specifications of information technology and this basically requires a broad range of empirical investigations on that matter. The problems of specification of cost functions for a certain information technology often appear in discussions on advantages or disadvantages of decentralized or centralized economic organizations. In general, however, if we consider large organizations it is safe to argue that costs of information processing are roughly proportional to 'computational complexity' of the machines which is increasing with the dimension of the lattice of partition pairs measured from its zero element. This brings us closer to the concern of computer scientists representing a measure of computational complexity by costs of computation. The problem of computational complexity will arise later in another context.

One possibility for dealing analytically with the problem of costs of information processing should be pursued here explicitly in some general form.

DEFINITION. A partially ordered vector space is a cost space C if

(1) C is endowed with a tolerance relation R, saying that for any pair of elements $(c, c') \in R$. (Any costs should be feasible with the given tolerance R).

(2) For each $c \in C$ there exist $a, b \in C$ such that $a < c < b$ and $a < c' < b$ implies $(c, c') \in R$.

Now given a machine $M = \langle X, Y, Z, \lambda, \delta \rangle$ and its homomorphic image $M' = \langle X_\tau, Y_\omega, Z_\pi, \lambda_{\tau\pi}, \delta_{\tau\omega} \rangle$, and a cost space C associated to Z_π, a cost function for M' is a function $\phi : X_\tau \times Z_\pi \to C$ with representation $\phi(x_\tau, z_\pi) = \sum_{\pi \in P} \phi(x_\tau, z_\pi)$. We could then formulate an optimal control problem in a tentative way.

PROBLEM. Let z_0 and z_1 be two states of Z_π and $Z_{\pi'}$ respectively, called the initial and the terminal state. We say that $x_\tau = (x_1, \ldots, x_n) \in X$ transfers M' from z_0 to z_1 if $\lambda(z_0, x_\tau) = z_1$ for all x_τ, whereby $\lambda(z_0, x_1, \ldots, \ldots, x_k) \neq z_1$ if $k < n$. Among all such x_τ in X_τ find that sequence $z_{\pi_1}, \ldots, z_{\pi_n}$ for which $\phi(x_\tau, z_\pi)$ is a minimum.

Let then $M' = \langle X_\tau, Y_\omega, Z_\pi \times C, \lambda_{\tau\pi}, \delta_{\tau\omega} \rangle$ be the machine with cost function ϕ and cost space C. We define the machine $(M', \phi) = \langle X_\tau, Y_\omega, Z_\pi \times C, \lambda^c_{\tau\pi}, \delta^c_{\tau\omega} \rangle$ by $\lambda^c_{\tau\pi}(z_\pi, c, x_\tau) = (\lambda_{\tau\pi}(z_\pi, x_\tau), \; c + \phi(z_\pi, x_\tau))$, and $\delta^c_{\tau\omega}(z_\pi, c, x) = \delta_{\tau\omega}(z_\pi, x)$.

7.7 A SIMPLE MACHINE MODEL

To the extent that organizational designs resemble designs of microprocessors, as presented by Zissos [15] we subsequently try to establish such analogy by linking hardware considerations of human organizations (structures) to software considerations of human behavioral rules (procedures).

As mentioned in Section 8.2 the organization member 'processes' x_j into y_k. This processing may be deterministic or stochastic. In the first instance, the organization member produces the same output symbol y_k whenever he receives x_j and transmits it to the same destination, in the second he does so only with a given probability.

We are emphasizing that the organization is 'task-oriented' and that every member is coping with the difficulty of properly processing input into output symbols, depending on the nature of the task as well as on his competence for its execution. As a proxy measure for the level of difficulty we could use the (average) processing time (or the number of computational steps in time) which he needs to perform a given task.

It will be convenient to visualize an organization member, a machine, as being composed of an input machine and an output machine – hooked in serial connection as illustrated in Figure 9. The reason for this distinction is that an organization member may be called upon to do two quite different tasks, and may have difficulties of different kinds when performing them. One is the acquisition and sorting out of input symbols, the other the production and dispatching of output symbols.

The processes which are needed for one usually differ significantly from those for the other, and their processing times accordingly depend on quite different parameters.

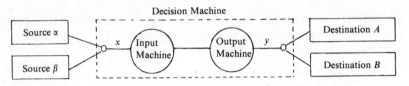

Fig. 9

The decision machine is then characterized by two sets of processing times. Thus, $t_j^{(i)}$, i for input, is the processing time of the input machine for symbol x_j, and $t_k^{(o)}$ is the corresponding time of the output machine for the symbol y_k.

The performance of the two machines can be measured by their average processing times $\tau^{(i)}$ and $\tau^{(o)}$, given by

$$(1) \qquad \tau^{(i)} = \sum_i P_j^{(i)} t_j^{(i)}, \ \tau^{(o)} = \sum_k P_k^{(o)} t_k^{(o)}$$

where P_j and P_k are the probabilities with which the processing of x_j and y_k is called for.

The *processing load* of the organization member is measured by the sum of $\tau^{(i)}$ and $\tau^{(o)}$, i.e. by

$$(2) \qquad \tau = \tau^{(i)} + \tau^{(o)}$$

The individual processing times $t_j^{(i)}$ and $t_k^{(o)}$ may depend only on the symbols x_j or y_k that are being processed, but they may depend also on other parameters, for instance, length or number of symbols, not explicitly considered here.

All these parameters may reflect the *complexity* or difficulty of a processing task for a particular organization member.

By the assumption that an organization is required to meet its schedule we see immediately that the average processing time τ of each member must not exceed the average time between the arrivals of input symbols, namely one time unit. Therefore,

$$(3) \qquad \tau = \tau^{(i)} + \tau^{(o)} \leq 1$$

must be assured for every member of the organization. If this bound is violated for some member, he will be considered 'overloaded', in an intuitive and technical sense.

7.8 ORGANIZATIONAL MALFUNCTIONING, AND DESIGN

An organization member is considered *malfunctioning* if he (she) cannot keep up with the schedule on which the organization works but falls progressively further behind. This will be the case when

$$(*)\tau = \tau^{(i)} + \tau^{(o)} > 1$$

where $\tau^{(i)}$, $\tau^{(o)}$ are the mean processing times of his input and output machines. The only way in which an overloaded member can react to this predicament is to make mistakes.

It does not matter for the moment how an organization member makes his errors, i.e., whether he does so deterministically, stochastically or in some other, less well defined manner. All that matters here is that on occasion an overloaded organization member will generate an output other than the one that is called for, and as a result, will jeopardize the *expected payoff* to the organization. What are the conditions under which such an over-overload occurs?

The issue that will matter most is the intuitive notion that overload should develop in most cases of interest when the complexity of processing tasks for either or both of the machines of an organization member increases beyond some critical point. Start with the simplest case of a single decision-maker (or decision machine), labeled DM, how can he manage the processing task under a SOR. Suppose

$$x_j = \{x_j^1, x_j^2\} \quad \text{input symbols}$$
$$y_k = \{y_k^1, y_k^2\} \quad \text{output symbols}$$

are processed in such a way that the (mean) payoff is largest.

EXAMPLE. We consider a set of behavioral or procedural rules which governs the relationship among the organization members and forms the 'standard operating routine' (SOR) of the organization. In practice, these procedures are sometimes laid down in elaborate detail embedded in a systemic environment (say in an organizational handbook), sometimes they are left entirely to tradition and common sense among the members.

Let the SOR generate the rule: DM $: x_j \to y_k$ with probability 1.

Here, j and k range over the DM's input and output alphabets, respectively. If it develops that the DM can actually manage this SOR without overload, the designer's job is done. He has specified the organizational structure which is trivial in this case, namely a graph consisting of a single node (the DM), and has drawn up the SOR for it. However, the designer may find that the DM is badly overloaded, and hence that he is error-prone. In general, this will entail a deterioration of performance, in the sense that the mean-payoff is decreased by the incidence of error. The question is then how performance can be improved by using an organization of more than one member. In fact, there are quite a few options available to the designer, but, if we confine ourselves to centralized, bureaucratic-type organizations, the designer can basically do only two things: he can interpose an organizational unit between the DM and the sources, which is intended to reduce the *input load* of the DM somehow, and another one between the DM and the destination, intended to alleviate his *output load* (see Figure 11, Section 7.7).

The two units do quite different work. The first will be referred to as 'staff'. Its function is to preprocess information and to present it to the DM in a form to make further processing possible. The second is called the 'line' used in an analogous manner to accept signals which the DM is best capable of generating.

The load reduction can be achieved in the following way:

The staff can, for instance, take on the job of searching for necessary inputs, and the line that of producing the outputs at appropriate locations. Both are often time-consuming tasks, involve long symbol processing times, and result in high loads.

The basic objective of the economics of organizational design as pertaining to line organizations is the reduction of the output load on the DM(s), without generating overload among the line members. As Arrow [1], p. 37 has remarked, 'the scarcity of information-handling ability is an essential feature for the understanding of both individual and organizational behavior' and it is to be explicitly dealt with by the organizational designer.

7.9 THE CASE OF LINE ORGANIZATION

We start with a brief discussion of a one-mh line, consisting of one buffer unit only, say γ, which accepts all instructions $d_1, d_2, \ldots, d_n$ from the DM, converts them to the desired outputs $y_1, y_2, \ldots, y_n$ and delivers

them to a dispatching agency, the Post Office, or else directly to their
destinations.

Then the SOR is specified by the table

$$\text{SOR}:\begin{cases} \text{DM}:x_k \to d_k, d_k \text{ to } \gamma \text{ with probability 1,} \\ \gamma:d_k \to y_k, y_k \text{ to P.O. with probability 1.} \end{cases}$$

Since the DM's input is unknown at this stage of organizational design
the effectiveness of this arrangement can only be judged by the extent
to which it reduces the DM's output load, without overloading γ. Avoidance of overload means that an organization is required to 'keep up with
the schedule'. Applied to an individual organization member this means
that his mean processing time τ must not exceed the average time, namely
one time unit. If this is not done, i.e., if $\tau > 1$ for some member, he will be
said to be 'overloaded'.

The DM's *mean output processing time* amounts to

$$\tau_{\text{DM}} = \sum_k t_{\text{DM},k} P_k.$$

Here $t_{\text{DM},k}$ is the processing time of the DM for the directive d_k and P_k
is the probability of having him do that.

In order for this design to be effective, that $t_{\text{DM},k}$ must be smaller than
they would be if the DM had to produce y_k himself. Otherwise there
would be no point in having a line unit. Also, overload must be avoided
by γ. That is,

$$\tau_\gamma = \sum_k t_{\gamma k} P_k \leq 1,$$

where $t_{\gamma k}$ is γ's intrinsic processing time for the conversion of d_k to y_k.

If the designer finds that a one-member line is not sufficient to solve
the problem of overload he will expand it to include additional members.
In that case, he must decide whether to use the line for *alternate* or *parallel*
processing. First we treat the alternately processing line. Under this
option the DM follows some procedural rule by which he issues directives
to the various line members once at a time, each instructing its addressee
to produce a certain output. The basic idea is that in this way every line
member can be given more time to do his processing at least on the average,
and therefore is more likely to avoid overload than one unit, γ, acting by
itself.

Thus, consider a multiple member line, starting with γ and δ and ending
with μ, i.e., $s = \gamma, \delta, \dots, \mu$. Let the DM, once during each time interval,

issue an instruction $d_k, k = 1, 2, \ldots, n$ to one (and only one) of the line members, directing him to produce the output symbol y_k. The DM can act according to his SOR, the most general and most flexible appears to be a stochastic or mixed rule which prescribes that the directive be issued to s with a certain probability P_{sk}.

The SOR for the DM and his line could thus be specified as follows:

$$\text{SOR:}\begin{cases} \text{DM}: x_k \rightarrow d_k d_k \text{ to } s \text{ with probability } P_{sk} \\ s: d_k \rightarrow y_k, y_k \text{ to P.O. with probability 1.} \end{cases}$$

The P_{sk} are the *assignment probabilities*, satisfying

$$P_{sk} \geq 0, \quad \sum_s P_{sk} = 1.$$

The probability that an arbitrary line member s receives *any* assignment is given by

$$Q_s = \sum_k P_{sk} P_k$$

The probability of s receiving the specific assignment d_k, to be denoted by $Q(d_k | s)$, is obviously the conditional probability

$$Q(d_k | s) = P_{sk} P_k / Q_s.$$

The SOR is considered to be successful if it reduces the output load on the DM and if it avoids overload on the line. Now the output load of the DM is represented by his mean processing time τ_{DM}. The line unit's load is

$$\tau_s = \sum_k t_{sk} P_{sk} P_k = Q_s \sum_k t_{sk} Q(d_k | s),$$

$$s = \gamma, \delta, \ldots, \mu.$$

The DM's individual processing time $t_{\text{DM},k}$ for the directive d_k may no longer be constant, because, in view of his operating mode, if his output machine is *load-dependent* the $t_{\text{DM},k}$ will be functions of the number μ of line members and the assignment probabilities P_{sk} prescribed for the DM by the SOR. On the other hand, s processes y_k to only one destination, e.g. the Post Office. Therefore, if there is any load-dependence it is due to his input machine. His mean processing time τ_s which comprises both his input and output processing will then depend on the probabilities with which he receives his inputs d_k.

Let us see whether the expansion of the line has actually overcome the problem of the one-member line. Is it always possible to avoid overload on the line? It can be shown that the answer is yes in general, provided the line is made large enough.

THEOREM 1. Suppose that the input machines of the line members are load-dependent and that their processing times t_{sk} remain bounded, $t_{sk} \leq T$, as μ increases. The assignment probabilities can be chosen such that no member is overloaded, provided μ is made sufficiently large.

Remark. The assignment probabilities can certainly be made equal, $P_{sk} = 1/\mu$. Overload will then be avoided if

$$\sum_k t_{sk} P_k/\mu \leq T/\mu \leq 1,$$

which certainly is possible if μ is made large enough. Load dependence would imply here that the line unit's mean processing time is a function of the size n of his input alphabet and of the probabilities with which he receives his input symbols. These probabilities may be interpreted in two ways here, namely as $P_{sk}P_k$ or as $Q(d_k|s)$. The second in effect assumes that his input machine adapts to the relative frequency with which d_k occurs among his assignments, while the first makes the machine adaptive to the relative frequency with which d_k is processed by him among all assignments.

COROLLARY 1. Let the input machine of the s-th line member be load-dependent:
  (a) if this dependence is on the probabilities $Q(d_k|s)$ Theorem 1 remains valid,
  (b) if it is on the probabilities $P_{sk}P_k$, Theorem 1 remains valid if also $\lim P_k t_{sk}(P) = 0$
as P_k goes to zero.
  Proof. (a) Let $Q_s = 1/\mu$ and $Q(d_k|s) = 1/n$. Since P_k can be safely be assumed to be different from zero,

$$P_{sk} = Q(d_k|s)/P_k = 1/\mu n P_k$$

can be made less than 1 in this way.

  (b) t_{sk} depends on $P_{sk}P_k$, put $P_{sk} = 1/\mu,$
Then

$$\lim_{\mu \to \infty} \tau_s = \lim_{\mu \to \infty} \sum_k t_{sk}(P)P_k/\mu = 0$$

and $\tau_s \leq 1$ is therefore assumed when μ is large enough.

This proves the corollary.

The organization designer who sets up a line for alternate processing can thus fully expect to avoid overload among its members if he makes it large enough.

He cannot expect the same for the DM, however. In fact, if the DM's output machine is load-dependent he must be prepared for the opposite, for as the number μ of line members is increased, the DM is liable to become overloaded. The best the designer can do is to minimize his overload, while avoiding overload among the line members. The solution of this design can then be visualized as a sequence of programming problems. For every $\mu \geq 1$ determine a set of assignment probabilities $P_{sk}, s = \gamma, \delta, \ldots, \mu$ such that

$$\tau_{\text{DM}} = \sum_k t_{\text{DM},k} P_k \rightarrow \text{Min},$$

subject to the constraints

$$P_{sk} \geq 0, \sum_s P_{sk} = 1 \quad \text{and}$$

$$\tau_s = \sum_k t_{sk} P_{sk} P_k = Q_s \sum_k t_{sk} Q(d_k | s),$$

$$s = \gamma, \delta, \ldots, \mu$$

If a smallest $\mu_* = \mu$ is found at which the problem has a feasible solution, then the most economical line has been determined, as well as an SOR which minimizes the DM's overload while completely avoiding overload among its members.

7.10 THE PARALLEL PROCESSING LINE

Consider again a multiple-line organization. The organization is again expected to produce n output symbols, $y_k, k = 1, 2, \ldots, n$. Each of these symbols is decomposable into m subsymbols

$$y_k^\sigma, \text{ i.e.} \qquad y_k = \left[y_k^1, y_k^2, \ldots, y_k^m \right].$$

The procedural rule laid down for the output machine of the DM, first of all, will be a parallel processing rule of the following kind. This rule will first of all require him to issue a directive d_k^σ to a line member, once on the average per unit time interval, instructing him to produce the subsymbol y_k^σ. The line member to which that directive is issued, and the probability with which this is done, will also be prescribed by the rule. In particular, it will specify first a permutation P_{uk} for the superscripts $[1, 2, \dots, m]$

$$[\sigma_1, \sigma_2, \dots, \sigma_m] = p_{uk}[1, 2, \dots, m]$$

with the understanding that $d_k^{\sigma_1}$ is to be issued to γ, $d_k^{\sigma_2}$ to δ, etc. The rule will furthermore prescribe which among all $(m!)$ possible permutations the DM may use, and finally with what assignment probability P_{uk} satisfying $(*) P_{uk} \geq 0, \sum_u P_{uk} = 1 (k = 1, 2, \dots, n)$ it is to be used. The rule would constitute the SOR for the DM.

A line member, on receipt of his instruction d_k^σ would turn out the subsymbol y_k^σ and transmit it to the Post Office. There, the subsymbols would be packaged into the complete symbol y_k and dispatched to the proper destination. The SOR for this arrangment is tabulated as follows

$$\text{SOR} : \begin{cases} \text{DM} : x_k \rightarrow P_{uk}[d_k^1, \dots, d_k^m], d_k^\sigma \text{ to } s \text{ with probability } P_{uk} \\ s : d_k^\sigma \rightarrow y_k^\sigma, y_k^\sigma \text{ to P.O. with probability } 1 \end{cases}$$

$$\sigma = 1, 2, \dots, m, k = 1, 2, \dots, n$$

where u is the number of allowed permutations.

What can be said about the effectiveness of such an SOR? So far as the DM is concerned, it will be successful if it reduces his mean processing time as far as possible, with $t_{DM,k}$ now interpreted as the time needed by him to generate the m-triplet of instructions d_k^σ, and to address them to the proper line members with the prescribed probability. As far as the line members are concerned, the SOR will be successful if it eliminates overload among them. The conditions for that can be obtained as follows. Among the permutations which the DM may use there will be a certain subset which assigns the subsymbol d_k^1 of d_k to unit s, for example. The probability of this happening is

$$P_{sk}^1 = \sum_u P_{uk},$$

with the sum extended over all u that belong to that subset. In analogous manner one defines $P_{sk}^2, \dots, P_{sk}^m$. Then if

$$(**)\,\tau_s = \sum_k \sum_\sigma t_{sk}^\sigma P_{sk}^\sigma P_k \le 1 \qquad \begin{aligned} \sigma &= 1, 2, \dots, m \\ k &= 1, 2, \dots, n \end{aligned}$$

s is not overloaded. The factor t_{sk}^σ is his intrinsic processing time for the conversion of the instruction d_k^σ into his contribution y_k^σ to the line output. Under these circumstances, the designer can approach the problem of the design of a parallel processing line in several ways, most naturally in two ways.

(1) He may try to increase the size of m of the line, member by member, and for each m perhaps also increase the number of allowed permutations. He may continue this process, if necessary, until he reaches the limitt of the practical decomposability of the symbols y_k. At each such step he could also attempt to minimize the mean processing time τ_{DM}, subject to the constraints (*) and (**). This procedure again would require the solution of a sequence of programming problems very similar to (though a little messier than) that discussed in the previous section. Under this set-up a line could be established which can avoid overload, as well as an SOR that actually does so.

(2) A second possible approach for the designer is to go directly to the limit of the decomposability of the symbols y_k. If that limit is m, he can enquire whether an m-member line can avoid overload among its members if he allows u permutations in the assignment of subsymbols among them. This will evidently be so if the largest among the mean processing times τ_s is less than 1. He can determine this by finding an SOR which minimizes the largest τ_s, on the premise that SOR will avoid overload on the line if overload is avoidable there in the first place. Such an SOR will be called a Minimax SOR for reasons we will show next.

THEOREM 1. *Minimax SORs have the property that they equalize the mean possessing times τ_s of the line members. Such SORs always exist, regardless of whether the input machines of the line members are load-dependent.*

Proof. For simplicity consider a three-man line, consisting of $\gamma, \delta, \varepsilon$. It will be shown first that a Minimax SOR, if it exists, is among those which equalize the t_s, $s = \gamma, \delta, \varepsilon$, the existence of equalizing SORs will be proven thereafter.

(1) Note that the constraints

$$P_{uk} \ge 0, \sum_{uk} P_{uk} = 1 \qquad k = 1, 2, \dots, n)$$

define a convex polyhedron CP in the space of the variables P_{uk}. Consider the subset of CP on which

$$\tau_\gamma = \tau_\delta = \tau_\varepsilon$$

and assume for the moment that it is non-empty. Select a point in that subset on which the common value assumes its minimum τ^*. It is claimed that this is a point at which the largest of the τ_s, $s = \gamma, \delta, \varepsilon$ is as small as possible. For suppose not, one could find another point of CP at which the largest τ_s is smaller than τ^*. However, it would then also be larger than any other τ_s at that point for if they were all equal, τ^* would not have been the smallest. It follows that τ^* minimizes the largest τ_s.

(2) It now remains to be shown that there exist equalizing SORs, i.e., that the subset on which $\tau_\gamma = \tau_\delta = \tau_\varepsilon$ is non-empty. Here we can use a line of reasoning by Nash as exposited by Luce and Raiffa [6], p. 391. Suppose that some mixed SOR has been chosen by the designer but that τ_γ, τ_δ, and τ_ε are not equal. In that case he can choose a new SOR which is the same except for the assignment probabilities of two symbols, d_i and d_k, say. Consider the change in probabilities

$$P'_{ui} = \left[P_{ui} + \frac{|\tau_\gamma - \tau_\delta|}{u} \right] \Big/ [1 - |\tau_\gamma - \tau_\delta|];$$

$$P'_{uk} = \left[P_{uk} + \frac{|\tau_\gamma + \tau_\delta|}{u} \right] \Big/ [1 + |\tau_\gamma - \tau_\varepsilon|].$$

The transformation from the P_{ui} and P_{uk} to the P'_{ui} and P'_{uk} is a continuous transformation, and it carries CP into itself. By Brouwer's fix-point theorem it has a fixed point, i.e., a set of assignment probabilities for which P_{ui} and P'_{ui}, as well as P_{uk} and P'_{uk} are the same. Evidently for this particular set,

$$|\tau_\gamma - \tau_\delta| = |\tau_\gamma - \tau_\varepsilon| = 0,$$

it follows that there exist equalizing SORs.

Note that the proof is valid regardless of whether the input machines of the line members are, or not, load-dependent. If they are not, the problem of determining the Minimax SOR is of a well-known type which is called an 'assignment problem', and more particularly, of the variety of 'bottleneck assignment problems'. Algorithms exist by which pure SORs can be determined, at least in principle (e.g. Ford and Fulkerson [2], p. 57).

Pure SORs, however, may produce overload on the line in case in which mixed ones still avoid it. The determination of a best mixed SOR, can be formulated as the following LP problem: determine values for the assignment probabilities, subject to the probability constraints, and to $\tau_\gamma = \tau_\delta = \tau_\varepsilon$, such that τ_γ, say, is minimized.

This type of programming problem assumes u fixed, for instance, at $u = m$! The designer, on finding that the Minimax SOR avoids overload on the line, may wish to investigate the possibility of a smaller line or at least a smaller number u of permutations, on the expectation that the load on the DM will be reduced in this fashion. He can do this by solving a sequence of programming problems which is in one respect the reverse of the one discussed earlier in this section. He would proceed as follows: decrease u stepwise for every m until you find a pair (m, u), for which even the Minimax SOR no longer avoids overload.

The designer has two fundamental options of how to use the line. He can do its processing alternately or in parallel. He can also use mixtures of the two. If alternate processing is chosen, overload can always be avoided among the line members, in making the line large enough. Moreover, if the output (machine) of the DM is not load-dependent, all line members can receive their instructions from him directly without adverse effect on his output load. On the other hand, if his output is load-dependent, additional line echelons must be introduced as the size of the line is increased, to keep the DM's output load under control.

Similar remarks apply, in principle to a line that does its processing in parallel.

Overload among the line members however, may not be avoidable unless the production of the organizational output can be resolved into sufficiently many subtasks.

Here SORs have been established that require the optimal solution of programming problems to avoid overload: in possibly more realistic situations, by setting up SORs for large organizations we may face difficulties in obtaining explicit analytical solutions. In these cases it might be advisable to establish more sophisticated SORs, namely those which are derived from 'allocation of effort' models or related models of bounded rationality (Radner [11], Radner and Rothschild [10]). For example, 'putting out fires' (damage control), or, 'staying with the winner' rules could be superimposed on such SORs and be more adequate for decision-making in complex organizational environments.

The choice between alternate and parallel processing, on the basis of this theory, should strictly be made after the programming problems have been solved. In practice, however, the choice often seems to be made on the basis of which mode enables a multiple-member line to get the job done faster. The comparison then frequently favors parallel processing because its processing times t^σ_{sk} are typically shorter than their counterparts $P_{sk}t_{sk}$ for alternate processing. This will lead to shorter mean processing times, and – what appears to be even more important – in practice, to shorter delays in the delivery of the output products.

Neither processing mode is used in practice to the exclusion of the other. In many organizations parallel processing seems to be exploited as far as it can be, i.e., to the limit of decomposability of a task into subtasks. Beyond that alternate processing is applied, as the only remaining alternative.

This appears to be true for 'natural' as well as 'artificial' organizations, e.g., computer networks, (Slotnick [14]). In practice, organizations use 'pure' SORs most of the time. But occasionally supervisory reasonings lead to a mixing, such as considerations of justice and personal matters to equalize load among subordinates. The effect is an SOR resembling a (mixed) minimax SOR.

7.11 THE CASE OF STAFF ORGANIZATION

By trying to alleviate the load of the decision-maker, we first looked at the output side and investigated in the design of the 'line organization'. We now concentrate on the input side and investigate the role of the staff in the organizational design. The function of the staff is to *pre-process* information and present it to the decision-maker (manager) which he can best use as a basis for his actions. There are a few possibilities how the staff can alleviate the overall input load. The staff can be used to convert the nature of the signals which reach the decision maker in a form that is more easily managed by him. The staff can for instance, take on the job of searching for the necessary inputs, and when they come in, to sort those out which are relevant to the organization's tasks. This is often a time-consuming task, hence, makes for long symbol processing times and results in high loads.

7.12 THE STAFF ACTING AS AN INPUT FILTER

As explained in the preceding section, it is often convenient to employ a staff to relieve the decision-maker of certain time-consuming tasks that are connected with the organizational inputs, such as their acquisition, interpretation and collation. In other words, it is often convenient, and in fact adequate, to use the staff merely towards a reduction of the decision-maker's input load $\tau_{DM}^{(i)}$. Employed in this way, however, it cannot affect his output load $\tau_{DM}^{(o)}$. It will therefore be assumed in this section that $\tau_{DM}^{(o)}$ has been sufficiently reduced by the design of the line and in any case that $\tau_{DM}^{(o)} < 1$.

A staff that is used in the above way performs a function that is completely analogous to that of the line. It will be said to be acting as a "filter".

Define the SOR for the staff with symbols $x_j, j = 1, 2, \dots, n$ it receives from the various sources. Each staff member is then expected to process the symbol conveyed to him via a collecting unit and relay it to the decision-maker. Let r be a staff unit and m be the message (alphabet) produced. The SOR for this would have the algorithm, e.g. the SOR

$$\begin{cases} \text{Collector:} & x_j \to x_j, x_j \text{ to } r \text{ with prob. } P_{rj}, \\ r & : x_j \to m_j, m_j \text{ to DM with prob. 1}, \\ \text{DM} & : m_j \to d_j, d_j \text{ to line with prob. 1}, r = v, \dots, \rho \\ & \hspace{5cm} j = 1, 2, \dots, n. \end{cases}$$

Most of the results derived for the line apply here as well. In particular, Theorem 1, Section 7.4 and its corollary hold. It is, in other words, possible to avoid in general overload on an alternately processing staff simply by making it large enough. One can clearly also formulate a sequence of programming problems in the present case with the objective of minimizing the input processing time $\tau_{DM}^{(i)}$ of the decision-maker. However, by contrast to the line, the staff size can be increased indefinitely, at least under the assumptions of this study, without adverse effect on $\tau_{DM}^{(i)}$ of the decision-maker. However, by contrast to the line, the staff can be increased indefinitely, at least under the assumptions of this study, without adverse effect on $\tau_{DM}^{(i)}$: the mean processing time of a load-dependent input channel is not a function of the number m of staff members but of the size n of the input alphabet.

The SOR for a parallel processing staff, by analogy to Section 7.5 would be the following.

$$\begin{cases} \text{Collector:} & x_j \to P_{uj}\{x_j^1, \dots, x_j^m\}, x_j^\sigma, \text{ to } r \text{ with prob. } P_{uj} \\ r & : x_j^\sigma \to m_j^\sigma, m_j \text{ to DM with prob. 1} \\ \text{DM} & : m_j = \{m_j^1, \dots, m_j^m\} \to d_j, d_j \text{ to line with prob. 1} \\ & \hspace{2cm} \sigma = 1, 2, \dots, m; j = 1, 2, \dots, n. \end{cases}$$

The number m of members of a parallel processing staff is seen to be determined by the number of sources. As on the line, therefore, the number cannot be arbitrarily large in general. Overload among the staff members may therefore not be avoidable in this case. If it is, a minimax SOR may be required.

In one way or another, therefore, the designer can avoid overload among the staff and at the same time expect to reduce the input load on the decision-maker. However, he may not be able to eliminate overload from the decision-maker altogether. The total mean processing time τ_{DM}, in other words, may still be greater than a unit time interval.

7.13 OPTIMIZATION PROBLEM OF THE STAFF DESIGN

The SOR for the decision-maker will then require him to treat every symbol m_k received by him as if it were an input symbol directly from the outside and to react accordingly. The SOR specified by the organization designer for the decision-maker and his one-member staff would then be the following.

$$(1) \qquad \begin{cases} r \quad : x_j \to m_k, \, m_k \to \text{DM with prob. } P(m_k | x_j) \\ \text{DM}: m_k \to d_k, \, d_k \text{ to line with prob. } 1, \\ \qquad\qquad j, k = 1, 2, \ldots, n \end{cases}$$

The SOR, i.e., the conditional probabilities $P(m_k | x_j)$, are to be so chosen that the decison-maker's overload is eliminated. This will be the case if his mean processing time

$$(2) \qquad \tau_{DM} = \sum_j \sum_k t_{DM,k} (m_k | x_j)_{P_j} \le 1.$$

Here, $t_{DM,k}$ is his total processing time, i.e., the time he needs to convert his input symbol m_k to the directive d_k which he then issues to the line, as prescribed by his SOR (1). The probabilities $P(m_k | x_j)$ characterize the errors which r intentionally commits in order to eliminate the decision-maker's overload, i.e., to insure that (2) holds.

The problem here is how to choose the $P(m_k | x_j)$. There are many choices which insure (2), but some are clearly superior to the rest: they are the ones which minimize the adverse effect of error generation on system performance. To be more specific, the mean pay-off to the organization, under any SOR of the type (1), is

$$(3) \qquad \phi = \sum_j \sum_k L_{jk} P(m_k | x_i) P_j$$

since neither the decision-maker nor the line make any further errors. Hence, the best SOR is one which maximizes ϕ.

The problem is then the following. Find the set of n^2 conditional probabilities which maximize (3) satisfying

(4) $P(m_k|x_j) \geq 0, \sum_k P(m_k|x_j) = 1,$ $(j, k = 1, 2, \ldots, n).$

as well as (2).

If the decision-makers' processing times $t_{DM,k}$ are constant or, in other words, if his input machine is load-independent, this is clearly a linear programming problem of a completely standard kind. In the present case, however, its solution has certain special properties which are summarized in

THEOREM 1. *Consider a one-member staff, and a decision-maker with constant processing times $t_{DM,k}$ satisfying*

(5) $t_{DM,k^*} = \min_k t_{DM,k} \leq 1.$

Proof. The constraints (4) define a convex polyhedron CP in the n^2-dimensional space of points representing the probabilities $P(m_k|x_j)$. The vertices of CP are more particularly the points at which, for each x_j, all but one of the $P(m_k|x_j)$ vanish. They therefore represent the pure SORs. The edges of CP represent mixed SORs but in any case mixtures in which, for each x_j, all but two of the $P(m_k|x_j)$ vanish.

Note first that, under the condition (5), the linear programming problem always has a feasible solution, namely

$P(m_k|x_j) = \delta_{jk}(j = 1, 2, \ldots, n).$

It is therefore necessary to characterize the optimal ones. To this end, let

$h \leq \sum_j \sum_k t_{DM,k} P(m_k|x_j) P_j = 1$

be the boundary of the half-space defined by (2), and distinguish the following three cases.

(i) *h does not intersect CP.* In this case, CP lies entirely within the half-space (2). All SORs are feasible, the pure ones included and none engage the decision-maker fully. Now, as is well known, ϕ attains its maximum ϕ^* at a vertex of CP. It follows then that a pure SOR is optimal, as claimed. (It is also well known that ϕ^* may be attained at more than one vertex in which case more than one pure SOR is optimal, and so are all mixtures of these.)

(ii) *h intersects CP at one of its vertices.* All the statements of case (i) apply here as well unless the intersection of *h* and CP occurs at a vertex of CP at which ϕ^* is attained. The pure SOR that is represented by this vertex is then still optimal but the DM is now fully loaded by it.

(iii) *h intersects one or more of the edges of CP.* In that case a new vertex is created at each such point of intersection and ϕ^* may be attained at one of these. If it is, the mixed SOR represented by such a point is optimal but since it lies on an edge of CP, all but two of the probabilities $P(m_k|x_j)$ still vanish. (Again, ϕ may attain this maximum at more than one of the newly created vertices. In such a case, the mixed SOR represented by each is optimal, and so are all mixtures of these.)

Theorem 1 is accordingly proven. One of the assumptions on which the proof is based is that the decision-maker's input machine is load-dependent. As will now be shown, it remains valid also when he suffers from load-dependence. The problem in this case is again a programming problem but it is no longer linear because one of the constraints, namely (2), is not. The decision-makers processing times $t_{\mathrm{DM},k}$ and their mean τ_{DM} are then functions of the probabilities

$$(6a) \qquad Q_k = \sum_j P(m_k|x_j)P_j$$

with which the symbols m_k arrive that this input machine. The condition for the absence of overload on him, written out explicitly, is

$$(6b) \qquad \tau_{\mathrm{DM}}(Q) = \tau_{\mathrm{DM}}^{(i)}(Q) + \sum_k t_{\mathrm{DM},k}^{(0)} Q_k \le 1$$

where Q is the vector of the probabilities Q_k. The first term in this expression for τ_{DM} is concave in Q, by the definition of load-dependence for an input channel; the second is linear (hence also concave) because the $t_{\mathrm{DM},k}^{(0)}$ are constants when the DM's output SOR is fixed, as it is by assumption. The result that holds now is the following

THEOREM 2. *Consider a non-person staff, and a decision-maker whose input channel is load-dependent but such that*

$$(7) \qquad \min_Q \tau_{\mathrm{DM}}(Q) \le 1.$$

If his output SOR is fixed the assertions of Theorem 1 remain valid, except that more than two of the conditional probabilities $P(m_k|x_j)$ may differ from zero, for each x_j.

Proof. The mean processing time τ_{DM} in (6b) is a concave function of the variables Q_k, and hence, also in the probabilities $P(m_k|x_j)$ which are related to the Q_k by (6a). The set defined by (8) is then convex, consequently it is its intersection with the convex polyhedron CP (using here the same notation as in the preceding proof). It follows that ϕ assumes its maximum ϕ^* at an extreme point of that intersection, provided only it is non-empty. The fact, however, is that it is non-empty because, by (7), $\tau_{DM}(Q) \leq 1$ for at least one vector Q. It can now happen that an extreme point at which $\phi = \phi^*$ is a vertex of CP, in which case the optimal SOR (1) is pure, If not, it must lie on the surface $\tau_{DM} = 1$ but possibly in the interior of CP. In that case the decision-maker is fully loaded, as was to be proven.

7.14 THE ALTERNATELY PROCESSING STAFF

In this section it is more narrowly assumed that the staff does its processing alternately. It will be shown that, as on the line, overload can always be avoided among the staff members simply by using a sufficiently large number of them. This statement, however, takes it for granted either that the sources are sufficiently cooperative to submit their input symbols according to an SOR which is specified by the designer, or else that a collector can intercept those inputs and retransmit them to the staff according to that SOR, without suffering overload.

An optimal one for the staff is then one that maximizes

(1) $$\phi = \sum_R \sum_j \sum_k L_{jk} P_r(m_j|x_j) P_{rj} P_j$$

subject to

$$P_r(m_k|x_j) \geq 0, \qquad \sum_k P_r(m_k|x_j) = 1$$

and

(2) $$\tau_{DM} = \sum_r \sum_j \sum_k t_{DM'k} P_r(m_k|x_j) P_{rj} P_j \leq 1.$$

The problem of determining an optimal SOR for an m-member staff is clearly very similar to its counterpart for a one-member staff. In fact, it becomes identical if one sets

(3) $$\sum_r P_r(m_k|x_j) P_{rj} P_j = P(m_k|x_j)$$

in (1) and (2). This, however, implies that the m-member staff will perform optimally if it can simulate, in the sense of (3), the function of a one-member staff that is not overloaded.

7.15 THE PARALLEL PROCESSING STAFF

The staff, by analogy to the line, can process symbols in parallel. The analogy, however, barely fits. It will become clear presently that parallel processing is done quite differently by staff and line.

In order for parallel processing to be possible, the symbols assigned by the collector to the staff must be of the kind that can be resolved into subsymbols, or, which happens more often in practice, that they are received from several sources simultaneously. They are than in a resolved form to begin with. Let it therefore be assumed that one or the other is the case and let the symbol x_j received by the staff, after having been processed in some way by the collector, be of the form

(1) $x_j = \{x_j^1, x_j^2, \ldots, x_j^m\}.$

The number m of subsymbols is then the maximum number of staff members who can be used to process the input symbols x_j in parallel. The staff in turn is required to relay to the decision-maker another symbol, namely

(2) $m_k = \{m_k^1, m_k^2, \ldots, m_k^m\}.$

If m_k is always related to x_j in a one-to-one fashion, the staff acts as a buffer; if not, it acts as a filter.

For optimal performance, the staff as a whole will have to act as a filter and will transmit to the decision-maker the symbol m_k with a probability $P(m_k|x_j)$ whenever it receives x_j from the collector or from the outside. Now, it is important to note that any optimal set of such probabilities must be among the optimal ones for a single-member staff, and vice versa: each can be determined as a solution of the same programming problem as the other, namely the problem described in 8.13. An immediate consequence is

THEOREM 1. *Under the assumptions of Theorem 1 a and 2 Section 13, regarding the decision-maker, there exists an optimal set of conditional probabilities $P(m_k|x_j)$ for an m-member staff as a whole. They have the* *same properties as those stated in Theorem 1 and 2 for a single-member staff.*

This statement, however, does not define the conditional probabilities of the individual staff members or, in other words, it does not characterize the SOR for a parallel processing staff. In fact, it does not even make quite clear just how the term 'parallel processing' is to be interpreted in connection with a staff. The interpretation given in this section is that individual staff members produce the subsymbols m_k^σ, $\sigma = 1, 2, \ldots, m$, of m_k in (2) from the staff input x_j, and transmit them individually to the decision-maker. An optimal SOR for a staff that does its processing in parallel in this sense can then be arrived at very quickly by the following reasoning.

The optimal conditional probabilities $P(m_k | x_j)$ for the staff as a whole can be written more explicitly in terms of the subsymbols m_k^σ:

$$P(m_k | x_j) = P(m_k^{\sigma_1}, m_k^{\sigma_2}, \ldots, m_k^{\sigma_m} | x_j)$$

with the understanding that x_j is the m-tuple in (1). The expression on the right is a joint probability, namely that v will transmit $m_k^{\sigma_1}$ to the decision-maker $om_k^{\sigma_2}$, and so on, all conditioned on the staff input x_j. This probability, however, can also be decomposed into conditional probabilities, for instance,

$$(3) \qquad P(m_k | x_j) = P_A(m_k^{\sigma_1} | k, \sigma_1; x_j) \ldots P_M(m_k^{\sigma_m} | k, \sigma_1, \ldots, \sigma_{m-1}; x_j)$$

in which $k, \sigma_1, \sigma_2, \ldots, \sigma_m$ have been used as conditioning variables rather than the equivalent $m_k, m_k^{\sigma_1}, m_k^{\sigma_2}, \ldots, m_k^{\sigma_m}$, for notational convenience. The last expression, however, already is a solution to the present problem: it in effect characterizes an optimal SOR for an m-member, parallel processing staff.

All optimal SORs for a parallel processing staff are seen to be quite demanding on load-carrying capacity of its members. The input machines of each must be able to accommodate the input alphabet of the organization as a whole, namely the symbols x_j, as well as the coordinating information which they receive from the Chief of Staff, and from the others that have preceded them in their choice of transmitted subsymbols m_k^σ.

The output machines are also loaded fairly heavily. The Chief of Staff distributes his outputs among m destinations, namely, the decision-maker and all $(m - 1)$ fellow staff members. However, only one transmission is governed by a stochastic SOR, namely the one to the decision-maker. The other staff members have it progressively easier; r, in particular, transmits to $(m - r)$ destinations, stochastically to one and deterministically to the rest.

The structure and the SOR that are best for a staff depend surprisingly strongly on what assumptions one can make regarding the capabilities of the collector and the procedures it can execute. In principle, one can assume that it can execute arbitrarily plex SORs without suffering overload. Such an assumption, however, is surely unrealistic, for if it were not, the collector himself could take on the function of the staff. This would be quite contrary to the notion of what such an agency could accomplish. One should probably assume it capable of executing only simple SORs, mainly pure ones. Among these will, no doubt, be the identity operation, in which case the decision-maker creates signals by himself as straightforward permutations, all of which carry the symbols from a given source directly to a given staff member. This list might be expanded to include SORs which provide for the transmission of symbols to several members simultaneously, and perhaps also for the resolution of symbols into a few subsymbols.

In what follows, it will be assumed that the collector is capable of executing only very simple SORs, namely, those providing for the transmission of all symbols x_j^σ from a certain source to one or more designated staff members.

The first special case to be discussed here under this assumption is characterized by the fact that staff members suffer mainly from output load. The designer can admittedly often reduce this. In the case of the Chief of Staff, he can relieve him of having to make transmissions to the decision-maker, and charge him merely with the issuing of the coordinating signal to the remaining staff members. Suppose this has in fact been done. A further reduction may be possible by supplying the Chief with a hierarchy of processors, analogous to the line, and charge those with the distribution of the coordinating signal among the staff. Suppose that this has in fact been done also, at least, to the extent to which it is useful. A similar arrangement can be considered for the coordinating signal issued by, say, r. It can, however, happen that the latter is unnecessary, as the following proposition shows.

THEOREM 2. *Suppose that the collector is capable of transmitting the input symbols* $x_j, j = 1, 2, \ldots, n$, *of the organization to any or all staff* *members. Regarding the latter, suppose that their input processing times are negligible, i.e., $t_{rj}^{(i)} = 0$ for $j = 1, 2, \ldots, n$ and $r = v, \ldots, p$. Assume that the Chief of Staff, v, transmits only the coordinating symbols m_k, $k = 1, 2, \ldots, n$ and that his processing times for these obey*

(4) $t_{vk}^{(0)} \leq 1$ $k = 1, 2, \ldots, n$,

regardless of the SOR that is prescribed for him. Regarding the remaining staff members, assume that each can be charged with the transmission of a subsymbol m_k^σ to the decision-maker, and furthermore that these transmissions can be so assigned among them that, for all k and all σ, there is at least one r for which

(5) $t_r^{(0)}(m_k^\sigma) \leq 1$ $\sigma = 1, 2, \ldots, m; r = v, \ldots, p$.

The decision-maker's input machine is assumed to obey either (4) or (7), Section 7.13, whichever applies. The staff can then realize the optimal SOR.

Proof. Let the collector be required to transmit every organizational input symbol x_j to all staff members. Under the assumptions of this proposition, the collector can do this without overload and all staff members can absorb x_j without input load. Moreover, there exist an optimal extended SOR for the staff as a whole, as Theorem 1 points out. Let the probabilities for that SOR be $P(m_k|x_j)$. According to (4) the Chief of Staff, say v, is safe from overload in any case, and therefore he designates m_k with probability $P(m_k|x_j)$ as the symbol to be transmitted to the decision-maker by the staff whenever x_j is received. Among the remaining staff members, r can avoid overload if, for a given m_k, he processes a subsymbol m_k^σ for which (5) holds, and every m_k^σ can in fact be so assigned among the staff that this is true. Let this assignment be the staff SOR. I.e., for every $k = 1, 2, \ldots, n$, and every $\sigma = 2, 3, \ldots, m$ establish a staff member $r = r(k, \sigma)$ such that (5) holds. Then

(6) $P_r(m_k^\sigma|k, \sigma_2, \ldots, \sigma_{r-1}, x_j) = P_r(m_k^\sigma|k, x_j) = 1$

for $r = r(k, \sigma)$ and zero otherwise. The mean processing time of a typical staff member will then be

$$\tau_r = \sum_j \sigma_j \sum_k P(m_k|x_j) \sum_\sigma P_r(m_k^\sigma|k, x_j) t_{rk}^{(0)}(m_k^\sigma)) =$$
$$= \sum_j \sigma_j \sum_k P(m_k|x_j) t_{rk}^{(0)}(m_k^\sigma) \leq \sum_j P_j \sum_k P(m_k|x_j) = 1$$

which shows that he is not overloaded. Moreover, the probability with which the decision-maker receives m_k, for given x_j, is $P(m_k|x_j)$. This SOR therefore realizes the optimal conditional probabilities. Moreover, as (6) shows, there is no need for coordination among the staff beyond that coming from the Chief. The proof is accordingly complete.

7.16 SOME PRACTICAL ASPECTS OF ORGANIZATIONAL DESIGN

The designer can utilize the staff in two ways. The first is as a buffer in which case the staff acts very much as a counterpart of the line. The second and more general way is for the staff to act as a filter. It then, in effect, commits the decision-maker's errors for him, but does so in an optimal manner. Alternate and parallel processing is possible in either case. The first can always eliminate overload from the decision-maker and at the same time avoid it among the staff according to certain well-designed *procedural rules* which will not always be realizable in practice. The second can also eliminate the decision-maker's overload, but may not be able to do the same for the staff. However, a broad range of structures and SORs exist among which the organization designer can choose, in an effort to find some that avoid overload throughout.

Optimal SORs for the staff are not as difficult to determine, in principle, as those for the line. They, too, require the solution of programming problems, some linear and some less so, but even the worst do not appear as formidable as their counterparts for the line. Explecit solutions, in fact, appear to be quite feasible in some cases, notably in those in which load-dependence can be neglected.[5]

The comparison between this theory and practice is more tenuous for the staff than for the line, partly because the term 'staff' is not clearly defined. The meaning that is attached to it here, namely, that of a group of organization members which is charged with the preprocessing of information for executives, may be more comprehensive than its usual interpretation.[6] It probably does include organizational units, such as military staffs, as well as advisory groups in industrial firms which are usually subsumed under the concept. The interpretation that is attached to it here, however, includes also others that are not usually considered staff groups. Intelligence agencies, sales departments, and purchasing agencies may be cases in point.

In many situations in practice, staff and line personnel coincide. Some of the most important inputs to the commander of an army unit in the field, for instance, come not so much from special agents as from the officers and soldiers of the line. In an organization chart a staff and a line person would then really be one and the same person.

Military groups probably do function roughly like a committee. Their outputs, namely the preparation of detailed plans of action, are typically very time-consuming business or, in other words, place high output loads on their members. The adoption of a committee-like structure would then be the best thing to do, according to this theory.

One should further be prepared to designate a Chief for such a staff who acts as a rather forceful committee chairman. This is in contrast to the line, which has no corresponding 'Chief of Line', a fact which also seems rather consistent with experience in practice. One can even speculate that the need for a Chief which emerges from the theory is essential to the avoidance of the kind of intransitivities which, according to Arrow's well known theorem[7], can block all effective action by a group of co-equals.

Industrial firms appear to favour hierarchical staffs, perhaps because input loads tend to outweigh output loads. Moreover, there never is a position that is designated as 'Chief of Staff' except for public and political bureaucracies. In some cases the position actually exists but, perhaps in recognition of its importance, it is then often the president of the company who occupies it. The position of the decision-maker goes to an executive vice-president or some equivalent. In either case, the staff itself usually consists of several echelons of pre-processors and thus assumes a structure resembling that of the line. The pay-off function for such organizations presumably exhibits, or at least approximates, the kind of zones of indifference which make hierarchical staff structures near-optimal.

NOTES

[1] The behavioral rules of organization members as embodied in the 'standard operating routines' (SOR) very much resemble rules of 'procedural rationality' according to Simon [13].

[2] See Hartmanis and Stearns [4].

[3] Recall from above that every partition pair constitutes by itself a feasible information technology. Thus every point of the lattice of partition pairs (or pair algebra according to 14 is itself a lattice, hence we can speak of a lattice of lattices. Instead of considering a pair (π, π'), for simplicity, we could take an n-tuple $(\pi_1, \ldots, \pi_n)$ (corresponding to a sequential process in n-stages) which itself forms a lattice.

[4] Furthermore, if D and D' are both dimension functions and exist, then D and D' are uniquely related up to positive linear transformations, hence dimension in a lattice is measurable on an interval scale. We consider the minimal dimension of the lattice as a measure of *computational* or informational efficiency.

[5] Some of the programming problems associated to SORs get so complicated that they have

to be solved by heuristic procedures, and fall into the very class of NP-complete problems (see Chapt. 5).

[6] Under this interpretation the staff consists of highly specialized professionals, see C. Perrow [9].

[7] K.J. Arrow, *Social Choice and Individual Values*, Yale Univ. Press, New Haven, 1951.

REFERENCES

[1] Arrow, K. J., *The Limits of Organization*, Norton, New York, 1974.

[2] Ford, L.R. and Fulkerson, D.R., *Flows in Networks*, Princeton Univ. Press, Princeton, N.J. 1974.

[3] Gottinger, H.W., 'Qualitative Information and Comparative Informativeness', *Kybernetik* (*Biological Cybernetics*) **13** (1973), 81–94.

[4] Hartmanis, J. and Stearns, R.E., *Algebraic Structure Theory of Sequential Machines*, Prentice Hall, Englewood Cliffs, 1966.

[5] Hurwicz, L., 'Optimality and Informational Efficiency in Resource Allocation Processes', Ch. 3 in *Mathematical Methods in the Social Sciences*, Stanford Univ. Press, Stanford, Calif., 1959.

[6] Luce, R.D. and Raiffa, H., *Games and Decisions*, Wiley, New York, 1957.

[7] Marschak, J. and Radner, R., *The Economic Theory of Teams*, Yale Univ. Press, New Haven, 1972.

[8] McGuire, C.B. and Marschak, T., *Design of Organizations* (unpublished notes), Univ. of California, Berkeley, 1972.

[9] Perrow, C., *Complex Organizations: A Critical Essay*, Scotts, Foresman & Co.

[10] Radner, R. and Rothschild, M., 'The Allocation of Effort', *Journ. of Economic Theory* **10** (1975), 358–376.

[11] Radner, R., 'A Behavioral Model of Cost Reduction', *Bell Journ. of Economics* **6** (1975), 196–215.

[12] Reiter, S., and Mount, K., 'The Informational Size of Message Spaces', *Center for Math. Studies in Economics and Management Science*, Northwestern Univ., Evanston, 122. Discussion Paper No. 3, 1972.

[13] Simon, H.A., 'On How to Decide What to Do', *Bell Journ. of Economics* **9** (1978), 494–507.

[14] Slotnick, L., 'The Fastest Computer', *Scientific American* **224** (1971), 76–87.

[15] Zissos, D., *System Design with Microprocessors*, Academic Press, London, New York, 1978.

INDEX OF NAMES

NOTE: Numbers in brackets refer to chapters; P means 'Preface'

Albin, P.S. (1) 12: 36n
Ando, A. (4) 114: 132n
Arbib, M. (1) 23: 35n; (2) 38, 40, 67: 75n
Arrow, K.J. (4) 132: 132n; (6) 164: 173n; (7) 197, 217: 218n
Ashby, W.R. (3) 78, 103: 111n
Aspvall, B. (5) 142: 156n

Beer, S. (1) 24: 35n
Bellman, R. (1) 10: 35n
Blin, J.M. (6) 164: 173n
Brainerd, W.S. (1) 5: 36n
Brewer, G. (1) 13: 35n; (4) 120: 132n
Brunner, R.D. (4) 119:132n

Casti, J. (1) 24: 35n
Clifford, H.H. (2) 67: 75n
Cody, M.L. (3) 84: 111n

Eilenberg, S. (2) 40: 75n
Ernst, G.W. (6) 158, 171: 173n

Ferguson, Th.S. (5) 141: 156n
Fisher, F.M. (4) 114: 132n
Ford, L.R. (7) 204: 218n
Fulkerson, D.R. (7) 204: 218n
Futia, C. (1) 39: 44n; (3) 89, 107: 111n; (6) 161, 172: 173n

Gaines, B.R. (6) 172: 173n
Garey, M.R. (5) 142, 146: 156n
Gardner, M. (3) 111n
Gause, G.F. (3) 76: 111n
Gottinger, H.W. (1) 16, 32: 35n; (7) 186: 218n

Hardin, G. (P) xii; (1) 20; (3) 79: 111n
Hartmanis, J. (1) 5: 35n; (7) 217: 218n

Hayek, F.A. (4) 113, 128: 132n
Heisenberg, W. (1) 9
Hildenbrand, W. (1) 30: 36n
Hopcroft, J.E. (1) 5: 35n
Hurwicz, L. (1) 6: 36n; (7) 179, 180: 218n

Isnard, C.A. (1) 24, 26: 36n

Johnson, D.S. (5) 142, 146: 156n

Kahnemann, D. (5) 147: 156n
Karp, R.M. (5) 143: 156n
Keeney, R.L. (5) 135: 156n
Kemeny, G. (3) 82: 111n
Krohn, K. (P) xi, xiii; (2) 39: 75n; (3) 87, 88: 111n

Landweber, L.H. (1) 5: 36n
Leibenstein, H. (6) 158: 173n
Luce, R.D. (6) 159: 173n; (7) 204: 218n
Lynch, K. (3) 86: 111n

Marglin, S.A. (4) 131: 132n
Martin, J. (4) 125: 132n
Marschak, J. (1) 16: 36n; (5) 135: 156n; (6) 159: 173n; (7) 182: 218n
Mateosian, R. (2) 75n
May, R.M. (4) 114: 132n
McCarthy, J. (5) 138: 156n
McCorduck, P. (P) xv
McCulloch, W.S. (P) ix; (1) 8
McGuire, C.B. (7) 182: 218n
Minsky, M. (1) 16: 36n; (2) 38: 75n
Moiseev, N.N. (4) 128: 133n

Newell, J. (5) 136, 139, 151, 153: 156n; (6) 158, 171: 173n
Neumann von, J. (P) ix, xii; (1) 1, 9, 12: 36n

Oniki, H. (4) 131 : 133n

Papert, S. (1) 16 : 36n; (2) 38 : 75n
Pearl, J. (4) 132 : 133n
Perrow, C. (7) 218 : 218n
Pitts, W. (P) ix; (1) 8
Preston, G.B. (2) 67 : 75n

Radner, R. (1) 16, 31 : 36n; (5) 135 :
    156n; (7) 206 : 218n
Raiffa, H. (5) 135 : 156n; (7) 204 : 218n
Raphael, B. (5) 138 : 156n
Rapoport, A. (3) 76, 77 : 111n
Reiter, S. (1) 6 : 36n; (7) 180, 192 :
    218n
Rhodes, J. (P) xi, xiii; (2) 39, 75 : 75n;
    (3) 87, 88 : 111n; (6) 170 : 173n
Roberts, F.S. (6) 158 : 174n
Rosen, R. (1) 10 : 36n
Rothschild, W. (1) 31 : 36n; (7) 205 :
    218n

Sandell, N.R. (4) 111 : 133n
Scarf, H. (1) 30 : 36n
Schelling, T. (3) 84, 94 : 111n
Schmidbauer, P.L. (1) 7 : 36n; (4)
    129, 131 : 133n
Schmidt, A.G. (4) 128 : 133n
Selten, R. (6) 172 : 173n

Shannon, C.E. (P) xv; (5) 137 : 156n
Shaw, P. (5) 136, 139, 153 : 156n
Simon, H. (1) 4, 11, 15, 16, 32 : 36n;
    (5) 136, 139, 151, 153 : 156n; (6) 157,
    158, 160, 173 : 174n
Slotnick, L. (7) 206, 217 : 218n
Smale, S. (3) 108 : 111n
Stearns, R.E. (7) 217 : 218n
Steinbruner, J. (5) 135 : 156n
Stone, R.E. (5) 142 : 156n
Strassen, V. (5) 143 : 156n
Suppes, P. (6) 172 : 173n

Thom, R. (1) 24, 28 : 36n; (3) 106, 107 :
    111n
Thompson, G.L. (5) 142 : 156n
Tilson, B.R. (2) 75n
Turing, A. (P) ix, xiv; (1) 5; (7) 175
Tversky, A. (5) 147 : 156n

Ulam, St. (3) 82 : 111n

Varian, H. (6) 163 : 174n

Weaver, W. (4) 113 : 133n
Whitney, H. (1) 25 : 36n
Wooldridge, D.E. (3) 110 : 111n

Zeeman, E.C. (1) 24, 26 : 36n
Zissos, D. (7) 194 : 218n

INDEX OF SUBJECTS

NOTE: Numbers in brackets refer to chapters

adaptability (1) 10
algebra,
   pair (7) 189
algorithm,
   approximation (5) 146
   Khachiyan's (5) 142
   polynomial-time (5) 146
analysis,
   means-end (5) 154
array,
   Pascal (2) 66
approximation,
   successive (5) 151
assessment,
   technology (5) 153

balance,
   tradeoff (5) 153
 breakdown (2) 38; (3) 104

catastrophe (3) 93
circuit (1) 8; (3) 96
choice,
   social (6) 163
class,
   complexity (5) 145
   equivalence (2) 42, 44
combinatorial (2) 62
communication (2) 37
complexity,
   algebraic (3) 107
   algorithmic (5) 142
   analytic (1) 13
   computational (1) 5, 8; (4) 117,
    127; (6) 171; (7) 193
   control (1) 13, 19; (3) 92, 94, 106,
    110
   disorganized (4) 113
   design (1) 19; (3) 92, 94, 106, 110;
    (4) 131; (6) 167

differential (1) 28
evolution (1) 20; (3) 92, 111
intermediate (1) 30
mathematical (2) 39
structural (1) 21; (4) 127; (5) 137;
   (6) 162, 171
system (4) 112
thresholds of (1) 3
time (5) 145
topological (1) 28; (3) 106
computability, (1) 23; (5) 134; (6)
   160; (7) 179
   practical (6) 160
computational (6) 171
computation (2) 37
   costs of (7) 193
   real-time (7) 192
configuration (3) 82
connectedness,
   structural (4) 120
controllability, (1) 10, 23
   level of (1) 10
controller,
   artificial (4) 129
   centralized (4) 127
   human (4) 129
costs,
   computational (1) 31
criteria,
   multiple (5) 135

decentralization,
   information (7) 175
decision,
   social (6) 164, 165
decomposition,
   cascade (7) 185
   parallel (7) 184
   serial (7) 183
design,

221

organizational (7) 197
dilemma,
  prisoner's (3) 79

efficiency,
  information (7) 180
eggbox (2) 68
equilibrium (7) 179
  competitive (3) 93
equivalent,
  certainty (5) 135

fix,
  technological (3) 109
flip-flop (3) 80, 88
form,
  organizational (7) 178
function,
  recursive (1) 6
function,
  social decision (6) 165
  social welfare (7) 179

game,
  Schelling's (3) 84
  sequential (6) 168
game-playing (5) 137
goal,
  organizational (7) 178
group,
  cyclic (2) 68
  simple (2) 55

Heisenberg's uncertainty (1) 9
heuristics (4) 129

ideal (2) 42
  principle (2) 42
  principal left (2) 42, 43
  principal right (2) 42, 43
intelligence,
  artificial (5) 139
interacton,
  external (1) 2
  internal (1) 3
  man-machine (1) 33, 34

intractability (5) 142
itinerary (5) 151

Jacob-Monod model (3) 93
Jordan-Hölder theory (3) 88

Khachiyan's algorithm (5) 142
Krohn-Rhodes theory (3) 88

length,
  computational (6) 162
  program (1) 6

machine,
  decision (2) 37
  delay one (3) 88
  finite state (1) 8; (2) 37
  sequential (1) 6, 7; (3) 76, 95; (7)
    175, 180
  social choice (6) 162
  Turing (1) 5, 6; (5) 147
malfunctioning (7) 196
mathematics (1) 1
mechanisms,
  homeostatic (3) 77
model,
  Jacob-Monod (3) 93

network, (2) 38
  element of a (2) 37
  McCulloch-Pitts neural (1) 8
NP-hard (5) 142

optimality,
  Pareto (3) 93
organization,
  human (7) 194
  line (7) 197
  multiple-line (7) 201
  staff (7) 206

partition (7) 187
Pareto optimality (3) 93
Pascal array (2) 66
payoff,
  expected (7) 196

planning,
  means-end (5) 154
  strategic (5) 137
points,
  fixed (1) 30
principle,
  Heisenberg's uncertainty (1) 9
problem,
  assignment (7) 204
  ill-structured (5) 135; (6) 159, 173
  social choice (6) 158
  travelling salesman (5) 142
  well-structured (6) 159, 173
problem-solving (4) 128; (5) 134
process,
  social decision (6) 164
product,
  direct (2) 48
  partial (2) 58
  wreath (2) 40, 46
program,
  chess playing (5) 136; (6) 167

rationality,
  bounded (4) 129; (5) 134; (6) 167
  global (6) 157
  limited (6) 157, 170
redundancy,
  information (7) 191
Rees matrix representation (2) 70
Rees matrix semigroup (2) 74
regularity,
  statistical (4) 121
relation,
  equivalence (2) 49
resources,
  computational (4) 112
rules,
  complexity of decision (6) 165
  decision (4) 129; (6) 161
  minimax control (1) 14
  sequential decision (6) 162
  social decision (6) 167
  transition (3) 81
rule-of-thumb (6) 160

satellite (4) 118
search,
  breadth first (5) 138
  in depth (5) 138
semigroup,
  cyclic (2) 57
  irreducible (2) 55
  Rees matrix (2) 74
  right transformation (2) 40
  transformation (2) 41, 44
Schelling's game (3) 84
space,
  cellular (3) 82
  problem (5) 135
stable,
  quantitatively (3) 93
  structurally (3) 78
staff,
  alternately processing (7) 211
  parallel processing (7) 212
structural (6) 171
structure,
  hierarchic (1) 4
  information (3) 101
survival, (2) 38
systems,
  artificial (1) 4, 13, 17
  competitive (1) 7
  control (4) 112
  decomposable (4) 114
  linear dynamic (4) 114
  finite complex (1) 2; (4) 113
  infinitely large (1) 2
  natural (1) 4
  satellite (4) 118
  small (1) 2

technology,
  information (7) 180, 186, 217
theorem,
  prime decomposition (2) 62
theory,
  catastrophe (1) 24
  Jordan-Hölder (3) 88
  Krohn-Rhodes (3) 88

Thom's program (3) 106
tradeoff,
   complexity (4) 127
transformation,
   semigroup of (1) 6, 18; (3) 98

Turing (7) 175
Turing machine (1) 5, 6; (5) 147

undecidability (6) 165